D1367359

Road to Ruin

Also by A. Q. Mowbray

THE THUMB ON THE SCALE
OR THE SUPERMARKET SHELL GAME

Road to Ruin

A. Q. Mowbray

J. B. LIPPINCOTT COMPANY
Philadelphia and New York

Contents

Road to Ruin

The Asphalt Shroud

The measure of a modern, industrialized nation can be taken by observing the quality of its works in the two extremes of its environment—cities and wilderness. The quality of the city and of life within its borders bespeaks the attitudes of that nation toward the human being; the quality of a nation's wilderness bespeaks its attitude toward the living earth. The United States is swiftly destroying its cities and its wilderness with highways.

Americans are a restless, moving people. Before the land was ours, we leaped upon her virgin wealth to invade, rend, and devour her, expelling the hot energies of our youth against the raw wilderness. Now the frontiers have gone, but still we tear at the land with giant machines and thrust black tentacles of asphalt through the living flesh of our cities. We will not rest until the last remnants of wild spaces are open to the rubber tire, until the last clear mountain stream is bridged, until the last cathedral grove of redwoods is visible from the back seat of a Chevrolet.

The city was once envisioned as the place where a man could find his highest expression as a human being, where he could find rewarding labor, go to a concert, exchange philosophies in his neighborhood bar or on a park bench, grow in wisdom through exposure to human diversity, listen to the teachers at a great university, assuage his loneliness with crowds, and find protection from the iron forces of nature.

But the highest function of the city has become the efficient moving and storage of automobiles. The fine-grained, human-scale diversity of shops and homes and bars and parks and newsstands and shoeshine parlors is being wiped out by freeways, interchanges, boulevards,

9

and parking lots. The bustle, the color, the friction, the exuberance of human contact are giving way to the sterile ooze of steel automata moving along the corridors between high-rise monuments to insurance companies and towering ghettos for their clerks, and marking their passage with the stench of fumed rubber and burned hydrocarbons. At night, the lights of the monumental city blaze down on streets empty of humanity, silent except for the whisper of rubber against asphalt, as the rear guard of the daytime clerks escape along the freeways to the suburbs.

What of the hundreds of thousands of residents and small businessmen whose homes and businesses are destroyed when the highway rips through the city? That's too bad, but that's the price of progress, says John C. Kluczynski, congressman from Illinois. "I thought we had a lot of problems in Chicago, but the Chicago problems are all over the country, especially where there are old cities—relocation. We had a problem in New York City, when we were there last year, where they were going to condemn a lot of property, and put out 260 small business people because of a new road. Well, we are not against progress. I am for better roads. We need more of them. I am chairman of the Subcommittee on Roads in the Public Works Committee. We want more roads."

If the city was envisioned as the place where man could find his place among men, the wilderness and open spaces were believed to be the place where man could find his place in Nature. And the preservation of that wilderness should testify to man's reverence for the earth from which he comes and to which he will return. By his very act of preservation he acknowledges his humility before his creator. By staying his destructive hand, he disavows the arrogant notion that he is the be-all and the end-all of creation; he surrenders to the wolf and the lizard that which is rightfully theirs; and he preserves for future generations some unturned bits of earth far beyond road's end, beyond the ordered geometry of man's works, beyond the last outpost of man's concerns.

But land is money, and Americans are nothing if not commercially enterprising. In the "developer's" eyes, the way to make the wilderness more attractive for the sightseer is to improve it with hamburger stands, souvenir shops, motels, and barbered "scenic overlooks" complete with coin-operated binoculars. And the key to the success of all this endeavor is roads. Hiking is for the birdwatchers and other such nuts. "See the U. S. A. in your Chevrolet." If the developers have their way, it will some day be possible for Mom, Pop, Junior, and Sissie to spend two weeks touring the scenic spots of the United States without leaving the car except to drain and de-sludge their innards. Even the drive-in mortuary has come to pass.

If something is worth seeing, it's worth getting an automobile close enough to see it. U. S. Rubber Company executive H. E. Humphreys, Jr., complained to the Eleventh Highway Transportation Congress about the "anguished cries from some about 'paving the countryside.' Ladies and gentlemen, if 'beauty is in the eyes of the beholder,' where is it if people cannot go to see it? If our generation and succeeding ones become—as seems likely—more and more conscious of beauty, it will be because every road that is built can and should make more beauty accessible to more people. In a year's time, a few hundred people may be able to afford the time and the energy to *hike* through a woods or a park. But every day, hundreds of *thousands* may *drive* through those woods and parks, when carefully designed highways unfurl the whole, lovely view."

If the military-industrial complex threatens to destroy the quality of our lives through costly foreign adventures, the highway-automobile complex threatens to destroy the land we live in, by burying it under a shroud of asphalt.

Slowly—perhaps too slowly—the bitter truth of limited resources is penetrating the profligate American frontier consciousness. The forests are not limitless—they must be husbanded. Our mines are not bottomless—we must make efficient use of scrap and search for substitutes. The atmosphere is not unbounded—we can poison it beyond redemption. The tolerance of our rivers is not without end—they can swallow only so much of our noxious effluent before they die.

And now we must look to the land. It, too, is limited. If our automobile population doubles and doubles again, and doubles again (as their manufacturers so happily predict), and if we continue our futile efforts to provide for their free and rapid movement throughout the land (as the highway builders so fondly wish), the day will come when every lake will be encircled, every woods invaded, every park bisected, every trout stream bridged, every mountain tunneled, every city block cut, filled, viaducted, overpassed, interchanged, hard-surfaced, clover-leafed, its citizens isolated in a sea of asphalt and smothered in an ocean of exhaust fumes.

There are 3,600,000 square miles of land in the United States. There are 3,600,000 miles of roads and streets in the United States: one mile of road for every square mile of land. The land area covered by roads and their rights-of-way is estimated to be about 24,000 square miles—equal to the area of the state of West Virginia. But apparently we have only begun. California alone has completed 2,700 miles of freeways, but its master plan calls for an eventual 12,500 miles. Every mile of freeway consumes about 24 acres of land; every interchange eats up about 80 acres. The 41,000-mile Interstate system now under construction will gobble up more land than the state of Rhode Island.

All this says nothing of the area needed for storage of the automobiles. Los Angeles, which apparently will not be satisfied until it is solid concrete, devotes an estimated two-thirds of its downtown land area to the storage or movement of automobiles—about one-third for parking lots and garages and the rest for roads and freeways. It is estimated that by the year 1980, Los Angeles will have given up 34 square miles to its freeways—an area equal to a city the size of Miami.

These statistics, staggering as they are, say nothing of the destruction of the environment along the edges of these strips of asphalt. For some distance to either side of a freeway, life is not worth living. The noise, the stench, the pounding of rubber on bitumen, the incessant glare at night do little to improve the quality of life for ordinary flesh and blood. So perhaps the statistics just cited could easily be doubled to arrive at an estimate of the land area in America that will be rendered unfit for human habitation.

In the National Parks and other recreation areas, the destruction of values that accompanies the intrusion of a highway is even more widespread. Suppose, for example, that a square mile of wilderness is occupied by four separated parties of hikers. The chances are that each party could hike all day through the woods without being aware of the others—each party is left at peace to enjoy the solace of alone-ness in the wilderness. Suppose, now, we put each party in an automobile traveling at 60 miles per hour, with the occupants gazing in rapture as their highway "unfurls the whole, lovely view." Peace and solace have left the scene. Indeed, if two of these cars happen to be moving toward one another the drivers have no more than 30 seconds to avoid collision. The capacity of recreation land to absorb people is sharply reduced by highways.

Responsible voices already are warning us of the imminent destruction of our National Parks by highways. The creation of the Great Smokies National Park, says naturalist Michael Frome, "though designed to preserve natural resources, brought forth roads and more roads, people and more people." President Johnson's budget for fiscal year 1969 provided $122 million for the National Park Service, $27 million of which is earmarked for more road construction. "The National Park Service," says *The New York Times,* "has become increasingly acquiescent in recent years to automobile and highway pressure." Former park ranger Edward Abbey predicts sadly that any untouched area of natural beauty "is sure to be, someday, another national park complete with police, administrators, paved highways, automobile nature trails, official scenic viewpoints, designated campgrounds, Laundromats, cafeterias, Coke machines, flush toilets, and admission fees. If you wish to see it as it should be seen, don't wait— there's little time."

"Why," he asks, "is the Park Service generally so anxious to accommodate . . . the indolent millions born on wheels and suckled on gasoline who expect and demand paved highways to lead them in comfort, ease, and safety into every nook and corner of the national parks?"

An excellent question. We might expand its scope. Why, in the face of the imminent disappearance of our land under a carpet of asphalt, and with it all hope for an environment fit for human habitation, do we continue to spend some $10 billion per year on building highways? It is as though we were a nation of Frankensteins using our national treasure to create the monster that will destroy us.

Why? One answer is money.

Money for the land developers. Jack Goodman, travel writer for *The New York Times,* tells it like it is: "Palm Springs, Calif.—The bulldozers are busy along State Road 111. They are lumbering through the sunny groves of date palms, flattening portions of the lush Coachella Valley into graded areas for motels and resort lodges. The scene along the traffic-clogged highway linking the valley's major resort cities is a familiar one. The orange groves around Los Angeles disappeared in much the same way and for much the same reason: There is more money in harvesting winter-season vacationists in the luxurious desert center that sprawls from Palm Springs 30 miles south to Indio than there is in raising dates. While those familiar with this resort area—it is situated in the midst of the Agua Caliente Indian Reservation—may have reason to lament the steady disappearance of the giant Deglet Noor palms, travelers will find no cause to object. For them, the changing scene represents a boon. Resort hotels, motels, clubs, and spas in the area now number more than 1,000. And these accommodations will increase still further as the date groves disappear under the crunch of the bulldozers."

Money for the road builders. The National Highway Users Conference has estimated that, for every million dollars spent in the 41,000-mile interstate system now abuilding, materials are consumed at the rate of:

16,800 barrels of cement
694 tons of bituminous materials
485 tons of concrete and clay pipe
76,000 tons of sand, gravel, crushed stone, slag
24,000 pounds of explosives
121,000 gallons of petroleum products
99,000 board feet of lumber
600 tons of steel
57 new bulldozers and other construction machinery

Money for the automotive and petroleum industries—more roads, more cars and trucks, more gasoline pumped. The statistics are astronomical: One of every four retail dollars spent in this country is spent for the automobile; 75 billion gallons of fuel are consumed each year on our highways.

Money for the government. State and federal taxes on automobiles, trucks, and gasoiine totaled $17 billion in 1966; the states derive nearly one-fourth of all their tax revenues from motor vehicles and fuel.

Money for the banks and insurance companies. Americans borrow $30 billion *each year* to buy automobiles, and put out $6 billion in insurance premiums.

Money for everybody. Nearly 13 million people—1 person out of 6—are employed in manufacturing, selling, maintaining, or driving motor vehicles. The United States contains 60,000 car dealers, 211,000 service stations, 114,000 auto repair shops, 40,000 motels, and God only knows how many nickel-and-dime parking lots. The manufacture of automobiles consumes 20 per cent of all the steel, 12 per cent of the aluminum, 10 per cent of the copper, 51 per cent of the lead, 15 per cent of the nickel, 35 per cent of the zinc, and 60 per cent of the rubber used in the United States.

Any doubt as to the commercial importance of highways and the need for commercial interests to build even more of them is dispelled by scanning the survey of U. S. industry, "National Economic Review," published annually as a supplement to *The New York Times.* The January 8, 1968, issue is full of advertisements by chambers of commerce attempting to entice industry to build new plants in one location or another. Here is a sampling from those ads:

Northeast Pennsylvania: "A dynamically modern network of express highways . . . to provide swift access to the major markets of the United States—to the north, east, south, and west."

Daytona Beach, Florida: "Located at the heart of Florida's Interstate Highway System—the junction of I-95 and I-4."

Middlesex County, New Jersey: "Position at the hub of superhighways such as Interstate Route 287, New Jersey Turnpike, and Garden State Parkway."

Randolph Township, New Jersey: "Located on Route 10, just minutes from Interstate 80, Interstate 78, and Interstate 287."

Kansas City, Missouri: "New and improved roads and highways— $108,385,000 worth! The bonds passed. The largest portion will go for the new South Midtown Freeway."

Indianapolis, Indiana: "Seven Interstate Freeways connect Indianapolis to the Nation."

The other major theme in these advertisements is the wealth of recreational amenities in each locality:

Columbus, Georgia: "There's an abundance of fresh, fresh air . . . Recreation? Columbus boasts of wide fairways with easy roughs. Big lakes with hungry fish. Fat quail that fly slowly."

West Virginia: "Dozens of Blue Chip giants have found a fresh outlook in West Virginia. They've discovered that industry and people thrive in the clean, pure air of the Mountain State."

Williamsport, Pennsylvania: "There isn't an industrial plant anywhere in our Lycoming County located more than fifteen minutes from beautiful mountain trout waters. That's why we aren't surprised to see a dapper fisherman, in white shirt and tie, by a stream over the noon hour."

The irony of these advertisements is that the more successful they are, the less true they become.

Another reason for our permissive, even indulgent attitude toward the ravages of the bulldozer is love—our tenacious love for the automobile, the symbol of power, independence, freedom, and sexual prowess for which the average American spends as much each year as he does for the food to sustain his life. It amounts, according to Lewis Mumford, to a religion, and, says he, ". . . the sacrifices that people are prepared to make for this religion stand outside the realm of rational criticism."

The first thing that a young man buys, as soon as he has shoes on his feet, is an automobile. This he often does at considerable sacrifice to himself—he may scrimp on lunch money, forgo another suit, cut down on booze or cigarettes, even force himself to ration those pleasurable hours with the young ladies. No matter. When he slips behind the wheel, he is King of all Creation.

Once these sacrifices are made, he will defend with the ferocity of a mother lion his native-born right to drive his car anywhere, at any time, over any route, and to park it when he arrives. Any attempt by anyone to infringe these rights is, in his eyes, a serious blow at individual freedom and the American Way. Nor is this sentiment a youthful peccadillo that vanishes with sober maturity. On the contrary: the passion for this American freedom burns even more fiercely in the breast of the gray-templed, bay-windowed motorist. If he wants to go

from point *A* to point *B* and there's no road between, then, God-
dammit it, they'd better build one!

The crime we are committing is no less than the murder of our
once-lovely land. The dual motives: money and love, or, rather, community greed and individual selfishness. Congressman Kluczynski recently wrapped them up in one brief statement: "Our highways are
the basic element in the national transportation system. They are the
physical plant upon which the continued economic and social strength
of this country depends. I am convinced that we are going to have to
develop new and different kinds of transportation . . . but I am equally
convinced that *all* of these revised or added transportation forms will
have to be built around the highway networks. Americans are not
going to give up their cars."

Perhaps so. But if we go down that road, and we are well along
it already, the land is doomed.

Magical Highway Trust Fund

There are those who say the American Dream is a split-level in the suburbs with a half-acre, a guaranteed annual income, and membership in the Best Club. Others maintain it's just a matter of all the booze and broads you can handle. Not so. The American Dream is to drive from coast to coast without encountering a traffic light.

Most people believe the dream was born with Henry Ford, but the seed was planted long before that. It was at about the time of the American Civil War that a self-taught German engineer named Nikolaus August Otto began to fiddle with the idea of an engine in which the burning process took place inside the cylinder, instead of outside, as was the case with the very inefficient steam engines of that day. Otto tinkered with the steam engine cylinder and illuminating gas, trying to obtain combustion of the gas without an explosion that would wreck the engine. In 1876, he succeeded. The result was the first four-stroke-cycle, internal combustion engine, which developed in its single cylinder the impressive total of 3 horsepower at a speed of 180 rpm. It was so much quieter than the noisy steam engine that folks called it the "Silent Otto." For those who would wish to pay obeisance to that unprepossessing piece of hardware, which, over the next ninety years, wrought changes upon the lives of mankind more sweeping than any single device ever conceived before or since, it is on display at the museum of Klöckner-Humboldt-Deutz near Cologne.

A few years later, another German, named Gottlieb Daimler, put the internal combustion engine on wheels to produce a self-propelled vehicle. Then in 1909, twenty-seven years after the Silent Otto, Henry Ford announced his intention to put the nation on wheels, thus setting

18

the scene for the great love affair of the American for his car, a passion that has culminated in an attempt to hard-surface the entire nation. Said Henry: "I will build a motor car for the great multitude. It will be large enough for the family but small enough for the individual to run and care for. It will be constructed of the best materials, by the best men to be hired, after the simplest designs that modern engineering can devise. But it will be so low in price that no man making a good salary will be unable to own one—and enjoy with his family the blessing of hours of pleasure in God's great open spaces."

And Mr. Ford did so. And he saw that it was good. And the citizens were pleased, and they bought the Ford cars, and later the Chevrolets, as fast as they could be made. They had found the ultimate toy. But one thing more was needed—the toy required a playground, the larger the better.

At about the time Mr. Ford made his ominous pronouncement, there were only 190,000 miles of surfaced (stone, brick, gravel, macadam) rural roads in all the United States, but work was going forward on many fronts to increase this as rapidly as possible to give the machine ample *Lebensraum*. The first rural road of portland cement concrete was laid that same year, just outside Detroit, Michigan, a 1-mile stretch that was opened to traffic, appropriately enough, on Independence Day, 1909. Experiments were already afoot to smooth and stabilize the macadam roads by pouring asphalt and other bituminous materials upon the crushed-stone roadway.

In 1909, total sales of passenger cars in the United States were just under 125,000. By 1916, just seven years later, this had increased more than tenfold: sales of passenger cars that year exceeded 1,500,-000, and the demand to build more roads was in full voice. It was in this year that the magic formula was found—the first Federal Aid Road Act signed by President Wilson, July 11, 1916, put the federal government in the road-building business in a big way. This Act provided that half the funds used for road-building in the states would be supplied by the federal government, provided the states agreed to bear the cost of maintenance once the road was built. The Act also stipulated that the federal contribution was not to exceed $10,000 per mile. Typical cost of a modern urban expressway easily is a thousand times as much.

Injection of federal money was a marvelous tonic for the road
builders. In 1916, the total expenditures for construction of state-
administered highways was about $50 million. Only four years later,
in 1920, this figure had mushroomed to nearly a quarter of a billion
dollars. But the real secret for building roads was discovered in 1956,
and since then this figure has risen to exceed $10 billion each year.
Best of all, the magic formula discovered that year guarantees that
the money will continue to be available every year; in fact, the more
roads we build, the more money becomes available for building yet
more.

The magic formula is known as the Highway Trust Fund. It was
invented in 1956, when the nation entered on the greatest spree of
highway building in the history of the world, a program that has
justifiably been called "the greatest public works program in history."
Launched by legislation signed by President Eisenhower in June,
1956, the National System of Interstate and Defense Highways will
be a 41,000-mile system of super roads connecting 90 per cent of
all the cities in the nation over 50,000 population. The system is
designed to handle the traffic expected in 1975; and 90 per cent of
its cost will be paid out of federal funds, only 10 per cent by the
various states. This program is superimposed upon the regular, continuing federal-aid highway programs, which have built a million
miles of roads financed by the states and the federal government on
a 50-50 basis.

This ambitious highway measure, passed by a voice vote in the
House and an 89-1 roll call in the Senate, projected a total cost for
the system at about $40 billion, to be spent over the next thirteen
years. (The estimated cost for the program has since increased to
something like $55 or $60 billion, and the completion date has crept
up by stages from the original target of 1972 to something more like
1975 or 1976.) After much wrangling in Congress about how to pay
for this monumental program, a scheme was devised that not only
assures a steady flow of funds, but also renders the flow all but im-
mune from the year-to-year whimsies of a fickle legislature. Under
this scheme, a Highway Trust Fund was established, into which pour
in an unceasing stream tax money from the sale of gasoline and other
motorists' necessities such as spare parts and tires. At the outset one

cent of the federal tax on every gallon of gasoline fed the Trust Fund; this has now increased to four cents. ✔

This self-perpetuating fund simply grows—independent of any new authorization by Congress. Each year the Administration doles out the bounty to the states as their highway departments come up with plans that seem reasonable to the Federal Bureau of Public Roads. As the road mileage increases, more cars take to the roads and drive more miles, burning more gallons of gasoline, wearing out more tires, and feeding more money into the inviolate Trust Fund. A perfect closed loop calculated to keep smiles on the faces of the highway builders.

During the decade following enactment of the Interstate Highway Act, all went smoothly. The money poured into the Highway Trust Fund in a golden stream. Engineers across the land drew lines on maps, and the bulldozers followed, in increasing numbers. While each year Washington budget-makers strained to find the money for a thousand crying needs, and Congressional committee rooms echoed to the voices pleading for funds to pour on this or that hurt, the inviolable Highway Trust Fund plowed ahead under its own power, the money pouring into one end and out the other, as though regulated by an immutable law of nature.

The pork-barrel aspects of this gigantic operation gave it apparent immunity from the tug and haul of all other earthly endeavors. "We want more roads," the nation had said, and more roads it was getting. The bill had providentially been paid in advance. It remained only to dole out the largess year by year.

It took a major land war in Asia and the threat of runaway inflation to cast the first faint shadow of doubt over the operation. In the fall of 1966—with war costs mounting, spending levels rocketing above $100 billion, and heavy federal borrowing pressing prices upward—President Johnson looked about for ways to reduce federal spending without curtailing vital programs. By mischance, his eye fell on the highway program.

Federal grants to the states for highway building had been running along at about $4 billion per year, and highway builders anticipated an allocation of $4.4 billion for fiscal year 1967. On the day before Thanksgiving, however, the Administration announced that

the states would receive only $3.3 billion. This was not a cut in allo-
cations, it was simply a "freeze" of money already allocated, a delay
in handing it to the states for use.

The announcement had been cagily timed. Election day was safely
past, and the long Thanksgiving weekend might provide a cooling-
off period for any Congressional or gubernatorial hotheads.

But the President had underestimated the power of the highway
lobby. No sooner had the freeze been announced, than White House
wires began to buzz with messages from the state capitals expressing
the displeasure of the various state highway departments and governors; letters and telegrams from road contractors rained down upon
the congressmen, and they, in turn, rose upon the floor of Congress
to denounce the President.

"Illegal" and "unwarranted" were some of the terms used to describe the freeze. The chairmen of the Public Works committees of
the House and Senate announced angrily that they would hold joint
hearings to investigate the cutback in highway funds. Representative
George H. Fallon, chairman of the House Committee on Public
Works, said "the cutback and freeze makes it impossible to maintain an orderly highway construction program. The failure to do so
is not only economically shortsighted but puts us in the highly questionable position of acceding to an action that must spell death and
injury to the thousands of people who will be involved in accidents."

Engineering News-Record, the authoritative weekly construction
magazine, echoed the life-and-limb argument: "Delayed completion
of new highways claims a high price in lives and property lost in
traffic accidents, as well as in the economic losses caused by traffic
congestion. Individuals and groups concerned with highway construction should do their best to make [their wishes known] to the Administration, and to Congress."

The individuals and groups concerned with highway construction
needed no prodding. Their wishes were flowing to Washington in
abundance. Robert S. Holmes, president of the politically potent
American Road Builders Association, burned the midnight oil preparing testimony for the joint Congressional hearings on the fund
freeze. As general manager of highway construction for U. S. Steel

Corp., Mr. Holmes was quick to announce that the freeze would eliminate a half-million tons of steel from highway construction.

Massachusetts Governor John Volpe, himself a one-time road contractor, charged that the President had designs on the frozen highway funds, that he intended to use them for other purposes. This, said Volpe, would be a "misuse of gas tax money" and a "direct violation of the intent of Congress." The full $1.1 billion in frozen funds, he said, should be restored at once.

On February 13, in a move to take some sting out of the rising storm, Secretary of Transportation Alan Boyd announced that the frozen funds would be released just as soon as economic conditions permitted. But his words were as effective as a meat ball thrown to a hungry lion. Representative Fallon and Senator Jennings Randolph went busily ahead with plans for their joint hearings. The Building Trades Department of the AFL-CIO adopted a resolution demanding restoration of the frozen funds, warning that the slowdown in construction would seriously jeopardize the industry and cause substantial increases in unemployment.

On February 27, Secretary Boyd was up on Capitol Hill testifying at the joint Public Works hearings. He had brought with him a large chunk of rich, red meat to throw to the lions: the Administration had decided to release $175 million of the frozen $1.1 billion immediately, and promised $225 million more before the end of June, which was the end of the fiscal year. Further, he promised that the Administration would release to the states the full $4.4 billion authorized by Congress for the coming fiscal year, starting July 1. As though unwilling to let his transportation secretary get all the credit, Mr. Johnson, back in the White House, made the same announcement, at almost the same moment.

The President said the partial release of funds was prompted by an easing of the inflation threat, but many in Washington saw it as a bending to the will of an irresistible political force. Even so, the lions were still hungry. Senator Randolph said the hearings would continue. Representative William C. Cramer, ranking Republican on the House roads subcommittee, demanded that the President release the entire $1.1 billion. "This is nothing more than a token gesture," he said. "The Administration has converted the federal-aid highway

program from a stable program for which advance planning could
be undertaken with the assurance of orderly construction financed
by an inviolate trust fund to an 'iffy' program which goes up and
down like a Yo-Yo depending upon the policies and economic theo-
ries of the Administration."

On February 28, President Johnson sent his budget director,
Charles L. Schultz, down to the joint Congressional hearings to capi-
tulate. In his testimony, Mr. Schultz hinted broadly that very substantial sums of money would be restored to the highway program
within a few weeks. When Representative Fallon asked how good a
bet this was, Mr. Schultz smiled and replied that, although he was
not a betting man, he would be willing to put a substantial stake on
the probability. This satisfied the congressmen. Although several
days of hearings still were scheduled, they were abruptly ended.

On March 17, Mr. Johnson made good his promise: he released
an additional $350 million. Three months later he released the re-
mainder of the $1.1 billion. Said the President, "Inflationary pres-
sures have subsided." *Engineering News-Record* believed there might
be another reason. "Administration officials soon realized they had
a tiger by the tail," said the construction weekly. And they loosed
their hold on the highway funds "before the aroused beast mauled
them severely. . . . Contractors, equipment dealers and manufacturers, material suppliers and others lost no time in complaining to
their congressional delegations in no uncertain terms. The clamor
came through loud and clear at the White House."

This, the magazine said, should be a lesson to the President and
also to his new Secretary of Transportation: "Never underestimate
the raw power of the federal-aid highway program. Politically, it
contains something of benefit to every member of Congress, something he can show the home folks that he has got for them. Practically, the vested interests with a major stake in the program are
strong, vocal and well organized; they pack tremendous clout."

The great highway battle of 1967 ended with a clean victory for
the forces of highway construction. By spring it was apparent that,
even with the very temporary setback occasioned by the President's
imprudent shenanigans, 1967 would be the biggest year the road
builders had ever had. The states planned to spend more than $5.2

billion during the year, an estimate that would increase to record-breaking proportions when the unfrozen funds swelled the flood. And 1968 promised to be even better; the President had already stated his intention to release $4.4 billion to the states.

Although there had been some slippage in the Interstate Highway program, great things had been accomplished. By mid-1967, 23,756 miles of new highway were open to traffic, 5,668 miles were under construction, and 10,070 were in the process of design or right-of-way acquisition. The total of 39,494 miles was 96 per cent of the projected final figure of 41,000. A total of $28.6 billion had been spent. Estimated completion date had moved back from 1972 to 1975.

For several months, during the summer and early fall of 1967, all was serene on the highway front. The battle had been won, and, seemingly, the principle of the untouchableness of the Highway Trust Fund established. But inflation, despite the President's pronouncement, had not subsided; war costs continued to mount; budget deficits continued to widen. In belated response to these pressures, Mr. Johnson finally went to Congress with a request for a 10 per cent tax surcharge. But Congress was adamant; no tax increase until the President cut spending.

The resulting protracted pull-and-haul between the President and Congress was not one of the more heroic chapters in American political annals. Frustrated in his attempts to get a tax increase, furious at what he felt to be irresponsible yammering from Congress about spending cuts, Johnson countered with a right cross to the body, a blow that the men on Capitol Hill felt below the belt. They wanted spending cuts? All right, he would give them spending cuts. He proceeded to freeze funds for certain low-priority military construction projects and for the time-honored "pork barrel" construction involving rivers and harbors and flood control. Further, he instructed Transportation Secretary Boyd to send a telegram to each of the fifty governors warning that massive cuts might be necessary in federal aid for highway construction. The telegram asked the governors to give their estimate of the economic effects on their states of a freeze in highway funds amounting to as much as $2.2 billion, or half the program for the year. The telegram went out on October 9.

The reaction was swift and intense. Within two days, replies were in from no less than sixteen outraged governors. Typical was that from Governor Ronald Reagan of California, who fumed that a cutback in highway money would be a "dishonest and a grave mistake on the part of the Administration, since under federal law, highways are built with gasoline tax funds placed in trust for highway purposes. They cannot legally be diverted or used as a tool for fiscal gimmicks." This response ignored the fact that Boyd's proposal had been merely to "freeze" the money, that is, to delay spending it. When the economic storm had passed, the funds would be there in the Trust Fund, waiting to lay asphalt.

Flak from the governors descended upon the White House and the Transportation Department, and it was accompanied by heavy bombardment from congressmen and the highway lobby. According to a close associate of Secretary Boyd, incoming fire directed at him included a rocket from the President, who was fuming because the Secretary had released a copy of his telegram to the press.

The telegram, said *Engineering News-Record,* was "intended to give Congress a taste of what it means to demand that the Administration make sweeping reductions in the federal budget as the price of a tax increase." Most other observers agreed that the move was an attempt to put pressure on Congress rather than a serious effort to cut spending. In Congress, it rankled. "It looks to me," said Representative Charles S. Gubser, Republican of California, "as if the President were trying to use these popular programs to put the screws on Congress." Other congressmen accused the President of trying to "badger" them. Said Representative William C. Cramer, Democrat of Florida, Johnson's move was "an obvious sledgehammer tactic to bludgeon the Congress into passing the tax surcharge . . . instead of reducing unnecessary federal expenditures." Representative Fletcher Thompson, Republican of Georgia, accused Mr. Johnson of "trickery," "chicanery," and "blackmail."

Grumbling in the Senate was more discreet. Senator Jennings Randolph, chairman of the Senate Public Works Committee, said that "nearly every senator" had complained to him about the proposed highway fund cutback. He noted that, interestingly enough, the complaints about cutbacks in other construction projects had been very light by comparison. "A dam that helps prevent a flood can be vital," he said, "but there's a detachment about that kind of project that you don't get with money for highways or schools. Those things are more personal to people than regular public works."

A few days later, Congress responded. On October 18, the House whooped through a bill, by a vote of 238-164, demanding that President Johnson cut nonmilitary spending by a minimum of $5 billion. The bill specifically exempted a number of activities from budget cuts, to wit: Social Security, old-age assistance, veterans' pensions, the Post Office, Internal Revenue department, Medicare, payments on the national debt, all military and related operations, and, last but not least, highway construction. Debate on the bill was often raucous, undisciplined, irrelevant, and even downright ludicrous. At the end of it all, the oldest member of the House, eighty-five-year-old Barratt O'Hara, Democrat of Illinois, was heard to say, "For the first time in all the years I've been here, I'm ashamed of this House."

Such was the immunity of highway spending that it ranked with Social Security and payments on the national debt. Some other less essential programs were chopped. A record $1 billion was lopped from foreign aid, poverty funds were slashed by $300 million, model cities by $350 million. The rent supplements program was cut from $40 million to $10 million, which left it just barely breathing. All these cuts the members of Congress seemed to bear with equanimity, but, said Representative George H. Fallon, "Any cutback in the federal-aid highway program would amount to breaking faith with the states, and with the motorists who are paying the bill."

As luck would have it, one week after the controversial Boyd telegram, the 53rd annual convention of the American Association of State Highway Officials (AASHO) opened in Salt Lake City. One of the most politically potent organizations in the nation, AASHO includes in its membership the top officials from state highway departments as well as the top highway people from the federal government. At the Salt Lake City convention, meeting rooms and lobbies buzzed with the voices of incensed highway engineers speculating on the outcome of the Boyd message. In an action that *Engineering News-Record* termed "unprecedented," the highway officials adopted a resolution warning that any cutback in federal highway funds would have "great adverse effect upon the program and would not be in the public interest." The AASHO resolution demanded an end to "the atmosphere of uncertainty that has engulfed the federal-aid highway program" and assurance that the program continue "at the maximum level possible."

By now the outcry in the construction industry had reached such proportions that even the industry magazine, *Engineering News-Record,* felt constrained to question the sacrosanct position of highway building in the economy. "In a time of national economic strife, with defense expenditures soaring and the possibility of runaway inflation threatening the economy, should any federal spending program be sacrosanct?" asked the editor. "Should the highway program be spared? Are expenditures for roads more important than those for flood control, urban renewal, airports or conservation? Or, for that matter, for education, public health, the war on poverty, or any one of a host of other programs? . . . Can we really expect to build federal-aid roads at a normal rate when other worthwhile programs are being delayed, crippled, even cancelled? Are roads *that* important?"

Apparently the readers of *Engineering News-Record* thought they were. In a later issue, under the heading "The Road Program *Is* Something Special," the magazine published letters from several irate readers with the rueful comment that the editorial had "raised the hackles of some ENR readers." Typical was the letter from J. Anton Hagios, National Good Roads Association: "Your editorial prompts me to say to you, 'Et tu, Brute.' The editorial concludes with the question, 'Are roads *that* important?' Let me state here, categorically, emphatically and unequivocally: *'They are!' "* Highways, said Mr. Hagios, represent a "current, continuing and universal need, affecting and benefiting virtually all people from cradle to grave." And if the worst were to happen, he pointed out, and World War III were to break out, look at the mess we would be in with only a half-finished highway system on our hands.

But so far, the suggestion that road funds might be cut remained only a threat. At the beginning of January, 1968, three months after the Boyd telegram, the Department of Transportation notified the states that they would receive $1.1 billion for highways for the first quarter of the year, which was exactly one-quarter of the promised $4.4 billion for the year. The Administration had not followed through yet on its threatened cut. And, commented the UPI, "any such move would certainly encounter strong opposition in Congress. Several legislators threatened to introduce bills to prohibit Boyd from trimming the program."

By now the controversy was becoming a partisan issue. In a 13-page report issued January 7, the Republican Coordinating Committee charged that the Administration was using highway funds "as a tool for playing budget politics with the Congress, by repeatedly withholding and threatening to withhold construction funds from the states." The President, said the Republicans, should "stop using interstate highway funds for partisan political purposes."

Finally, two weeks later, the second shoe dropped. Secretary Boyd announced that $600 million in federal highway funds would be held back for 1968 as a "modest but essential move to combat general inflationary tendencies in the economy." This was a far smaller cut than the $2.2 billion he had hinted at in his telegram to the governors more than three months before, but still it was a substantial sum of money.

The outraged response from the states this time was an echo of the reaction the year before. In Pennsylvania, Secretary of Highways Robert G. Bartlett said, "This is a black day for highway construction in Pennsylvania." With the announcement of the cut had come rumors that the Administration had nefarious plans to use the Trust Fund money for other purposes. This would be illegal, said Bartlett. "Congress set up inviolate—and I underscore inviolate—rights where monies that go into the highway trust fund must be used only for highways."

Pennsylvania's Governor Raymond Shafer, charging that the cutbacks made a "complete farce" of highway planning, sent telegrams to the entire Congressional delegation of his state, two senators and twenty-seven representatives, urging them to "join with me in a direct appeal to the President that the cuts be restored." Further, asked Shafer, each legislator should support the legislation that had been introduced in Congress which would restrict the President's freedom of action to "manipulate" the Highway Trust Fund.

"The motorists and the economy of the area need the highways," grumbled the Philadelphia *Bulletin,* "and more than a placing and passing of blame is required."

In the midst of their travail, the highway builders could take comfort from the knowledge that the freeze was, after all, only a temporary measure to take some of the steam out of a dangerously overheated war economy; it was not prompted by an aversion to building highways. The four pennies from the sale of every gallon of gasoline would continue to pile up in the Trust Fund, and, once the economy cooled, it would be there, waiting to buy more bulldozers and pay engineers to draw more lines on maps.

While the funding squabble continued, however, the highway establishment was beginning to feel pains in other quarters.

Gasoline Alley

There are about 3,600,000 square miles of land area in the continental United States. That is all. Unlike the human population, the gross national product, and the number of registered motor vehicles, this number does not increase each year. In the land, and only in the land, does the wealth of our nation reside. Each acre that we cover with asphalt is no longer available for building a home, a school, or a hospital; it is no longer available for a tennis court, a swimming pool, a bicycle path, a farm, a factory, or an airport; nor can it serve as a bird sanctuary, a wildlife refuge, or a wooded grove.

We have now constructed a mile of road for every square mile of land in this country. How many will be enough? Two miles? Three?

To build highways, we are consuming land and other irreplaceable resources at a staggering rate. When completed, the Interstate system will be thirty times as long as the Great Wall of China. The Bureau of Public Roads has estimated the enormous wealth that we are pouring into that 41,000-mile system: "The pavement area of the system, assembled in one huge parking lot, would be 20 miles square and could accommodate two-thirds of all the motor vehicles in the United States. New right-of-way needed amounts to 1½ million acres. Total excavations will move enough material to bury Connecticut knee-deep in dirt. Sand, gravel, and crushed stone for the construction would build a wall 50 feet wide and nine feet high completely around the world. The concrete would build driveways for 35 million homes. The steel will take 30 million tons of iron ore, 18 million tons of coal, and 6½ million tons of limestone. Lumber and timber requirements would take all the trees from a 400-square-mile forest. Enough culvert and drain pipe is needed to equal the combined water and sewer systems in six cities the size of Chicago." In acquiring the rights-of-way, 750,000 pieces of property will be taken.

All this in a day when millions of Americans live in crumbling tenements and ramshackle huts unfit for human habitation.

No land in this country is merely lying there useless. Even the swamps, the deserts, and the wilderness areas have their uses in nature, and their existence is indispensable to the well-being of man. When a highway is built, therefore, the land that it gobbles up must be withdrawn from other uses. To serve the motorist, cornfields disappear, homes are destroyed, redwoods are leveled. Further, the state may take the land regardless of the wishes of the owner. The power of eminent domain, which has been called the most drastic of all governmental powers, permits the state to take private property for public use, provided only that the owner is given a fair price for it.

Not only is *private* property vulnerable to acquisition by state highway departments, but, in many states, the highway department also has the power to take *public* lands, such as parks, schools, recreation areas, historical sites, without the permission of the governmental unit administering that land. And, when the state does not have the power, it can turn to the federal government for help. The federal government can, and does, condemn such land for highway use. Municipal parklands and even cemeteries have been acquired for road-building in this way.

One cynic claims that the California Highway Commission could build a highway right through the state capitol building in Sacramento, and no one could stop it, including the state legislature and the governor. An exaggeration? Perhaps. But clearly the power over the land that resides in our state highway departments reflects the highest priority of our society—highways.

Expressways swallow precious urban land at a monstrous rate. In Chicago, five freeway interchanges alone have consumed 275 acres of irreplaceable ground—lost to human uses and lost to the city tax rolls. Planners in Arlington County, Virginia, eying 300 acres of underdeveloped land just a few miles south of the Pentagon, see it as "one of the hottest pieces of property on the Eastern seaboard," with potential for perhaps three-quarters of a billion dollars' worth of building development. But all these buildings would need so many lanes of expressway to handle the traffic to nearby Washington that there would be little room left for the buildings. A pretty dilemma.

When the buildings are already there, the problem is simplified: you evict the occupants, smash the buildings to rubble, and bring the highway through. The resulting ribbons of asphalt and spaghetti-like tangles of ramps and interchanges may present a breathtaking geometrical pattern from the air, and they may bring a swell of pride to a highway engineer's breast, but they destroy human lives as surely as a plague, and they destroy the city as surely as bombs.

No one knows exactly how many people have been forced out of their homes by highways. D. R. Neuzil, of the Institute of Transportation and Traffic Engineering, University of California, cites studies estimating the present rate at 90,000 persons per year for the nation as a whole. He estimates the displacement rate to be 15,000 per year for the state of California alone. Neuzil cites another study estimating the number of homes to be demolished for highways in California during the period 1947-1969 to be 98,000. A report of the House Committee on Public Works, published in July, 1967, estimates that, during the three-year period from 1967 to 1970, federally aided highway construction will displace 146,950 households, 16,679 businesses and nonprofit organizations, and 5,000 farms. The editors of *Fortune,* in their book, *The Exploding Metropolis,* report that so many highway-displaced houses were being moved through the streets of Los Angeles that the chore of shifting the overhead traffic lights out of the way became burdensome. That problem was solved by designing an arm on which the lights could be hung and swung out of the way as the houses went by.

Building the Hollywood Freeway required the demolition of 90 buildings and the moving of 1,728 others. When the New Jersey Turnpike swept through Elizabeth, 240 buildings were destroyed or moved. The Crosstown Expressway planned for the heart of Philadelphia will displace 6,500 persons, mostly Negro. The Hudson River Expressway in New York, also still on paper, will displace more than 800 residents of North Tarrytown alone, or nearly 10 per cent of the population. And so it goes, in town after town, city after city.

Human beings are made of flesh and blood, not asphalt and concrete. When they are displaced from their homes and forced to re-
establish their lives elsewhere, they suffer. Marvin G. Cline, in an
article in the *Highway Research Board Record*, notes that displacement strikes at the very foundations of the resident's sense of psycho-
logical well-being: "When the residents of the West End [in Boston]
were forced out, many of them exhibited . . . the clinical syndrome
of grief. A depression similar to the experiences one has at the loss of
a loved one seems to have persisted in some cases over a period of
years . . . and it is the feelings that the residents have for their neighborhood which are the most important determinant of the social and
economic value of the area. Social disorganization almost inevitably
results in physical and economic disorganization, which ordinarilly
can be expected to spread to adjacent areas." This study, incidentally,
is rare. The library shelves are full of reports on the *economic* impact of highway building; reports on the *human* impact are all but
nonexistent.

When a highway slashes through a city, it is usually the low-income
housing areas that suffer, often the Negro ghetto. This does nothing
to improve the attitude of the Negro toward the white power structure. This brutal, unjust shoving aside of black human beings to make
highways for white motorists no doubt has played its part in nurtur-
ing the outrage against society that fires the black revolt. Payment for
property confiscated by the state means nothing to these residents,
since most of them are renters. They must simply move from slum
to slum, with conditions worsening at every move as the supply of
low-income housing diminishes.

An unsigned letter, postmarked Newark, New Jersey, received by
urban expert Daniel Patrick Moynihan and published in *Time* magazine shortly after the Newark riots, should be required reading for
all highway builders:

"Dear Sir we are writing you all for help and justice here in New
Jersey. We are asking you all to go forward and help us. . . . We
need peace and justice here in Newark and all over New Jersey.
They are tearing down our homes and building up medical collages
and motor clubs and parking lots and we need decent private homes
to live in. They are tearing down our best schools and churches to
build a highway.

"We are over here in provity and bondage. There are supposed to be justice for all. Where are that justice? Where are justice?"

Compounding the injustice being done to human beings is the illogic of destroying low-income housing in the face of a growing shortage of low-income housing. The reason for the shortage, aside from the fact that we are destroying the houses, is that we do not seem to be able to find the money to build low-income houses. One reason for that failure is that we are spending our money on other things, such as highways. Ten million dollars a *mile* is cheap for a city expressway these days.

Another reason for the lack of housing funds is the declining tax income of the center city, and, according to a study made by Wilfred Owen for the Brookings Institution, "One of the most significant factors in the declining tax base of the city is the liquidation of properties being absorbed by major highway projects." Which seems to bring us full circle.

Highway engineers, given the choice of buildings to destroy, will naturally choose the low-income areas. The community hardly notices the loss of these undesirable structures, and, of course, the land costs less to acquire. Since every dollar saved in right-of-way acquisition is a dollar more that can be spent in placing asphalt, highway engineers are naturally careful about whose land they condemn.

This is not to imply that the highway engineer is insensitive to the pain he causes. Indeed, his awareness of that pain, coupled with considerations of economy, often lead him to select city land that is uninhabited—park lands and waterfront areas. A 1957 statement by the American Association of State Highway Officials, titled "Policy on Arterial Highways in Urban Areas," gives highway engineers helpful hints on where to find land in the metropolitan areas for highway building:

"Most cities have land areas outside the central core that lend themselves to the location of new highways. The improvement of radial highways in the past stimulated land development along them and often left wedges of relatively unused land between these ribbons of development. Such wedges resulted, perhaps, from steep slopes, valleys, or streams, or the absence of adequate street connections. These undeveloped land areas may offer locations for radial routes.

"Favorable location may be found within or along the boundaries of parks and other sizeable tracts of city or institutional property that disrupt the regularity of a rectangular street pattern. These locations have the advantage of minimum property damage and few intersection problems. Such open and possibly wooded areas, however, are valuable assets to a community, and opposition to their use for highways will develop. Narrow strips along the edges of sizeable parks might be used for highways. Where more park space is desired, these strips might be replaced by acquiring other areas for parks."

The report does not indicate where such other areas might be found in a densely populated urban area. So, at a time when urban planners are scrabbling for every bit of open green area to assuage the asphalt-blunted senses of city dwellers, we find the highway builders eying the pitifully few remaining acres of green as probable corridors for new expressways.

Even in the midst of the city—*especially* in the midst of the city—the spirit of man craves a glimpse of green, a small open space innocent of the works of man. Ann Louise Strong, a land-use expert, puts it clearly: "Genetics may in time produce a race able to subsist solely and happily on concrete and steel, asphalt, plastic, chrome; content to breathe smog and fumes; asking only superhighways, superchargers, and fuel stations with juke boxes for its delight. The eventuality is not imminent. For health and a sense of well-being, people need frequent contact with nature. They will look for reality and meaning in rivers and clear streams, in the ebb and flow of tides along clean shores, in a few trees and a patch of green along the towering structures of their cities. Open space fulfills a present and future human need, and that need should be satisfied."

If the highway builders have their way, the only ebb and flow available for the citizen to observe will be the diurnal rhythm of motor traffic on the expressway—toward the city center in the morning; outbound in the evening.

In Memphis, Tennessee, the six-lane Interstate Route 40 will run right through Overton Park, 340 acres of urban greenery containing playgrounds, baseball fields, a golf course, art gallery and academy, and a shell for music and drama. Business groups in town support this desecration. The local paper says it will make the park "far more accessible to visitors." Says Spencer M. Smith, Jr., secretary of the Citizens Committee on Natural Resources (a national organization),

"It will kill one of the most beautiful city parks in the country. It is one of the greatest evidences of stupidity in modern times."

According to San Antonio city planner S. P. Zisman, the proposed North Expressway in San Antonio deserves mention for the variety of damage it threatens to produce. The expressway, says he, "curves and winds its way through virtually every element" of a system of park lands and recreation areas. It crosses "an Audubon bird sanctuary and Olmos Creek, a tributary in its natural state to be converted into a concrete ditch; it moves along a picnic ground and recreation area obliterating a Girl Scout Day Camp and a nature trail; it stretches across the Olmos Basin and rises to enormous height, roller coaster fashion, to go over Olmos Dam; it severs the campus of Incarnate Word College, forcing the closing of an elementary school; it cuts through the lands of the San Antonio Zoo; it blocks off the half-built public school gymnasium, slides along the rim of the famous Sunken Garden, hovering over in cantilever the edge of the outdoor theater, squeezes itself between this and the municipal school stadium, blocking a major entrance; it slashes through residential areas, shaves a municipal golf course, and then brutally cuts across a wooded portion of the San Antonio River's natural water course, one of the few remaining wilderness touches left within the city."

According to the magazine *City*, the only opposition in the nine-year fight to prevent construction of this expressway has been the San Antonio Conservation Society, "which has spent $50,000 and worn out three presidents in the course of battle."

Fairmount Park in Philadelphia is the largest city park in the world. It includes 4,000 acres, running for about 8 miles along both banks of the Wissahickon Creek and the Schuylkill River, right through the heart of the densely populated city. Several years ago, the Schuylkill Expressway, Interstate 76, was built along the west bank of the Schuylkill for a distance of about 4 miles, knifing through the center of the park, and, for long stretches, effectively cutting off residents of the city from the banks of the river. ✓

In Wilmington, Delaware, Interstate 95 horribly mutilates what was once a beautiful, quiet park along the Brandywine Creek. In its course through the heart of the park, the expressway changes from a trench scar to a viaduct scar.

Again in Philadelphia, a new expressway is proposed to connect a proposed new bridge across the Delaware River to the northeast section of the city. The route will follow the course of two creeks, the Frankford and the Tacony. Only 4.69 miles long, the Tacony Expressway will plunge through the heart of Tacony Creek Park. In the words of the engineer, it will "preempt" a portion of a golf course, which the city has every intention of patching up. In the words of another apologist, although the expressway "usurps a substantial area of a very beautiful park, it does preserve the 'more active parklands.' "

Another citizen of Philadelphia was not so gentle in his appraisal. Writing to *The Philadelphia Inquirer* several days after the official hearings announcing the proposed course of the Tacony Expressway, he expressed his disgust as follows: "The proposed destruction of this irreplaceable stream valley park is an outrage. While no significant additions have been made to our park system since the early part of this century, the parks we have are rapidly being nibbled away by highway construction. A vast area of Fairmount Park was despoiled by the Schuylkill Expressway; Fernhill Park was cut up by the Roosevelt Expressway; Franklin D. Roosevelt Park will soon be ravaged by the Delaware Expressway; much of Cobbs Creek Park will be taken for the Cobbs Creek Expressway; well over 50 acres of Tacony Creek Park will be destroyed for the Tacony Expressway, and so the list grows. Are any of our parks ultimately safe from such destruction?"

In Milwaukee, Juneau Park and Lagoon along the shores of Lake Michigan are the pride of the city. There, mothers sun their children on fine spring mornings, lovers gaze together at the red evening sky, and occasional touch-football scrimmages add zest to nippy fall afternoons. In Juneau Park, concrete-weary citizens of Milwaukee can fly a kite or roast a hotdog. For those less gung-ho, duck-feeding in the lagoon is always in season, especially in winter. In the words of one reliable observer, "Those mallards must be the most overfed flock of wild game in the Midwest; they feast daily on stale bread, sweet rolls, and popcorn."

But soon they will feast also on unburned hydrocarbons and other select exhaust fumes. The city has decided to cut through the park with a six-lane freeway. In the words of *The Milwaukee Journal*, this

Lake Freeway "involves the front door of the city, a front door that is beautiful because Milwaukee's leaders 50 years ago had the foresight to preserve the lake front from private exploitation and develop it for the public.

"They did it when other Great Lakes cities were building on their beaches the blight of steel mills and coal docks. Instead of coal heaps and smokestacks pumping black clouds into the sky, Milwaukee has beaches, pleasure drives, and parks."

When the freeway goes in, the Juneau Park Lagoon will be completely surrounded by highway—the freeway on the west, and the relocated Lincoln Memorial Drive on the East. This situation does nothing to facilitate access of the lagoon to the citizen of Milwaukee. If he does make it inside the concrete noose, his enjoyment of a quiet hour on the lagoon will not be enhanced by the fact that he is completely surrounded by the roar of internal combustion.

The Lake Freeway will be built into a 60-foot bluff between the city of Milwaukee and the park along the lake shore, thus turning what is now a wooded bluff into a concrete retaining wall. In addition, the freeway will usurp about 12 acres from the 100-acre park. The county engineer is attempting to soften this blow by adding a marina to the park, which will increase its area by 60 acres. But this marina, even if it comes to pass, will do nothing to restore the tranquillity to a park invaded by high-speed, heavy-truck traffic.

The destruction and the threat of destruction to irreplaceable urban parklands is repeating itself in many cities throughout the country, but perhaps one of the most horrendous examples is in Shaker Heights, Ohio, a suburb east of Cleveland. Interstate Route 290, the last remaining uncompleted link in Ohio's Interstate system, is shown on the engineers' maps as running right through Shaker Lake Park, a 275-acre park that was bought by John D. Rockefeller in 1895 and later given to the city of Cleveland.

The Shakers, the religious sect that settled this area in 1882, built two dams to form two large lakes that now dominate this park in the midst of one of the nation's more affluent and lovely suburbs. Not only does the proposed east-west I-290 (the Clark Freeway) run right through the park, and through Horseshoe Lake, but another proposed freeway, the Lee Freeway, runs north-south, and the

interchange between the two sits smack in the middle of Horseshoe
Lake, thus forming a 60-acre obscenity in the midst of this lovely
park.

The citizens of Shaker Heights are still battling to save their community, with the outcome in doubt. In 1963, when the plan was first
announced, *Cleveland Plain Dealer* columnist Howard Preston was
bitter. He stated flatly then that the opponents of the freeway were
destined to lose. "Don't get me wrong," he wrote. "I am in their
corner all the way, at least until the battle is lost and the bulldozers
begin to knock down trees, fill in lakes, and otherwise desecrate the
landscape. We live today for the convenience of the motorist, and if a
new bridge or highway will get him to his destination five minutes
faster, then hang all nature and down with her leafy sentinels. What
possibly can be more vital than getting a motorist home from work
five minutes earlier so that he can fall asleep before dinner or possibly catch part of a canned television show?"

People and parks are not the only sufferers in the city. Not even
the dead are safe from the bulldozers. In the path of the proposed
Tacony Expressway in Philadelphia is the Greenwood Cemetery.
According to the delicate euphemism of the assistant district engineer,
several hundred burial plots in the cemetery will be "affected."

On the banks of Horseshoe Lake in Shaker Lake Park is the grave
of Jacob Russell, a soldier who fought in the Revolutionary War. His
solitary grave is surrounded by a little iron fence and marked by a
bronze plaque donated by the Western Reserve Chapter of the DAR
in 1929. If the Clark Freeway comes through, soldier Russell will
have to go.

Not all highway builders are ghouls. The contractor on a $12-
million improvement of the interchange between the Long Island and
Brooklyn-Queens expressways turned handsprings to keep off the
graves in Calvary Cemetery. Even if the state of New York had
preferred to "relocate" the graves, the land costs would have been
prohibitive, so the state chose instead to design a complex system
of viaducts to carry the interchange ramps over and around the
graves. The work site between the highway and the cemetery was
such a tight squeeze that the contractor had to build a 22-foot-wide
timber platform overhanging the cemetery to hold his cranes, pile
driver, and concrete-delivery trucks.

Some years ago, when the world was just a little younger, it was not an uncommon practice for city-pent people to wander down to the waterfront, if their city was blessed with a waterfront, to gaze at the water and watch the slow movement of the ships. Man never ceases to yearn for the soul-healing quality that accompanies the idle contemplation of ships and water.

Now, of course, even if the city resident is foolhardy enough to make his way among the grimy warehouses, skid-row derelicts, roaring trucks, filth-spewing industry, and rotting wharves of the typical city waterfront, he is rewarded by the sight of scum, oil slick, and garbage floating on the surface of the noisome waters.

Pennsylvania's former governor William Scranton says that it does not have to be that way. "It never fails to amaze me," he says, "to travel around the world, and particularly in Europe, and you see what the cities in Europe have done with their rivers and then you come back to the United States and you go through our towns and cities and see what we haven't done with them, or what we've done *to* them. It seems to me that we put all the worst things of our cities along the rivers, and they put all the best."

Philadelphia is going to do something about the blight along its Delaware River waterfront. The city has an ambitious plan, known as the Penn's Landing project, to remake the central mile of the downtown waterfront, where William Penn landed in 1682. The plan includes a promenade, a marina, a science park, a port tower, apartment houses, plazas, and "selected" commercial structures.

But the plan looks more like a monument to the automobile than a facility for use by humans. The mile-long area is, first of all, cut off from the city by the six-lane Delaware Expressway. It is bounded on the north by the vast interchange connecting the expressway with the Benjamin Franklin Bridge, and on the south by the interchange network connecting the Delaware and Crosstown expressways. Further, of the six areas delineated in the plan, by far the largest is the parking area for 2,150 cars, stretching the entire mile length of the project. The land area to be devoted to parking is 636,000 square feet, which is nearly 40 per cent of the total area of 1,622,000 square feet in the project.

And that's not all. Says the seventy-six-page brochure prepared by the consultants on the project: "Multiple turnouts must be provided

from Delaware Avenue, together with ramps on the east end of the
Market Street Overpass; and a substantial north-south service road
must be provided for vehicle circulation. Plazas at Dock, Chestnut,
and Arch Streets will permit vehicle access as necessary to the inte-
riors of the project elements.

"Primary parking will be at street level in a 200-foot-wide tree-
lined strip just east of Delaware Avenue. The 2150 spaces thus provided can be more than doubled by selective second-decking in the
parking area and by the inclusion of parking space within the project
structures themselves. Substantial overflow parking space will be
available just west of the Expressway."

So it seems the automobile will not be restricted to the parking
areas provided for "primary" parking; they will also be permitted
to park "within the project structures themselves," and, if necessary
(and who can doubt it *will* be necessary), the parking strip can be
"second-decked," thus cutting the project off from the city not only
by an expressway but also by a two-story wall of parked automobiles.

If the view for the city resident will be somewhat restricted, the
planners have not forgotten the view to be provided the motorists on
the expressway: "Over 62 million people a year will be passing this
area on the Expressway by 1970," say the planners, "and to accommodate spectator speeds of up to 60 miles an hour, the visual presentation of the entire complex must be carefully organized into an intri-
guing 60-second experience."

One would hope that the experience is not too breathtaking for too
many motorists: there is still that 60-mile-per-hour speed to be reckoned with.

The desecration of our riverfronts was begun, of course, many
years ago by the railroads. Riverbanks offered excellent rights-of-way
for the railroads—the land was cheap and the grades were gentle.
The expressway builders are continuing a well-established tradition.
But, as one conservationist has observed, there is no reason why
we should permit the expressways to compound a felony by perpetu-
ating a mistake made a century ago by the railroads.

There is always the possibility that cities with waterfronts might
some day awaken to the needs of the people who live there and open
up the waterfront areas to recreational use. But if those areas are to

be subjected to a new wave of blight—the noise, the fumes, the nerve-jangling destruction of repose introduced by a high-speed express-way—they will be lost to human uses for more generations to come. And that is precisely what is happening in city after city throughout the land.

Our homes and schools, our park lands, our shorelines, even our buried dead, must give way to the overriding needs of the automobile. This nation has apparently dedicated itself to the proposition that there is no higher good than the unimpeded movement of automobiles, and there is no higher use of our land than to provide for that movement.

4

A Man's Home Is His?

Lee street was a quiet, narrow, lower-middle-class street tucked away in the southeast corner of Philadelphia, a few blocks from the big produce terminals along the Delaware River. The street was just wide enough to accommodate two lines of cars—one parked and one moving—so the traffic was very light, and the kids could play in the street with little fear of being run down. About a mile to the south towered the enormous suspended structure of the Walt Whitman Bridge across to New Jersey, and beyond that was the sprawling, bustling complex of the Philadelphia Naval Base. The row houses along Lee Street were tiny, neat, clean, each with its vest-pocket front porch. The half-dozen or so concrete steps up to the porches were always swept clean, and on trash day the cans were aligned in orderly fashion along the curb. The people along Lee Street owned their homes, and they were proud of that, because they had worked hard all their lives to pay for them.

The people on Lee Street were not transients. Most of them had been born there, had lived there all their lives, and in the case of many, their parents before them, and some, even their grandparents. These were hard-working, decent people, whose men worked along the docks or in the shipping terminals or warehouses, or down in the Navy Yard. They had names like Lynch, Davis, and Bevans; Cavanaugh, Green, and Short; Myers and Mitchell. Lee Street was a neighborhood, with loyalties and memories rooted in the very beginnings of the old city of Philadelphia.

Mr. and Mrs. Francis (as we will call them) were relative newcomers to the neighborhood; they had moved to Lee Street thirty-five years before, just after their wedding. Mr. Francis was looking forward to retirement in a few years, and Mrs. Francis would be glad of that, because his being home more would make it easier to take care of their grown daughter, who was mentally retarded. She was a sweet girl, but Mrs. Francis could never really let her out alone. Luckily, the neighbors on Lee Street were very kind and understanding. "Everybody looks out for her," Mrs. Francis would say to her husband, with a smile of gratitude. It warmed her to see how helpful and sympathetic people could be.

Mrs. Carol, a widow of eight years, lived alone on Lee Street, in a house that she had first entered as a bride, forty years before. Now she was getting along in years, and her health was not as good as it had been, but living there with her friends of many, many years made it all a little easier. Some of the families on her block had been in the neighborhood for three and four generations.

Mrs. Hill had undergone a breast-cancer operation just a few years ago, and with three small children in the house, it had been a worrisome time. But the neighbors had come in to do the housework, do the marketing, and watch after the children. They had practically taken over the running of the household until she was back on her feet. "I don't know how I ever would have made it if I hadn't had those wonderful people helping me," Mrs. Hill would say, with a wondering shake of her head.

Mrs. Roberts had been born on Lee Street, in her grandmother's house. Now she lived in the same house with her grandmother, her husband, and two sons. Over the years, the two women had loved to fuss over the house, changing little things here and there to get things arranged just to their liking. Mrs. Roberts' grandmother had been a widow for many years, and had made the last payment on the house nearly ten years before, and the feeling that they owned it entirely was part of their pride in keeping the little place clean and comfortable for their family. Mrs. Roberts still remembered with a warm thrill the day they had put venetian blinds in every window in the house. What a difference it had made in the way the place looked! Their good friends in the neighborhood had all come in and oohed and aahed very satisfactorily.

Mrs. Fitzgerald and her husband were each sixty-four, and he had less than a year to go to retirement. They had lived on Lee Street all their married life. Their children were all long since grown and married and moved away, and she and her husband were looking forward to his retirement. They had a little money put away, and with his pension, maybe they could at long last do some traveling.

But the fates of these families, and of hundreds of others like them living along the Delaware River, had been sealed on the day in 1956 that President Eisenhower signed the bill authorizing construction of the 41,000-mile Interstate and Defense Highway System. More than ten years before that, an engineer in the Pennsylvania Department of Highways had proposed an elevated expressway along the western shore of the river, and consultants had been hired and plans drawn and studies made, but the project had looked much too expensive and it seemed nothing would ever come of it until 1956, when suddenly 90 per cent of the cost became available in federal money for just such projects. In December of that same year, the Federal Bureau of Public Roads had adopted the Delaware Expressway as part of the Interstate system, and in that same month, the Pennsylvania Department of Highways started serious work on the project, and assumed full responsibility for location and design. This was a story that was being repeated all over the country, as the promise of big federal money blew the dust off long-dormant projects like a fresh breeze in a long-shut room.

Soon after the passage of the 1956 Highway Act, the residents of Lee Street, and, indeed, of scores of neighborhoods more or less like theirs all up and down the Delaware River, began to hear rumors that the expressway would come through and they would have to get out. At first, they were alarmed and agitated, but the years went by and nothing happened, and gradually they took the rumors less and less seriously.

Then, one bitter day in November, the official notices came from the highway department. The Delaware Expressway was, indeed coming down Lee Street, and the Commonwealth of Pennsylvania planned to take their homes. They would receive fair compensation.

The thought of moving made Mrs. Francis ill. Those days and weeks of looking for another home were a nightmare of worry about her husband, her retarded daughter, and her own health, which seemed to have broken at the news of their dislocation and had never really mended. She and her husband had simply not been able to find another home in the vicinity, so finally their married son, who lived nearby, had given them his home, and he had moved to New Jersey so that they would not have to move too far from the neighborhood in which they had spent all their adult lives. The puzzled, uncomprehending look in her daughter's eyes on moving day tore Mrs. Francis apart. Even now, three years after the move, Mrs. Francis chokes up when she talks about the old neighborhood on Lee Street. "Every time I think about it or talk about it, it makes me cry," she says. "It was a shame to make us people move." Her husband had still not retired, and it was a good thing, because living was more expensive now, and they needed the money. But he missed the old neighborhood, too. After work, these days, "he comes home and just sits in his chair. He doesn't try to get out and socialize with the people on the block, like he did in our old house." Mrs. Francis says she knows several of the older people on Lee Street, who, when faced with moving from the houses that they had lived in and paid for over so many years, had simply given up and died. She and her husband, she says, sort of died inside, in a way.

When Mrs. Carol first heard the rumors that she would have to move, she determined to get to the bottom of them and to fight if it was true. She had been very active in the protest groups organized in the neighborhood. They had got together and hired a lawyer to intercede for them. She had gone, with various civic and religious groups, to see the mayor numerous times. They had even gone to Washington. The strain and worry had aggravated her asthma and her heart condition, and she had been in and out of hospitals during this grievous time.

Gradually, she came to realize that protests would be of no avail, and that despite all they could do, the expressway was coming through. The people on Lee Street, says Mrs. Carol, were wonderful through it all; they were "just like one big family." But, she says, the payments they had received for their homes were not sufficient, "the estimates were unfair all around." Her own home had been appraised during one of her stays in the hospital, and when she returned home, she simply didn't have the stamina to fight it. Mrs.

Carol also says she knows some elderly people who died when told they would have to move. "It was a heartbreak having to leave the homes in which they had planned to live out the rest of their lives." She had not been able to find a suitable home near the old neighborhood, so she had moved in with her married, forty-eight-year-old son. Although she says the people in her new neighborhood are pleasant enough, it will never be the same.

Mrs. Hill, whose neighbors had been so kind to her and her family during her long siege with the breast-cancer operation, had been too tied down with her family to do much to help the protest groups, but she had given them money to help pay for the lawyer. Now, after nearly four years in her new neighborhood, she still misses her old friends. "The people on this street speak to you but they aren't as friendly and as close-knit as the people where I used to live. It's just not the same." Mrs. Hill is bitter about the fact that the real estate agents in the area, once the eviction notices had been delivered, raised prices on the few homes that were available in the area, to take advantage of the increased demand from those who didn't want to move too far from the old neighborhood. Finally, after she and her husband did find a suitable house and committed themselves to buying it, "I went home and cried. We would probably never have moved if this hadn't happened. I wouldn't have wished this on my worst enemy."

Mrs. Roberts, who, with her grandmother, had lavished so much love and care on her house, says now that her family was "pressured" by people from the State Highway Department to vacate their house promptly. So they had bought another house hastily, and they are now sorry they did not look around more before buying. Also, they had been told they were not to move any venetian blinds, electrical fixtures, or the stove. Says her grandmother, "I wish I had taken that gas stove. It was only two years old, and it broke my heart to leave it there. And what we found here, and have to use, is in such terrible condition we can hardly cook on it." Even after three years in the new block, Mrs. Roberts' teen-age son, in the afternoons after school, still goes back to the old neighborhood to seek the companions he knew there.

Mrs. Fitzgerald's husband, less than a year from retirement, had been badly shaken at the prospect of eviction. He had walked around the house in a state of great anxiety, saying over and over to his wife, "Where will we go?" "What will we do?" But this had not lasted for very long. One day he fell down dead from a heart attack, and then Mrs. Fitzgerald, after making the funeral arrangements, started looking for another place to live alone.

Very shortly after her husband's death, and before she had located another house, Mrs. Fitzgerald was told by a few of her neighbors that there was a new rumor that the route of the expressway had been changed, and she would not have to move after all. To make sure, she visited the offices of the highway department to inquire. The man she talked with brought out a map of the area, which showed the route of the expressway and the houses to be demolished. "Is my house going to be taken?" she asked the man. "It's on this map, you figure it out for yourself," he answered. After a good deal of study, because she was not at all familiar with maps of this kind, she concluded that her house was, indeed, among those to be demolished. She resumed her search for another place to live.

"I was the first one to move from Lee Street," she says. "And the day I moved, it was so sad for me and my neighbors." However, Mrs. Fitzgerald says now she was one of the luckier ones. She is glad she moved when she did, because many of her friends waited and hoped until the last minute, and by the time they were forced out of their homes, they couldn't find a house to buy at a reasonable price, because prices had gone up in the meantime. Mrs. Fitzgerald says that a number of the more elderly people on Lee Street were unable to withstand the shock of uprooting themselves.

Being the last to leave the block was a harrowing experience for the Meyerses, who had a corner house on Lee Street. Says Mrs. Meyers, "As soon as the residents moved out, the vandals moved in. It was frightening. The breaking in of the empty houses all around us was terrible. As fast as the houses emptied, the scavengers would come in and strip them, then children would break all the windows and start fires in the empty houses." The sounds of breaking glass and the glare of fires at night kept her in a constant state of anxiety about her home and her children. It had been a terrifying and tragic thing to see her once-happy neighborhood turned into a block of ghost houses, empty and broken and waiting for destruction.

The Delaware Expressway is a link in the chain called Interstate
95, which, when completed, will enable a motorist to speed from
Maine to Florida without a stop. It will be a great engineering achievement. Some day, a government accountant will be able to sit down
and arrive at a grand total for the cost of Interstate 95. It will be well
up in the billions of dollars. But no one will ever be able to write
down the total cost in human tragedy.

The stories of this handful of families on Lee Street must be multiplied by the thousands, by the tens of thousands.

Here is a sixty-five-year-old Italian-American who, with his son,
has owned and operated an auto-body repair shop for many years.
They cannot find another place to set up their business, except places
they can't afford. The father is too old to get a job, so he will just have
to give up working, and his son will have to find another job. There is
a seventy-nine-year-old woman whose whole life was visiting with
neighbors up and down Lee Street. Now she lives with her niece and
she never leaves the house. Although her health is still good, she feels
very lonely, and has "crying spells" that she never had before. Down
the street is a couple in their late sixties whose home on Lee Street
had been paid for. The state had given them $7,600 for the house,
but they had to pay $8,200 for the place they are in now, and it had
cost another $4,000 to fix the place up so that they could live com-
fortably in it. That has just about wiped out their savings. The wife
says she has been "in and out of the hospital with a nervous condition" ever since the news came that they would have to leave. A block
away is a woman whose husband, an alcoholic, suffered brain damage
in a fall. The neighbors on Lee Street had understood his condition
and had helped her with sympathy and understanding. But her new
neighbors are suspicious and shun the family.

Not all of Lee Street was destroyed. The expressway, eight lanes
of steel and concrete sitting 20 feet in the air on massive concrete
columns, comes sweeping down from the north and then begins curving gently toward the river. That gentle curve "saved" two blocks of
Lee Street. Every morning, these lucky home-owners walk out their
front doors and look up Lee Street directly into the jaws of the overwhelming monster that destroyed their neighbors. It is like living constantly in the path of a charging express train that always swerves off

at the last instant. Once the highway is opened to traffic, these residents who were spared will be treated daily to the spectacle of a hundred thousand cars and trucks roaring by just at their rooftops at 60 to 70 miles per hour, destined, perhaps, even for fabled Florida. The people on what is left of Lee Street will be treated to the full effect of every thundering trailer-truck. Their children will be able to play among the concrete piers in the shadow of the expressway. At night, the cavernous spaces beneath the viaduct will be a cheery gathering place for the local bums and winos.

If displacement from their homes is the tragedy of a lifetime for some of these unfortunate residents in the way of progress, the highway builders view the disaster with some equanimity. R. G. Palmer, former New Jersey state highway commissioner, told a subcommittee of the House of Representatives: "We in the highway department are old hands at the business of making urban improvements and at facing the tragic problem of uprooting people which any such improvement in a congested area always produces."

Not only the highway builders, but the entire community, has become inured to the widespread tragedy and destruction in its midst. It has been a recent phenomenon. Before the signing of the Interstate Highway Act, and the contemporary urban renewal acts, a man could feel secure in his home, whether he owned or rented it. Dispossession by the state was relatively rare. The eviction of thousands of families from a single neighborhood would have been unthinkable. Now, it is not only countenanced by the community, but the leading members of the community become irritable when the evictees cause any delay by their opposition.

Some members of the community are able to be incensed by the process, however. Writes Jane Jacobs, "People who get marked with the planners' hex signs are pushed about, expropriated, and uprooted much as if they were the subjects of a conquering power. Thousands upon thousands of small businesses are destroyed, and their proprietors ruined, with hardly a gesture at compensation. Whole communities are torn apart and sown to the winds, with a reaping of cynicism, resentment, and despair that must be heard and seen to be believed."

In theory, at least, this blind, ruthless destruction of human lives

shows no discrimination as to race or economic and social status—
the road must go where the engineer's pencil draws the line. In practice, as we have noted, land is cheaper in the poorer sections, and
that is where the highway usually goes. Thus we find our nation, with
a desperate shortage of low-income housing, destroying low-income
houses by the thousands and throwing the occupants out on the street
to look for housing that doesn't exist. The sordid cycle of eviction and
demolition has become a familiar one to many ghetto dwellers. If it
isn't a highway, it's urban renewal. For one reason or another, the
poor find themselves being driven by the pursuing bulldozer from
one marginal slum building to another, denied all hope of a stable
family life or permanent ties to neighbors, schools, stores, churches.

Students of the social scene who seek causes for the increase in
violence, the decrease in compassion, the hardening of attitudes in
the city dweller might ponder the effects of wholesale destruction of
families and neighborhoods and the uprooting of human beings from
old, familiar territory. Such widespread damage to the community,
when caused by a natural disaster such as a flood or a hurricane,
usually brings men together in mutual acts of compassion and succor;
when the damage is the result of considered action by the state, however, the result is just the opposite—an increase in cynicism, hatred,
and despair. "Even a ghetto," Harrison Salisbury quotes a pastor as
saying, "after it has remained a ghetto for a period of time, builds up
its social structure and this makes for more stability, more leadership,
more agencies for helping the solution of public problems." Take that
away, and you take away about all they have left.

The destruction of the familiar scenes and routines of life are
especially distressing to the elderly. To many of them, the boundaries
of existence have narrowed to the familiar faces of a few old friends
who are left, perhaps a faithful relative or two, a chair in a certain
position on a worn porch, the pattern of the sidewalk from the house
to the corner, and the smell and feel of a corner store. Destroy these,
and you destroy a human life. How many such lives is a new expressway worth?

The resulting shortage of decent low-income housing is very real.
For example, Lynwood F. Blount, a director of the Philadelphia
Housing Association and chairman of its relocation committee, has

reported that, because of displacement caused by public programs in the coming years, there will be a shortage of 50,000 low-income housing units in Philadelphia by 1972. Mr. Blount has urged the Philadelphia Planning Commission to demand that displaced persons be properly relocated before any more public acquisition of property is permitted.

Some victims of the shortage find themselves moved from one substandard house to another, only to be evicted again by code enforcement. In one period in Philadelphia, 70 per cent of the dislocated families were forced to move to houses that violated the housing codes. This results in a second loss of residence when the code authorities crack down on the offending landlord.

Another result of the shortage caused by demolition for highways is that rents increase in the remaining housing, so the displaced families find themselves faced with higher rents in their next slum dwelling. When several blocks were razed in New York City to make way for an approach to the Triborough Bridge, rentals for the slum dwellings in the area went up by 25 per cent. A study of one hundred home-owners displaced by Interstate Route 20 in Dallas, Texas, showed that the average payment by the state for their homes was $9,695. The average paid for replacement homes was $12,175. The author of the study stated that there were two major reasons for the increased cost of the replacements. First, the owners were attempting to compensate for the loss of a "familiar and cherished dwelling" by going into debt for the replacement. Second, there simply were not enough houses available at the prices given by the state as compensation for the original homes.

Although the Interstate Highway Act was passed during President Eisenhower's first term, it was not until six years later, in 1962, that the first provision was added to the federal law requiring some assistance to displaced families and businesses. In a special message to Congress in 1961, President Kennedy asked for legislation to provide help to those who were being evicted by the highway builders. This was done the following year. The Federal Aid Highway Act of 1962 requires that, before the federal government will approve a proposed highway in a given state, that state must first show that it is prepared to offer advisory assistance to the displaced families in finding another home. This does not mean the state must find a home for the family, only that it must offer information about homes available on the open market, about available public housing, what help might be offered by welfare agencies, and so on. The Act also provides that, if the state helps to pay moving expenses, the federal government will consider that a legitimate part of the construction costs, up to a maximum of $200 for a family and $3,000 for a business. This does *not* mean that the state is required to pay moving expenses; it means only that if the state *does* agree to pay these expenses, the federal government will bear its share of those expenses up to those maximums. At the time this legislation was enacted, only eight states had any provision for paying moving expenses.

One additional provision of the 1962 Act was in response to the growing indignation about evictions and a demand that the government owed the victims at least the assurance that they were being displaced not because of the whim of some highway engineer, but because it was part of a long-range plan for the betterment of the community. This provision stated that, after July 1, 1965, the federal official would "not approve any program for projects in any urban area of more than 50,000 population unless he finds that such projects are based on a continuing comprehensive transportation planning process carried on cooperatively by States and local communities."

Senator Jennings Randolph, chairman of the Senate Public Roads Subcommittee, and staunch highway builder, recognized the widespread injustice. He told the state highway officials in 1964 that the relocation assistance provisions were "inadequate." He pointed out that federal assistance in paying moving expenses was limited to those states that provided such aid under their own statutes. "In addition," he said, "both Federal and State laws have largely ignored the responsibility to provide low-income rental housing for the impoverished inhabitants of the blighted areas which so often are the corridors for freeways." Since the vast majority of such residents were renters, the result was thousands of the poor made homeless by the government, with no assurance of finding another place to live, and with no compensation for their distress.

A 1965 report of the Advisory Commission on Intergovernmental Relations condemned the treatment of highway evictees in these words: "Provisions of the Federal Aid Highway Act with respect to payments and services to persons and businesses displaced by federally aided activities clearly provide less assurance than similar Federal provisions on urban renewal that displaced individuals and families will be spared hardship and will be 'made whole.' No assurance is required of State officials to show that there is a 'feasible method' of relocating families and individuals and an adequate supply of standard housing available or being made available and within their means. An advisory service is required, but it applies only to families, not individuals and businesses, and is far short of the requirement of the Housing Act for a positive relocation assistance program, applicable to all three categories of displacees. Relocation payments are authorized, not required, with the result that in 28 States displacees are not entitled to payments under the Federal Act, including such urbanized States as California, Illinois, Michigan, and Texas. Payments to business are limited to a maximum of $3000 for expenses of moving up to 50 miles and may not include payment for direct loss of personal property. Finally, the cost of administering the relocation program does not qualify for reimbursement by the Federal Government as part of the project cost."

A business faced with eviction encounters the same problems as the family in finding new quarters—reduced availability and higher rentals—plus the losses incident to the interruption of business operations and the need to start over in a new location, with little if any carryover of the good will that is vital to success. The typical business displaced in a low-rent district is the small retail or service store run by the owners on the premises, the so-called "Mom and Pop" store. For them, business starts to decline as soon as their neighbors begin to move out to make way for the demolition crews. Then business income ceases altogether during the packing, moving, and resettling process. Finally, there is the uncertain period of six months to two years during which the business must be re-established in a new location. For all these losses, the government has provided no compensation. If the owner was lucky enough to be doing business in a state that offered moving expenses, the federal government assumed its share of this burden to the maximum of $3,000, but only if he made the attempt to re-establish. Usually, about one-third of such small business operators have given up in the face of these difficult obstacles and made no attempt to re-establish the business. Of those that made the attempt, another large but unknown percentage failed. These unlucky business owners, who are usually elderly, then have had the options of trying to find a job or going on welfare.

Understandably, the small businessman faced with eviction reacts with anger and disgust. He has been told over the years of the favorable attitude of government toward small business, and of the many governmental programs designed to nourish it. Now, here comes the government throwing him out of his place of business—if he is renting, and lives in the wrong state, he gets no compensation whatever. His business will be severely hurt, possibly destroyed. He feels that, at the very minimum, if it is truly in the best interest of the community that he be evicted, then the community should compensate him fully for the damage done to him.

Leon Seidel, a small businessman in New York City, told a House small business subcommittee, "If the community says to a man, 'We need your property and your business because it is for the good of the community,' they should not ask this man to lose it. This man from the Port Authority had the unmitigated gall to say . . . they will offer a man up to $3,000 for moving. This is pure nonsense. . . . If they want to put an expressway through, by God, the community should pay this businessman his rights. That is what we need in this country."

Often, when the small grocery store, drug store, or newsstand is plowed under for a highway, the surrounding neighborhood is also destroyed, and thus a clientele developed over the years disappears. In this situation, starting again is usually out of the question. But even if the store owner is the only one displaced, the result can still be catastrophic to his only means of livelihood. A small businessman in the South told the House subcommittee: "If I had to move my store just four or five doors away, it would be just like starting a new business, in spite of the fact that I've been at this same spot for about 20 years."

In his book, *Rebuilding Cities,* Basil G. Zimmer reports the plight of 350 small businesses in Providence, Rhode Island, that were forced to move because of highway construction or urban renewal. Typical was a sixty-five-year-old shoemaker, an Italian immigrant, who had been in business in the same place for thirty-five years. "The loss was more than just a building," he complained; "my work is gone forever, too. All of my customers have moved away." He said the whole experience was a "nightmare" that "shook my confidence in my city and country—I never thought they would do such a thing." His means of livelihood completely destroyed, he simply gave away his small stock and equipment and quit.

Another man, who had a small grocery store, also gave up. "My wife died because they forced me out," he said bitterly, "so I got disgusted and sick, so I just quit. The whole thing still makes me sick." Here again, as among the residents of Lee Street in Philadelphia, a number of the displaced attributed the death of friends or relatives to the shock of having their lives uprooted.

Feelings of bitterness and hostility among the displaced persons in Providence were widespread. The owner of a millworks and home building firm said he took "a terrible beating" from the "crooked" appraisers. "They had men appraise my property who worked for the state and therefore were not neutral or honest either. I would be fighting yet, but my lawyers talked me into giving up."

The owner of a welding business claimed "the appraiser didn't even look at my shop—all he did was walk in and walk out. I don't mind highways—we need them—but they took away my business and now I got nothing. It's not right. I used to have four men working for me, now I'm working for someone else—it's no good. I was making good money then and I was my own boss—now I'm broke."

A sixty-nine-year-old owner of a variety store said the "rotten" treatment he had received had put him into the hospital for five months. He claimed the price he received for his store and home was unjust. "They made one offer—take it or leave it—and it wasn't enough. We didn't have a lawyer to fight them, so they beat us. They told us to get out and we didn't like it. They acted as though they could tell us to do anything."

"It's a dirty lousy deal," was the way a tavern-owner put it. "The condemnation proceedings are communistic." The wife of a recently deceased owner of a jewelry electroplating and polishing firm echoed this sentiment: "We lost everything—it was a terrible thing—I can't understand how the city of Providence would permit it. The whole idea of forcing anyone out of a tax-paying business is like communism to me. The whole thing is un-American."

On the contrary, it's as American as apple pie. We have always been a nation of builders, and if a few fingers are smashed by the hammer, that's the price of progress.

In the 1968 Federal Aid Highway Act, Congress finally got around to liberalizing compensation for the highway-evicted. This Act provides that no one shall be displaced from his home unless there is available to him, "to the extent that can reasonably be accomplished," a "decent, safe, and sanitary dwelling." Also, a displaced home-owner will now be repaid the difference between the acquisition payment for his old house and the cost of a replacement house, up to a maximum of $5,000. A renter will be given up to two years' rental for replacement housing, or the down payment for buying a house, up to a maximum of $1,500. In addition, the displaced will be paid "actual reasonable expenses in moving himself, his family, his business, or his farm operation, including personal property." A business-owner may elect instead to receive an amount equal to the average annual net earnings of the business, up to a maximum of $5,000.

With the enactment of these provisions, twelve years after the beginning of work on the Interstate system, Congress belatedly acknowledged its responsibility to ensure justice for its citizens. Practically all the land for the 41,000-mile Interstate system had already been acquired, and to the uncounted hundreds of thousands thereby evicted the justice was like a reprieve for a man already hanged. The victims of future highway programs will benefit. It remains only for Congress now to assure them that the highways to be built are truly in the best interest of the community and that their eviction is a necessary sacrifice.

5

Erosion of the Cities

The city is the culmination of man's attempt to become civilized; it offers the individual the fullest opportunity to realize his potential as a human being. It is the repository of our faith in the possibility of achieving a humane society and the arena in which this faith is translated into action toward that end.

The city is the center of commerce, and only the great diversity of human skills to be found in the city can supply the many specialized talents that are needed to make the machine run.

The city is the center of ideas, and only the frictional heat generated by the rubbing together of diverse minds can throw off the sparks that illuminate our age—such minds as are drawn to the great metropolitan universities, newspapers, publishing centers, and lecture halls.

The city is the center of the arts, and only the mass patronage and wealth of the densely populated city can support the theaters, symphony orchestras, operas, and museums that preserve past glories and stimulate future ones.

The city is the crucible of democracy, and only the billion daily encounters in its small shops, great department stores, park benches, promenades, sidewalk cafés, riverfronts, penthouses, fountains, provide the marrow of our democratic society.

But a city can be none of these things if people do not wish to live as well as work there. A city abandoned every evening in a human exodus to suburban bedrooms is a city in name only—it has no heart, no spirit. It has degenerated to tall office towers whose feet stand in a tangle of freeways. The creation of a city requires what

Jane Jacobs has called the "fine-grained diversity" of human activity; it is a place where the stroll of a few blocks will take you to a fine home, a bar, a butcher shop, an apartment building, a theater, or an office. In *The Death and Life of Great American Cities,** Miss Jacobs tells in loving detail what it should be like to live on a vital, human-being-dominated city street:

"The stretch of Hudson Street where I live is each day the scene of an intricate sidewalk ballet. I make my own first entrance into it a little after eight when I put out the garbage can, surely a prosaic occupation, but I enjoy my part, my little clang, as the droves of junior high school students walk by the center of the stage dropping candy wrappers. (How do they eat so much candy so early in the morning?)

"While I sweep up the wrappers I watch the other rituals of morning: Mr. Halpert unlocking the laundry's handcart from its mooring to a cellar door, Joe Cornacchia's son-in-law stacking out the empty crates from the delicatessen, the barber bringing out his side-walk folding chair, Mr. Goldstein arranging the coils of wire which proclaim the hardware store is open, the wife of the tenement's super-intendent depositing her chunky three-year-old with a toy mandolin on the stoop, the vantage point from which he is learning the English his mother cannot speak. Now the primary children, heading for St. Luke's, dribble through to the south; the children for St. Veronica's cross, heading to the west, and the children for P. S. 41, heading to-ward the east. Two new entrances are being made from the wings: well-dressed and even elegant women and men with brief cases emerge from doorways and side streets. Most of these are heading for the bus and subways, but some hover on the curbs, stopping taxis which have miraculously appeared at the right moment, for the taxis are part of a wider morning ritual; having dropped passengers from midtown in the downtown financial district, they are now bringing downtowners up to midtown. Simultaneously, numbers of women in housedresses have emerged and as they crisscross with one another they pause for quick conversations that sound with either laughter or joint indigna-

---

*Copyright 1961 by Jane Jacobs. Quoted by kind permission of the publisher, Random House, Inc.

tion, never, it seems, anything between. It is time for me to hurry to work too, and I exchange my ritual farewell with Mr. Lofaro, the short, thick-bodied, white-aproned fruit man who stands outside his doorway a little up the street, his arms folded, his feet planted, looking solid as earth itself. We nod; we each glance quickly up and down the street, then look back to each other and smile. We have done this many a morning for more than ten years, and we both know what it means: All is well."

In short, the city is a place where men crowd themselves together in a small area in order to reap the enormous social and economic benefits that can be derived from density of population. Of course, not everyone derives the satisfaction from city life that Miss Jacobs obviously does. A major problem of our time is that these satisfactions are rapidly diminishing as the city is given over to the automobile. For just as the body of the city is being destroyed by freeways, so is its soul being destroyed by the automobile.

✓ It was intended to be otherwise. At the outset of the Interstate Highway program, in 1957, a conference in Hartford heard this glowing promise for the future: "This is the biggest public-works program in history. It will not only change the faces of the old cities, but will open up vast new areas of rural land for urban settlement. These expressways will become the skeletons of the new metropolis. Their location, and the location of their interchange points, will establish urban patterns for generations to come. They hold out the promise not only of solving critical problems of urban congestion but of setting in motion other related steps that together can help us realize the better urban communities we want."

City planning of the future, said this report, would be dominated by planning for the automobile. The shape of our cities would be determined by the freeways, which, in turn, delineated the routes along which automobiles would wish to travel, the so-called "desire lines" of the highway engineer. These lines would determine the shape of our cities "for generations to come." As for the "old" cities, where patterns had been set by other and earlier considerations, the expressway would change their faces. Indeed, their faces have been changed. With most city planners putting the welfare of the automobile first, the city is rapidly becoming unfit for human habitation.

The freeways are supposed to take much of the traffic burden off the city streets, and thereby relieve the rest of the city from the congestion that was beginning to strangle it. The result has been quite the opposite. One reason for this is that the freeways themselves have acted as generators of additional traffic. As soon as the freeway is completed, more people abandon public transportation to take to their cars. Another reason is that the existence of the freeway persuades more people to move from the city to the suburbs, thus increasing the commuting load on the freeway. As a result, the freeway is usually choked with traffic as soon as it is completed. This stimulates the demand for more freeways. As they are built, and as their construction makes center-city living even less desirable, the flight to the suburbs accelerates, thus adding to the demand for more freeways. And so on, apparently, until either all the habitable land surrounding the city is covered by freeways and suburban "developments," or until the center city disappears under a welter of interchanges and parking lots, and there is nowhere for the suburbanites to drive to.

The Hollywood Freeway in Los Angeles was designed for an eventual load of 100,000 cars per day. It opened in 1954, and one year later the traffic volume was 168,000 cars per day.

A Dade County Commissioner in Florida, speaking of a freeway near Miami, said that "traffic engineers told us it would be saturated the day it opened and that we would immediately need two additional lanes on each side which would cost another $100 million." Planners in Atlanta, looking at their freeway needs in 1958, estimated that one section of a six-lane expressway already had enough traffic to justify sixteen lanes during the peak rush hour, and that the traffic would demand thirty-six lanes by 1970. The Delaware Expressway in Philadelphia is not yet completed, but the finished section in the northern part of the city is jammed by bumper-to-bumper traffic every morning.

Edmond L. Kanwit, an official of the U. S. Department of Transportation, attests to the futility of attempting to keep up with traffic demand by building freeways: "As the peripheral suburban area expands, traffic continues to grow, and gains in speed are often offset by longer trips and traffic tieups at ramps and interchanges. Improvements to highways attract new residential and commercial building and often generate enough traffic within a few years to equal or exceed twenty-year traffic forecasts." Obviously, the construction of freeways is a self-defeating occupation. And do they remove traffic from the city streets by serving as a bypass? It would be nearer the truth to say freeways increase traffic in the city streets by attracting more automobiles in from the suburbs.

For it is surely clear that, ever since the end of World War II, there has been an exodus of city residents to the suburbs. A center-city resident may own a car, or he may not, but once he moves to the suburbs, a car becomes an absolute necessity. Many of those who move continue to hold jobs in the city. But there is also a movement of industry out to the suburbs. This means that, although the radial movement of workers between suburbs and center city is still substantial, the circumferential movement of suburbanites within their satellite rings is increasing. The result of this, of course, is a demand for circumferential expressways, or "loops," as well as radial expressways, and thus the metropolitan area is carved in two directions. As we attempt to handle the peak commuter load by building freeways, we surely set in motion the forces that will destroy the city.

Standing shoulder to shoulder with the suburban commuter in his demand for more freeways is the downtown merchant, who is told by the highway establishment that his survival depends on the city's being able to handle the automobile. This means freeways to get the shopper in town, and plenty of parking space after he gets there. In a speech a few years ago, Harry A. Williams, managing director of the Automobile Manufacturers Association, made this clear: "Far-sighted merchants, officials, and planners have read the statistics on the steady decline in mass transit riding, and the steady rise in urban motor trips —and they recognize that just as motor traffic built the suburbs, so now the central city's future depends primarily on adapting to motor transportation requirements. With downtown accessibility restored by the new urban freeways, major investors in downtown land—including large insurance firms—anticipate a healthy revitalization of our downtown areas. A key element here, they inform us, will be large-scale investment in multideck parking garages. The parking industry appears to be on the threshold of an era of unprecedented expansion within our downtown areas, as an adjunct of structural redevelopment of our central business districts. The net result can be a doubling or tripling of downtown parking spaces. . . ."

Many others have echoed this commercial plea for more parking space downtown. U. S. Rubber Company's Vice-Chairman, H. E. Humphreys, Jr., warns that "if you ban cars or effectively discourage their use in any area, people will stay away from that place in large and increasing numbers. Most downtown merchants are aware of this. *All* city planners *should* be aware of it."

Representative John C. Kluczynski agrees that parking space is a must for the merchant. "I know what it is to find places to park," he has said, "because without parking, you can't do any business. Let's not kid ourselves . . . automobiles have made people lazy. They get to a big parking lot and everybody wants to park right near the stores. They don't even want to walk that 500 or 600 feet."

True enough. Big-city department stores agree that each parking space near the store generates about $10,000 worth of business annually. Says a traffic engineer in Washington, "The typical small businessman wants meter parking outside his door or a parking lot across the street. If he doesn't get it, he howls." Professor Allan Goodwin recently performed a study of parking and shopping for the Highway Research Board. One of the possibilities he studied was the provision of "fringe" parking outside the central business district, with adequate mass transit into town. But the businessmen he questioned would have none of this. In reporting his study, he concluded that "Merchants tend to panic when they hear that people can't park near their places of business. They don't buy the notion that clearing up congestion will in the long run make downtown more attractive, lure more customers to it, and increase business all around."

Those who believe the city should serve primarily as a place for a man to work and live deplore the increasing use of precious urban land for the storage of automobiles. But the chambers of commerce disagree. Also Humble Oil executive George L. McGonigle, who told a meeting of city planners in Montreal recently that "they decry the urban expressway as a despoiler of the cityscape and a breeder of fearful congestion at the freeway's terminus downtown. They bemoan the use of valuable urban land for such an uneconomic commitment as parking. But I submit that they are dead wrong."

Mr. McGonigle went on to show that a properly run parking facility can net from $160 to $200 per year per space, which is profitable use of even the costliest downtown land. No doubt this argument will stand up, from a purely economic point of view. Another question, however, has to do with the quality of life in the city, which is not amenable to economic analysis. The quality of life for the urban resident is not improved by the proliferation of parking lots. Nor is the visit to downtown by the suburbanite likely to result in an exciting encounter with the infinite variety of human activity, if the only thing he passes in his walk along the boulevard is a succession of parking lots.

Wilbur Smith and Associates, a consulting firm which has made exhaustive studies and reports of the urban transportation problem at the behest of the Automobile Manufacturers Association, also says the city should "adapt" to the needs of the automobile. In a recent report, the firm concludes: "The nation's urban centers are striving for a new equilibrium attuned to the motor vehicle—an adaptation essential for their continued prosperity and dominance." One major problem, of course, is downtown parking. "Because more downtown travelers will come from auto-oriented suburban areas in future years, downtown parking space demands and space needs will continue to rise in all cities. Thus, it has been estimated that by 1970 over 6000 additional spaces will be required in Philadelphia's downtown core, as compared with 3000 in 1960."

Another study in Philadelphia, however, concluded that no matter how "auto-oriented" the suburbanites might be, the attempt by the city to "adapt" itself would end in its own destruction. This study concluded that if all the suburbanites were provided with all the expressways they demand to drive into town, parking spaces needed to accommodate them would cover three-quarters of all the ground area in the city.

One devourer of urban land is the shopping center, which is conspicuous for the great proportion of its total area devoted to parking space. The vast expanse of asphalt is, in fact, its characteristic feature. Mrs. Florence Scala, member of a citizens' housing committee in Chicago, told the House small business subcommittee that "in the city, this excessive use of scarce land for the convenience of the automobile is absurd; particularly when, at night these parking lots are huge empty places on the city's landscape. . . . If this keeps up, the city of the future will be a sterile haven for parking lots, shopping centers, high-rise luxury apartments, and tax-free institutions. It is largely the mediocre city planner who is not concerned with people, but who is oriented to cater to big business and other pressures, that practically insures the death of so many firms and shops."

Federal Highway Administrator Lowell K. Bridwell said recently that it is "wasteful, costly, and downright foolish" to continue permitting curb parking in the city. "On-street parking in core areas is a luxury most cities can no longer afford," he said. "It is crystal clear that if traffic congestion is to be relieved and traffic strangulation is to be averted, the need for more off-street parking must be met and met soon." Thus Mr. Bridwell, who does not have the reputation of a hard-line highway builder, joins the ranks of those who would tear down more newsstands, pawnshops, and used-furniture stores to make way for automobile storage space. Also, presumably, if curb-side parking is banned, the line of stationary vehicles along each curb will be replaced by a line of moving vehicles—thus doubling the pollution load on the city air and posing a grim threat to any pedestrians who might be left.

In his study for the Brookings Institution, Wilfred Owen concluded that the amount of available floor area devoted to off-street parking in a typical "mature" city such as Baltimore is about 8 per cent. For the nation's most highly "auto-oriented" city, Los Angeles, this figure is more like 15 per cent, which is higher than the space devoted to either hotels or retail stores. But even more interesting is the trend of land use shown by a study covering the years 1930-1960. During these three decades, the available floor space in the central business district of Los Angeles increased by about 10 per cent. The amount of space devoted to hotels was down 12 per cent, institutions down 12 per cent, manufacturing and wholesale down 11 per cent, retail down 16 per cent, services down 8 per cent, offices up 15 per cent, government and "quasi-public" up 80 per cent, inside parking up 40 per cent, and surface parking up 203 per cent. These statistics suggest that downtown Los Angeles is becoming an area of widely spaced office towers and massive government buildings adrift in a sea of parked and moving automobiles—a concept that any aerial view will confirm.

In any discussion of the effects of freeway building on the city, Los

Angeles is inevitably cited as the wave of the future. The metropolitan area, firmly dedicated to the automobile as the means of getting people from place to place, has now spent more than $1 billion for about 500 miles of freeways, but it is just getting started. Projections of future needs go to 1,500 miles by 1980 at a cost of $5 billion. Already, the downtown area has been eroded to the point that Los Angeles is ironically called a hundred suburbs in search of a city. The government buildings and the office towers devoted to banking, finance, insurance, and oil stand as isolated islands of splendor amid a spaghetti-like mass of freeways and acres of parked automobiles. A monument to commercial endeavor, but by no stretch of the imagination a city.

A hundred thousand or so persons make their living there, but, as Richard A. Smith wrote recently in *Fortune,* ". . . nobody 'loves' downtown, and to the average citizen it is just 4000 acres of parking lots, an abundance of bad restaurants, a paucity of good hotels. Downtown is something he and 380,000 other freeway drivers—68 per cent of those coming into the area—are pleased to hurtle by every day without stopping." Indeed, although the highway builders have done everything in their power to make it possible for everyone to drive into Los Angeles, and although they have tripled the available parking space in the past forty years, the number of people who go downtown in a given day is about the same as it was before this frenzy of asphalting began. There is simply very little to go there for any more, and few people do unless their job compels it. And for many of these, the rush-hour trip on the Los Angeles freeways is a daily nerve-shattering and soul-destroying experience. Yet, some doggedly insist that even more freeways will alleviate the jams.

Where do the freeway advocates suppose it will end? Our population continues to grow, the number of cars on the road continues to rise, the demand for moving and parking space moves ever upward. And in response, our cities are eroding like the victims of some disease, or some destructive act of nature. As the bulldozers plow through the city, buildings intended for human activities dissolve into rivers of asphalt. As the expressways bring more cars into the city, old theaters and hotels are smashed to rubble to make more parking space. Shops and homes give way to gasoline stations, drive-ins, and used-car lots.

Every city scene is dominated by automobiles, moving or standing, or facilities for their service. The only result is to increase the demand for more.

Called in by the city fathers to diagnose the sickness that was undermining the health of Rochester, New York, twelve years ago, Victor Gruen saw a classic case of auto-erosion: " The phenomenon of commercial blight, starting immediately behind a thin façade of productive buildings along both sides of Main Street, was a general occurrence. The life tissue of the city had been slowly loosened to a dangerous degree by the demolition of buildings that had once contained urban functions, and their replacement by parking lots, garages, used-car lots, widened roads and other automotive facilities. When photographed from the air, the core area of Rochester appeared like a sea of asphalt and automobile tin roofs, from which rose, in islandlike fashion, some structures holding out against the surf of slowly but incessantly moving waves of automotive traffic."

This process of auto-erosion has already proceeded far in most cities. In the large "mature" cities like Chicago, Detroit, and Minneapolis, about half of the total land area in the central business district is devoted to the movement and storage of automobiles. In Los Angeles, it is more like two-thirds. If the downtown is to be regarded as just another shopping center, just like the ones in the suburbs, only bigger, perhaps this makes sense. But if the city is to be regarded as a place for creative and stimulating social intercourse among human beings, this is insane. It would appear we have already made the choice. Center city is becoming a throughway and a garage for rubber-tired suburbia.

The supineness of all other considerations before the demands of the automobile is illustrated by a tiny but very significant change made recently to a street in Philadelphia. The Benjamin Franklin Parkway is a mile-long, twelve-lane, divided drag strip down which the in-bound commuters roar in the morning, headed for their center-city offices. A total of 40,000 cars a day charge down this urban raceway. The first obstruction near center city is Logan Circle. Some motorists charge around the circle and continue toward City Hall; others go around the circle only about a quarter of the way and then turn off on 19th Street, rounding the corner that is occupied by the Natural

Science Museum. Some difficulty arises from the fact that 19th Street is only two lanes wide, and the right-hand lane is often occupied by a block-long line of parked school buses that have brought children to visit the Museum. So three lanes of hurtling machines on a broad parkway must make the sharp turn into one lane of a narrow street. As a result, those who have corner offices in the Museum are treated to a day-long screeching of tires as vying motorists give it a good go. There is a light at the corner, but this simply adds spice to the game. From the standpoint of those who valued the welfare of the lines of children often seen on the sidewalk, waiting their turn to enter the Museum, the sharp corner was a blessing, since it forced the automobiles to slow down before charging past the line of parked school buses.

What steps did the city of Philadelphia take to change this situation? The answer is obvious. The city chopped away at the sidewalk and removed about eight or ten feet from the sharp corner, making a much more generous curvature. Now a car can take the corner at a somewhat higher speed. Now the lines of children are confined to a much narrower sidewalk, and their bodies are somewhat closer to the hurtling vehicles. The sound of screeching tires has not diminished, however; only the pitch is higher.

At the other side of Logan Circle, where the cars enter the circle from Benjamin Franklin Parkway, the city also thoughtfully carved away at the sidewalk to make it possible for the motorist to enter the circle at higher speed. Here, the bulldozers sacrificed a half-dozen or so sycamore trees, and part of a bit of green area containing a few park benches. The benches have been moved back a little to make way for the dragsters. Here, in Logan Circle, we have the whole story: the automobile is taking over, and man and nature must give way. Neither the safety of schoolchildren nor the quiet contemplation of park idlers shall stand in the way of achieving an increase of five miles per hour in the rate at which Logan Circle can be negotiated by the resourceful motorist.

As the overpowering presence of the automobile assumes domination of the city, the opportunities for human-scale activities and pleasures diminish. The bicyclist and the horseback rider are seen no more. Walking for pleasure gives way to a harried scurrying along a narrow strip of concrete with instant death no more than 6 feet away: one false step and the miscreant pedestrian is instantly chastened by the screech of brakes and the blare of horn. Where once there were trees for the pleasure of man, now there are parking meters for the service of automobiles. Where once there were green areas and benches to offer man an hour of quiet and rest, now there is a weedy patch beneath a roaring viaduct.

If the building of freeways destroys neighborhoods, eliminates the sense of community among urban residents, and breeds a rankling resentment of the Establishment among those displaced, the crush of automobiles that the freeway brings into the city destroys human values, eliminates those urban amenities that make city life worthwhile, and breeds an ugly blight that coarsens the human spirit. An impartial observer, Colin D. Buchanan of London's Imperial College of Science, told a National Conference on Beauty in America: "If I can be quite blunt, if you look at the American cities overall and you add up the total amount of excruciating ugliness associated directly or indirectly with the motor vehicle, then I think it is staggering."

A Task Force on Environmental Health and Related Problems reported to the Secretary of the Department of Health, Education and Welfare in the summer of 1967 that the effects of the automobile in the city might very well be damaging to the urban residents' health. "Today's urban environment is frequently placing severe physical and mental stresses on people," said the report. "Cities are cramped and depressing. They fail to provide for man's needs for space and privacy. Noise, crowding, odor and traffic hazards are facts of life to the urban citizen. We must stop to consider whether these facts are, in reality, insidious threats to his physical, mental, and social well-being.

"Vehicular traffic is one of the most serious and complex urban irritants, and one of the most difficult to control. Vehicular movement is being directly superimposed upon the small-scale environment of man's ambulatory activities. It is recognized that unencumbered pedestrian flow within a neighborhood is essential for community identity and cohesion, and for a healthy social environment."

The constant din of automobile engines and the occasional deafening roar of a heavy truck wear away at our limited reservoir of nervous energy; the engine exhaust fumes bring a noxious stench to our nostrils and poison our lungs with lethal gases; the sight of a typical city street has become one hideous scene of traffic signs, garish used-car lots, parking lots, trucking platforms, gas stations, automotive litter, and drive-ins. Our cities have become such horrors that most people who can do so are escaping to the suburbs. But many of these escapees continue to drive into the city to work, thus increasing the depredations of the automobile, thus increasing the ugliness and the menace to health, thus accelerating the flight to the suburbs.

Air pollution in most cities has long been a menace to health; now it is rapidly becoming intolerable. Some experts estimate that as much as 80 per cent of this airborne garbage comes out of the exhaust of automobiles—the total every *day* being about 250,000 tons of carbon monoxide, 25,000 tons of hydrocarbons, and 8,000 tons of oxides of nitrogen. This inflames eyes; corrodes noses, throats, and lungs; sickens and kills. The death rate from emphysema in Los Angeles County in the past eighteen years has multiplied by 1200 per cent, and it is still climbing.

Deaths from cancer among the outdoor animals in the Philadelphia Zoo shot up suddenly after completion of the Schuylkill Expressway, which runs past the zoo. Fumes from automobile exhausts are contaminating powdered milk produced in Columbus, Ohio. The plants may have to be moved out of the city. On Thanksgiving Day, 1966, residents of New York City with heart, lung, and upper respiratory diseases were warned to stay indoors. The Dean of Dartmouth College School of Engineering said in 1967, "We're on our way to a public catastrophe." Several months later, a prominent meteorologist, James P. Lodge, Jr., said that our wholesale burning of petroleum in engines comprises a radical disruption of the earth's chemical balance that is producing waste products many of which are "toxic to nearly every form of life." "If we are to survive on earth," he said, "we must consider such things as whether we can afford to burn a precious organic material . . . to move a 120-pound woman and a bag of groceries to and from the market. When we reach the point where 50 per cent of the United States is black-topped, will it make any difference where we go, if it's all the same thing?"

Finally, the urban *Lebensraum* is being usurped by the automobile. The pedestrian is disappearing. Certainly walking for pleasure in the

city is long ago a thing of the past. The only walking takes place between the parking lot and the destination, and this walk is taken at
some risk to one's safety. August Heckscher, former director of the
Twentieth Century Fund, believes that "the time is past when you
are going to have streets which fulfill the functions that have been traditional functions of bearing traffic, of carrying pedestrians, and,
ideally, of allowing those meetings and discussions with which one
associates democracy down from the days of the Greeks. The man in
the street, in other words, isn't going to exist anymore."

Apparently not everyone believes this is a loss. A letter to the editor, from "Wise Motorist," was published recently by *The Philadelphia Inquirer:* "All this concern over the supposedly neglected
pedestrians is a lot of sentimental nonsense. People who walk are
usually motorists who have gotten out of their automobiles and if
they do not have enough good sense to understand that if they get in
the way of a moving car they will be injured or killed then that is
just too bad."

Another letter-writer agreed that the pedestrian was probably obsolete, but he appeared less willing to blame it all on the hapless walker:
"People ought to be discouraged from walking nowadays because it
has obviously become entirely too dangerous," he wrote. "Even with
sidewalks on both sides of the street, shoppers during the busy time
of the day crowd into the streets in front of passing automobiles. Pedestrians cannot cross the streets at intersections except at great risk
because of the continuous stream of corner-turning trucks, taxis,
buses and passenger cars. Sidewalks only create a dangerous delusion
that a safe place has been provided for the walker, when in fact no
such has been done. I am for eliminating all sidewalks, except on
pedestrian malls where motor vehicles would be banned."

Car-free pedestrian malls are exceedingly rare in the United States.
There are a few, but in most communities where they have been proposed, the downtown merchants have erupted in horror at the suggestion that money-laden automobile traffic might no longer pass con-
tinuously in front of their stores. Better to ban pedestrians than automobiles. And so streets are widened while sidewalks are narrowed.
Meanwhile psychiatrists wonder why humans are becoming "alien-
ated" from our society.

In some communities, indeed, the sidewalk has completely disappeared. Many suburban "developments" are built without them, on the assumption that rubber tires have replaced feet. A pedestrian in such a community becomes an object of suspicion. He is stopped and questioned by the police. He must adopt the protective device of taking a dog on a leash. The community knows that dogs do not drive cars. "For the first time in history," says the Greek architect and urban planner Constantinos Doxiadis, "since he came down from the trees, man is losing the right to walk inside his cities."

As long as we continue to build freeways to dump automobiles into the city, man's urban activities will be increasingly circumscribed by the demands of the automobile. Already, in some cities, the automobile is driving man underground. In Philadelphia's Penn Center, often cited as a model of urban renewal, several city blocks have been dug out underground where people can walk and do their shopping, while overhead, the automobiles hurtle about on the surface taking advantage of the sunshine and spewing their filth into the city air. The same kind of solution to the vexing problem of separating automobiles and pedestrians has been devised in Montreal. Some urban planners advocate putting the *automobile* underground in the cities, but it seems much more likely that man will end up in the catacombs while the automobile takes over on the surface.

Explosion of the Suburbs

Not long ago, former Secretary of the Interior Stewart L. Udall took a good look at the town in which he lives—McLean, Virginia—a once-rural suburb now with a population of 11,500 and growing fast. "It's all rather dreary," he said. "Eyesores. I don't know what the supermarket builders are thinking about with their wastelands of asphalt. Businessmen who persist in uglification are going to find themselves bucking the tide. Everything, it seems, is arranged today to meet the needs of the automobile."

Mr. Udall had said it all in just a few sentences. What depresses him is urban sprawl, a monotonous sea of stamped-out dwellings on half-acre lots, heavily interlaced by roads and expressways, and clotted with gasoline stations, supermarkets, and shopping centers surrounded by thousands of milling automobiles by day and vast expanses of asphalt by night. The open fields, farmlands, rolling hills, and small towns that once surrounded our great cities are disappearing in the spreading blight of suburban slum that has followed the expressways outward from the city center.

The population of Westport, Connecticut, has tripled in the past twenty years. Boston Post Road, once a pretty, tree-lined suburban street, is now lined with honky-tonk stores; there are nine gasoline stations in a one-mile stretch. Says one resident: "It was a pretty New England town, with a camaraderie of artists, but now there are so many people, so many shopping centers, and so little taste, that the appearance of the place has become appalling."

By now the statistics of megalopolis are familiar to us all. In twenty years, it is estimated, more than half the population of the

United States will live in four huge regions of dreadful sameness stretching for hundreds of miles. The citizens of these vast smears of humanity will be unable to see open countryside without first taking a long day's trip to reach the edge of the suburban sprawl. One of these giant cities will cover the Atlantic Seaboard from Boston to Washington; a second will cover the Pacific Coast from San Francisco to San Diego; a third will stretch along the Great Lakes from the eastern tip of Ontario west to Chicago, then north along Lake Michigan to Green Bay; the fourth will cover a good part of the Florida peninsula. Open land is gobbled up without planning or control, guided only by the greed of the commercial developers, abetted by the road builders, and implemented by the insatiable thirst of the American citizen for gasoline. The noted scientist, Athelstan Spilhaus, in making his proposal that we plan and build new cities of limited size to house future populations, said, "The major trouble with present cities is that they just spread like cancers instead of being of controlled size and kept as an operating, clean machine for living."

Communities do, indeed, have planners, and many of them sport Master Plans. But the plans are, for the most part, useless, because the planners have no political power to shape the community to their plans. The zoning process bends under the economic and political pressures of local businessmen and real estate developers. Further, the crazy-quilt fragmentation of regions into quarrelsome political fiefdoms makes regional cooperative planning an impossibility. The result is unplanned chaos, presided over by the pursuit of profit.

To the "developer," the sight of a field or marsh brings visions of a natural chain of events that leads to profit. First, there must be roads. The pressure of an expanding population ensures that automobiles will move along those roads, and that the motorists will have the usual human desires: to build homes, to eat hotdogs, to trade-in their old jalopies, to have a bottle of beer, and so on. The end result is money. But first there must be the road.

Roads and automobiles mean money and power. As a result, no bit of open land is safe. Lost in this worship of economic growth is any means of providing for other human desires: solitude, quiet, the sight of green fields or clear running brooks. There is no profit in a wooded slope or the refreshing sight of a mountaintop.

The land speculator or real estate developer has very little interest in long-range community values or human spiritual welfare. His only wish is to buy the land and to sell at a profit. Yet his gentle hands shape the use of our countryside and, ultimately, our cities. Land is our most precious resource, and its distribution and use should be at least as closely regulated as the production and use of electrical power, or the distribution and use of water. Instead, we give no more thought to the use of an acre of land than we do to a bushel of potatoes.

Housing expert James W. Rouse asked the right questions a few years ago during a symposium on urban transportation: "How do we want the community to grow? In what direction? And for what purpose? Will industry be concentrated or dispersed? What use will be made of the streams, rivers, and waterfronts? Of the hills, valleys, forests, and open spaces? What will be the function of downtown? What is to happen to the gray areas around downtown? How is the future growth of the metropolitan area to be accounted for—by continuing sprawl? Along transportation corridors? In a series of satellite towns?"

If our metropolitan areas were being planned for human beings, these are the questions we would ask ourselves. But they are being planned for automobiles, and therefore we ask: How heavy is the traffic along this route? How many additional lanes do we need to handle it? How many cars will wish to get from point A to point B in 1980? What is the estimated future traffic along this desire line? What kind of interchange will produce the most efficient flow of traffic at this point? Shall we put an overpass here or dig a trench? Says regional planner C. McKim Norton, "Until we make up our minds about what kind of cities we want to live in and design our transportation system to serve the indicated needs, transportation will continue to be the master of our urban environment."

The result of giving the automobile the sole voice in how the urban areas will be shaped is shapelessness, chaos. Reuban Lovret, a member of the planning staff for Los Angeles, should know. He said recently that "if you have complete dependence on the automobile it can lead to nothing but change. As long as you are oriented toward the automobile, any location is subject to reorganization or redevelopment according to how the driver can exert pressure—for shopping centers or apartment houses. As long as unbridled fluidity exists, there can be no permanent pattern."

Urban planning and highway building—two occupations that intimately affect the quality of our lives and that shape the world that our grandchildren will inherit—should ideally be done by the best experts we can find, armed with the best goals we can devise for our civilization, and insulated from the hurly-burly of commercial honkytonkism and political hackery. Such, regrettably, is not the case. A prestigious consulting firm, Arthur D. Little, Inc., was called in to take a look at highway planning for the Washington metropolitan area. "We analyzed it from the best economic and technological viewpoints," the firm reported. "We remained unbiased throughout, but found none of this really matters. Whether or not highways are built, the technology and economics are comparatively irrelevant. It is an emotional question, a political question, a question of vested interests and countervailing forces."

As population and the gross national product continue to grow, the explosion of our cities can only accelerate. Already the suburbs have become impossibly congested with automobile traffic, and the space-seeking suburbanites have moved ever outward in a self-defeating effort to find air and space. The expressways lead the way, and the "developments," shopping centers, neon signs, and used-car lots follow close behind. Every year 2,500 square miles are swallowed up. In the New York metropolitan area, if zoning practices are unchanged, an addition of 6 million people to the present 19 million during the next twenty years will eat up more acreage than all the land that has been "developed" since the first Dutchman set foot on Manhattan. A frightening statistic. Equally frightening is the fact that in the cities the automobile population is growing twice as fast as the human. By 1980, our human population will increase to about 250 million, a rise of 39 per cent over the 1960 population. But automobile ownership is expected to increase by 64 per cent. And the number of miles driven will increase even faster. In 1960, total mileage driven in urban areas was 332 billion miles; this is expected to rise to 800 billion by 1980.

The further out suburbia spreads, the more it spends for roads. If the New York metropolitan area reaches the proportions predicted for it by 1980, the suburban areas will then be spending 38 per cent of their *total capital expenditures* for roads—38 per cent of all the money spent for water and sewerage, airports, port facilities, public transit, education, hospitals, welfare institutions, parks, and recreation facilities.

Southern California, the most automobile-oriented region in the nation, is again the horrible example. In Santa Clara County, 26 square miles of suburban subdivisions have sprawled across the countryside since 1947. These are arranged in a helter-skelter fashion throughout a 200-square-mile area in such a way that no sizable piece of usable open space remains. Park and recreation facilities for the residents of this subdivided horror are thus severely limited by their chaotic use of the land.

The two factors that promote urban sprawl are highways, which encourage the people to forsake all means of transportation for the automobile, and the uncontrolled commercial exploitation of the land, which results in the proliferation of expansive checkerboards of single-family, half-acre moonscapes. The cure for unbounded urban sprawl, then, consists of two things: First, provide fast, efficient, comfortable, economical public transportation that can compete with the automobile for the public favor. Second, control the use of land so that dwellings are arranged in clusters, leaving open spaces untouched for recreational uses. The dwelling clusters would naturally center on the public transit stops. Finally, good community planning would mix residential with commercial and industrial structures to reduce drastically the amount of commuter travel required.

These things can be and are being done, but not in the United States. Great Britain has curbed urban sprawl by establishing inviolate green belts around the cities, where no "development" may occur. In Scandinavia, public ownership of land, elected planning officials with genuine power to enforce their decisions, and the use of a reasonable share of resources to create a modern, efficient system of public transit have combined to produce an orderly environment designed for humans rather than machines. The suburbs of Stockholm, as one traveler has observed, have grown "where and how the authorities wanted them." They are clustered "like pearls on a string" at the stops along the mass transit lines. The result is this rhapsodic description of the Stockholm suburbs by a reporter for *Engineering News-Record:*

"A 25-mile trip from Stockholm's airport to the city acquaints a visitor with Sweden's planning. There are no hot-dog stands, chrome-trimmed diners, outdoor movies, used-car lots, automobile grave-yards, discount stores, beflagged gas stations, garish motels, or loan-shark offices, all united in scenic discord by billboards and signs screaming for attention.

"The ride from Stockholm airport takes you through natural open space, with vistas of stately cedars punctuated with pink rock out-croppings. The chief signs of human habitation are isolated farm-houses and, heralding the approach to the city, clusters of white-walled apartments from four to 10 stories high.

"This determination to preserve the amenities of the natural coun-tryside in close proximity to the densely settled areas pervades Swedish planning. Unlike the rapid, weedlike growth of American metrop-olises, Stockholm grows like a carefully tended garden. . . . In Sweden, urban transportation needs are anticipated instead of remembered; rapid transit lines are completed before development. Thus, unlike Los Angeles' commuters, Stockholm's commuters have a choice. And they patronize the subways heavily because of the speed, convenience, and comfort."

A few brave attempts are under way in the United States to estab-lish planned communities. The two "new towns" of Reston, Virginia, and Columbia, Maryland, both in the general Baltimore-Washington area, were designed as cluster communities to control urban sprawl. Since these towns are privately owned, the outcome of the experi-ment will depend upon their being a commercial success. But whether or not they succeed as isolated communities, their eventual fate is to be engulfed in the urban sprawl creeping outward from the nation's capital.

The 1967 R. S. Reynolds Memorial Award for community archi-tecture was awarded by the American Institute of Architects to the town of Cumbernauld, Scotland. This town was begun in 1956 and now is populated by 23,000 persons, with an eventual planned ca-pacity of 70,000. The AIA jury called Cumbernauld "the Western World's highest achievement in new urban design for modern human needs." What is so outstanding about the town? It "puts the automobile in its place—out of the way of pedestrians." Here is a radical idea in urban planning—design the city for use by humans, instead of automobiles. In Cumbernauld, vehicle and pedestrian traffic are completely separated, and no automobile is permitted to enter an area where people live except at the very beginning or end of its journey.

Transportation planning should be more than simply a spastic reaction to the pressure of automobile traffic. Since transportation modes exert a powerful influence on the shape and quality of the community, the transportation plan should be a primary part of the over-all plan for the use of the land. As Henry Fagin, professor of urban and regional planning at the University of Wisconsin, puts it, "People engaged in the comprehensive planning of urban transportation systems have two equally basic responsibilities. They have an obligation to plan transportation to *serve* the metropolis as it evolves. And they have a simultaneous obligation to develop the transportation system in ways that will help *shape* the metropolis as it evolves so as to fulfill better the objectives of the people."

The objectives of post-World War II America apparently are to live in the suburbs and work in the city. But if you live in the suburbs you must have a car. The automobile manufacturers are happy to oblige. And if you live in the suburbs and own a car, you want to drive to work in the city. The freeway builders are happy to oblige. The bulk of the pressure for building urban freeways stems from suburbanites who commute to work in the city. But this is precisely the kind of traffic that mass transit on steel rails handles most efficiently, and any prudent man would advocate building rail transit facilities rather than freeways for handling the commuter load.

The freeway advocate counters with two arguments. First, he says, most of the peak-load traffic in the city streets is not from commuters at all, but from cars and trucks that are just passing through. Second, he says, rail transit is regimentation, and the free-born American will have none of it. Given his choice, he will choose the rugged individualistic automobile every time. Let us examine these arguments for building freeways.

First, the "passing through" argument. This is exemplified in a statement made by Harry A. Williams, managing director of the

Automobile Manufacturers Association, in 1962: "Traffic surveys in our large cities show that over *80 per cent* of peak-hour morning and evening traffic on downtown streets is merely passing through to other destinations." The implication here is that urban traffic is so diffuse that no fixed rail route could possibly serve it, that only the infinitely flexible automobile could handle it, and that "by-pass" freeways would route most of this peak-hour traffic around and away from the city, where it wants to be in the first place. But other statistics, amassed by Mr. Williams' own Automobile Manufacturers Association in 1963, point to a different conclusion. These figures tell how people get to work in the metropolitan area, whether they live in the central city or in suburban rings. The survey covered all metropolitan areas with populations over 100,000. The results:

18,142,000 people lived in center city and worked in center city. Of these, 54.4 per cent commuted by car.

2,006,000 lived in center city and worked in the suburban rings. Of these, 84.9 per cent commuted by car.

525,000 lived in center city and worked outside the suburban rings. Of these, 74.9 per cent commuted by car.

6,330,000 lived in the suburban rings and worked in center city. Of these, 82.3 per cent commuted by car.

11,225,000 lived in the suburban rings and worked in the suburban rings. Of these, 74 per cent commuted by car.

1,058,000 lived in the suburban rings and worked outside the rings. Of these, 79 per cent commuted by car.

In light of these figures, can it be concluded that "over 80 per cent of peak-hour morning and evening traffic on downtown streets is merely passing through to other destinations"? Obviously not. A total of 9,870,000 plus 5,220,000, or 15,090,000 people are driving with downtown as their destination. This is 57.3 per cent of the total of 26,349,000 who are driving to work. Second, the only group of these six categories of commuters who could conceivably be "merely passing through" the city on their way to work would be those who live in the suburbs and work in the suburbs, and here we must assume that all of these live in the suburbs on one side of the city and drive through the city to a job on the other side. If we make this unlikely

assumption, we find that these constitute only 32.6 per cent of all
city drivers. Finally, even if we were to assume that the only logical
candidate for mass transit is the worker who either lives or works
in the center of the city, a wholly unsupportable premise, we find
that these workers constitute 69 per cent of the total population in
the AMA study.

Proponents of freeway-building like to portray the metropolitan
area as a featureless, amorphous spread of light gray, where a trip
could easily start anywhere and end anywhere—the conclusion being,
of course, that the free-wheeling automobile is the only form of transportation that can fill the bill. Anything like a "fixed" rail system,
they say, with a deprecatory emphasis on the horse-and-buggy,
locked-in sound of the word "fixed," could never hope to service
such a loose, free, unbridled, swinging scene as the modern metropolis. If we are all to live like gypsies, with no roots in either job or
home, perhaps they are right. But if the city—the culmination of
Western civilization—is to survive, and if we are to retain any note
of permanence and form in our lives, they must be proved wrong.
We must re-cement our exploding lives. We must plan our transportation to shape the metropolis to our desires. If we do not, the
centrifugal effects of the freeway will end in our disintegration.

Anyone who doubts that the urban freeway, and specifically the
"radial" freeway, is built primarily to serve the suburbanite commuter need only look at the statistics. True, there is a trend for
industry to move to the suburbs, and thus there is a growing "reverse"
movement of commuters who live in the city and work in the suburbs,
but this only reinforces the argument for rail transit in place of
freeways: railway cars will be occupied in both directions.

Almost all the population growth in this country takes place in
the suburban rings, and at least a third of those who live in the
suburban rings work in center city. An increasing number of those
who live in the city work in the suburbs. Both these groups are most
easily served by "fixed" rail transit. Further, and this is becoming
increasingly apparent, the job opportunities opening up in the suburbs are less and less available to those who live in center city, who
are more and more the disadvantaged minorities who own no automobile and therefore are dependent upon public transportation. Give

these people ready access to the suburbs and you increase the job opportunities that they need so desperately.

Several developments in the Philadelphia metropolitan area alone would discredit the argument that the suburb-to-city commuting crush is not a primary source of transportation congestion. First, a study just completed by the Delaware Valley Regional Planning Commission, covering Philadelphia and eight surrounding counties, concludes that twice as many people will be commuting to center city twenty years from now. Second, a six-mile, six-lane Lansdowne Expressway just approved by the same planning group is described by its proponents as a "direct link to Philadelphia from the western suburbs." No nonsense here about "just passing through." Third, the Schuylkill Expressway, notorious for its in-bound commuter jams in the morning and outbound jams in the evening, will be supplemented by a proposed parallel expressway to relieve commuter congestion. This parallel route, according to *The Evening Bulletin,* "would divert traffic from the stretch of the expressway where the congestion usually is worst," namely, near the center of the city where the commuters converge. Finally, the Pennsylvania Turnpike was built as a limited-access, high-speed, intercity highway between Philadelphia and Pittsburgh. It was *not* intended as a commuter road. But, although it was built as a through-traffic road, an overload of commuters in the Philadelphia area has created a traffic clog west of the city. So the Turnpike Commission is looking into the possibility of building parallel commuter roads on the 32-mile section just west of Philadelphia at an estimated cost of $500 million to siphon off some of the load.

When the eastern extension of the Pennsylvania Turnpike was built in 1954, everyone believed that it would serve to divert "just passing through" traffic from the west, around Philadelphia and onward to New Jersey. It has not worked out that way. The section has become largely a commuter road into Philadelphia. The route traversed by this section of the turnpike covers some of the most rapidly "developing" countryside in the nation. If parallel commuter roads are built, and who can doubt that they will be, the rate of "development" will be even faster.

So much for the "passing through" argument. It has been dismissed by Edmond L. Kanwit, head of the Social Impact Group in the Department of Transportation. He sees a future of "expanding streams of commuting in both directions," resulting from massive rebuilding downtown, new and rapid population increases following from the second population explosion, and growing employment in the suburbs. "Under these circumstances," he concludes, "it may become difficult to continue the present freedom in automobility so prized by Americans, lest central business districts, central city, and densely packed suburbs become involved in even worse traffic jams than we have thus far encountered."

What was the word used by Mr. Kanwit? Automobility? This goes to the second argument used by the freeway advocates, namely, that automobile transportation gives the U. S. citizen the freedom of movement that he must have in order to express his individuality—restriction to a "fixed" route defined by a railroad would inhibit his freedom and smack of collectivism. In this catechism, the chaotic growth of megalopolis under the influence of untrammeled freeway building is looked upon as an act of Nature that can never be channeled. Says AMA Director Harry A. Williams, ". . . the nature of modern urban-area growth is such that increasing reliance on individual motor vehicle passenger transportation will occur, and the nationwide down-ward trend in patronage of mass transit facilities is not apt to be reversed under any circumstances."

The automobile is the first transportation choice of the free American, and anything else is a "restriction," of his God-given rights. Says Humble Oil executive George L. McGonigle, "The tide is running toward greater choice in the modes of urban transportation, not toward restriction. And until a substitute can be found that duplicates the cost, convenience, and flexibility of the passenger automobile, we will continue to pay the cost of expressways to bring us downtown and back home in our cars."

Planning is inimical to the free movement of the individual, according to the freeway advocates. Says H. E. Humphreys, Jr., an executive of the U. S. Rubber Co. and chairman of the National Highway Users Conference, ". . . we do *not* feel that to the planners belongs the world. We do not feel that planners can convert freedom-loving, individualistic Americans into masses that fit the patterns. Rather, the patterns must fit freedom-loving, individualistic Americans." The patterns formed by that criterion are, of course, visible in every community.

In a study sponsored by the Automobile Manufacturers Association, Wilbur Smith and Associates came out hard against any attempt to force the transportation system into preconceived molds. "Because it serves citizens of a democratic society," concludes the report, "an urban transport system must recognize that rigid transportation criteria should not be imposed. It should reflect the importance of permitting freedom in the selection of mode of travel, type of trip, place of residence, place of work, and use of leisure time."

If this premise is granted, one can only conclude with Mr. Humphreys that urban sprawl is "the inevitable pattern." He happily concludes that "large areas" of our nation "will be constituted of one 'typical town' after another, with scarcely a break between." Our highway program, as at present conceived, says Mr. Humphreys, "recognizes that there must be provided ways for people to go, not just from a few radiating points to a central point—but that there must be ways for people to go in any and all directions, frequently, easily, economically." Mr. Humphreys concedes that, under certain conditions, public transportation is needed. But, as a representative of the rubber industry, he insists that "fixed" steel rails cannot do the job. "Flexibility is needed, and this is best provided by motor vehicles— automobiles that can go anywhere, and buses that can ride the freeways and spin off into suburban streets."

No one would deny that the demand for cars is real. The American *is* in love with his automobile. There are now in the United States nearly 100 million motor vehicles, or almost one for every two persons. By the year 2000, we will have an estimated 200 million vehicles, or one for every 1.6 persons.* Two-car families are now commonplace, and the three-car family is on the horizon. A recent survey of 10,000 families in California shows that many of them believe that a three-car garage will be a "must" in their next house. Says the managing director of Honolulu, "We're rapidly on our way to-

---

* "If you want to cross the street," goes the sick gag, "you'd better do it now."

ward becoming a three-car-per-family city. But when we do, two
of those cars are going to have to remain in the garage because they
won't be able to move."

This visceral passion for the automobile affects even those who
know better. In his book, *A Different Kind of Country,* which deplores many of the destructive aspects of highway building and automobile worship, Raymond F. Dasmann confesses, "Despite my knowledge of the problems that too many motor cars present, I find myself
reading the car ads wondering whether I should buy a cool, foreign
sports car, or some high-horsepowered Detroit production. I fight the
extensions of freeways in the wrong places, but feel a great sense of
relief when I leave a crowded avenue and spin onto the beltway. I
know there is a fairly reliable bus at the corner, but I drive to work
and pay dearly for parking. The national schizophrenia surrounding
the freeway-automobile problem is internally familiar to me." This
confession is reminiscent of the addict who is hooked on a narcotic
and has lost all hope of a cure.

Ownership of an automobile confers many blessings: unparalleled
freedom of action, opportunities for travel and home location, and
simply the pleasures of tooling around aimlessly. The possibilities for
movement seem infinite, and all with a degree of independence and
privacy never before achieved. Beneath the obvious surface attractions, of course, lie all the substrate and shadowy benefits in the
realms of sex, status, and power. Money is truly no object. When an
American buys an automobile, he is not making a purchase, he is
making a commitment. To tell him that the railroad might be a less
expensive way to commute is to bore him with irrelevancies. The
automobile gives him multiple choices in spades—he goes where he
wants to go, when he wants to go, and stops when *he* is ready, and
not before. The fact that he must follow the expressway or get
bogged down in a hopeless jam, that the timing of his trip is as rigor-
ously set by the surrounding traffic as that of any commuter train,
and that he stops an average of 14 times each trip for signs, red
lights, and the clog of cars ahead does not enter his calculations of
freedom.

The American has opted for the automobile. About 80 per cent
of all the families in the United States own at least one car. The

average urban family spends $400 per year for his automobile trans-
portation, which is more than one dollar in every ten spent for goods
and services. Most commuters realize that the trip to work would
cost less by public transportation, but they willingly spend more to
drive the car. Studies in many cities have shown that, even where
people believe it is more expensive to drive to work, they still choose
to drive.

Further, the higher the family income, the less use there is of
public transportation. There is a uniform, predictable relationship
between economic status and use of public transit: as economic
status goes up, use of transit goes down. As the editors of *Fortune*
said in an article some time ago, "Once a man has made a heavy
investment in a brand-new car, he wants to drive it. . . . If his wife
needs the car during the day, he may condescend to use public transit
to go back and forth to work. But the urge is strong to buy a second
car to drive to work—especially if public transit requires him to
transfer. Outside of business hours, mass transit has the dreariest
associations, and nothing dampens an evening in town quite so much
as going home by bus."

The attitude of the suburbanite commuter is typified by Karl Mos-
kowitz, assistant traffic engineer for California's Division of Highways. "At the present time," he says, "I consider myself auto-
oriented because there are two cars in my family of two people. I
have a ten-year-old car which I drive 4000 miles a year to and from
work, and my wife has a four-year-old car which she runs errands in
and that we use when we go out of town. Every time either of us
goes any place, we go by car.

"I live in the suburbs, 8.8 miles from where I work. It costs me
$317 a year, or $26.50 a month, to commute. I set my own time for
going and coming. I have a comfortable seat and privacy. I keep dry
in rainy weather, and it takes 24 minutes from my door to the door
of the office building where I work. When the freeway, which is now
underway, is completed, it will take only 18 minutes. It takes up to
5 minutes to get from the ground floor to the fifth floor of the building by mass transportation (elevators), including the wait.

"There is a freeway about four miles from where we live that does
not quite go downtown yet. This freeway is paralleled by a railroad

that does go downtown and is on an exclusive right-of-way. The railroad goes to the same place that the freeway goes (including the places where my neighbors and I work). All of us use the freeway from time to time; three of us use it daily, but none of us uses the railroad. We wouldn't use it even if there were some trains on it, and the reason why is that we don't want to live on the railroad, although four of us work near it."

This attitude—plus, of course, the undeniable fact that the service and accommodations on most rapid transit and commuter railroad systems in the nation are abominable—is responsible for a decline in patronage of public transportation, which results in further deterioration of service and further decline in patronage. Between 1955 and 1965, the number of people living in cities increased by 30 million and the number of automobiles by nearly as much—24 million. But the use of public transit decreased by 3,000 million rides, or about 25 per cent. The choice has been made, the results are all around us, and the future is clear.

Even those who derive their livelihood from transit turn to the automobile for their own transportation. One transit system manager notes gloomily that he must provide parking facilities for his employees who come to take out their transit runs. "How can we expect to sell this service to the public," he groans, "when we can't *give* it away to our own employees?"

The result of this unswerving faithfulness to the automobile is that, in vast areas of suburbia, the only convenient way to go anywhere is by car. Every family has a car. Many have two. If the suburb is lucky and forward-looking, there may be rudimentary public transportation service to the center of the city. But any movement within the suburb itself is possible only by car.

Any program to improve mass transit facilities either to guide suburban growth or to reduce automobile traffic congestion in existing suburbs must contend with the widespread belief that the suburbanite's devotion to his automobile is unshakable and that, rather than looking for ways to change his allegiance, we had better be looking for ways to cope with its results. At a 1962 symposium on urban transportation, AMA executive Kermit B. Rykken said the changes being wrought by the automobile are "inexorable" because they are dictated by the desires of the people. "They will not be altered by the construction of subways or fixed rail lines." This attitude is not by any means confined to the highway and automobile establishment. James W. Rouse, a Baltimore urban planner, maintains that any attempt to plan the growth and redevelopment of our cities so that maximum use can be made of rapid transit is "against the trend— against the real yearnings of American people," who will be "increasingly unwilling to be herded into public transit vehicles and will seek the flexibility of individual transportation in their own automobile." ⚡

Knox Banner, director of a private business and civic group concerned with the revitalization of downtown Washington, D. C., says that his group recognizes the strong preference of the American for his automobile, and therefore the needs of the automobile come first in any transportation planning, even though it might be evident that mass transit could do a better job. "We are not ivory tower planners," he says. "We live in a real world, with real people. We base our plans, not on our own personal preference, but on our professional judgment. We recognize the role of the automobile in contemporary America and the importance most Americans place on driving their cars. We do not have any reason to forecast any drastic changes in human habits and desires."

All highway engineers and most city planners seem to agree with U. S. Rubber Company's H. E. Humphreys, Jr., who says that people have proved beyond doubt, by the many financial sacrifices they make to own a car, that this is their preferred way to get around. Instead of trying to find ways to frustrate this desire, says Mr. Humphreys, we should be using our inventive genius to find ways to provide for it. Any people, he says, with the highly developed industrial civilization that is required to manufacture automobiles in such enormous quantities surely "must also be smart enough to provide highways on which to move and places on which to park."

We are certainly smart enough to do it, but we should first consider the consequences and decide whether we wish to do it. We should understand that the amount of land available for asphalting is static, that the population continues to grow inexorably, and that the number of automobiles per capita also continues to grow with rising affluence. If we assume, as we must, that some day the so-called war on poverty will be won, and all those millions who now are forced to walk or ride a crowded bus will be able to buy automobiles, it becomes clear that what Mr. Humphreys calls "one of America's great freedoms—automobility" must somehow be curtailed.

The logical consequences of unbridled "automobility" could be ludicrous. Suppose, for example, that all those who now commute to Manhattan by public transportation suddenly decided to exercise their God-given right to drive. If the city should attempt to accommodate this desire, the entire downtown area would have to be leveled just to provide parking space—something like five square miles of it. But a moving vehicle requires much more room than a parked one. If all these cars wished to move about on the island, the city would have to build six or eight levels of street facilities to handle the traffic. But then, of course, there would be nothing on the island but eight levels of automobiles in motion, and very little reason for them to be there.

New York, of course, is not typical. Such a high population density could not exist without an extensive system of public transportation, and especially "fixed rail" transit. But there is more than a casual connection between this high human density and the fact that this city, despite smog, garbage strikes, and monumental traffic snarls, is still unparalleled as the financial, intellectual, and cultural center of the nation. In addition, all other mayors and their chambers of commerce worship at the shrine of growth—if their prayers are answered, they will all some day have their own New Yorks. But if their transportation plans are fulfilled, they will end up with Los Angeleses instead.

Philip Harrington, former transportation chief for the city of Chicago, has conceded that the unquestioned ideal standard of travel would permit every individual to own a car, to drive it freely, quickly, safely, and unimpeded to any destination, and to have a doorman waiting there to park the car for him and to deliver it on request. But, he says, unless we are prepared to wreck our city, no such Utopia is possible, even if we could afford it. Mr. Harrington condemns the "excessive and uneconomical use of the private automobile for daily travel to and from home and place of work." Those who have no need for their cars for their daily activities, he says, should leave them home, and avail themselves of public carrier facilities.

The straightforward way to return the downtown area to the people is to close its streets to the automobile. The British Transport Ministry is studying a plan for charging a toll to each automobile entering a city center. Ideas such as these elicit cries of anguish and outrage from downtown merchants associations, parking lot operators, and others with a commercial interest in automobility. Such ideas are also condemned by many as an unwarranted, unpalatable, and possibly even unconstitutional restriction of freedom. H. E. Humphreys, Jr., says that the man who prefers to drive his car should never be restricted as to where or when he can drive. Washington's Knox Banner maintains that the central position of the automobile in our transportation system will never be threatened, "either by individual choice or by dictation. We couldn't keep automobiles out of downtown even if we wanted to." At first reading, this statement would seem to assign omnipotent qualities of inevitability to a machine, but Mr. Banner makes it clear that these qualities stem from the political realities rather from anything intrinsic to Detroit iron: "It is difficult to conceive how the use of automobiles could be limited within certain areas, such as downtown, without resorting to some form of total dictatorial controls involving special privilege or sanction. Surely our transportation problems can never be so serious that we would abandon our democratic and reasonable processes in order to cope with them. I would ask those advocates of rigid controls: Who shall make the decision as to who may drive and who must use mass transit to reach his destination?"

Who indeed? The idea is dangerously un-American. Even the advocates of mass transit shrink from suggesting any such infringement of our rights. Says George W. Anderson, executive vice-president of the American Transit Association, "I know of no officer of our Association or other person authorized to speak for the industry who has ever advocated that automobiles should be barred from the core areas of our cities; or that the production of automobiles or their sale should be prohibited or restricted. It would obviously be ridiculous for any responsible person to make such a statement."

Obviously ridiculous? One of the regrettable consequences of crowding an exploding population into urban and suburban masses of humanity is that behavior once harmlessly indulged in becomes antisocial and subject to restriction for the welfare of the community. The right to carry and freely use firearms was never questioned on the frontier or in the vast sweeps of the great prairie land, because a wild shot would hit nothing but buffalo grass. A man who lives on a farm can spit on the ground freely on impulse, but there is a law prohibiting it in the city. He can drink himself into a state of euphoria and run screaming through his wheat fields, and he will disturb only the crows. But such behavior in the city will result in his being jailed as drunk and disorderly.

It is becoming quite clear that the free passage of automobiles throughout the land is antisocial behavior. Further, the attempt to pave the land so as to accommodate and even to encourage such free passage is antisocial. Both activities must be curtailed. But the forces working to encourage them are strong, and hope for salvation is dim.

The Road Gang

To the most extreme opponents of the freeway builders, the highway-man appears as a Mad Paver, astride his bulldozer, trailing oceans of asphalt, imbued with a single-minded passion to hard-surface the world. Nothing is so beautiful to his eye as a flat, unbroken plain of black-top stretching in every direction to the horizon, the better to serve the limitless possibility for the movement of automobiles. In his zeal to make every point on earth accessible to the motorist, he will cover every other point with his bituminous carpet.

This view is exaggerated, but not much.

Take the rubber man, H. E. Humphreys, Jr. Citing the automobile as "the number-one mark of social success," Mr. Humphreys puts these words in the mouth of the typical American motorist: "I want to use my car. I want good roads to drive on. I want to see something when I am driving on these roads. I want to get where I am going conveniently and safely. And I want a place to park when I get there." What should we do for this citizen? Build more roads, of course. If we fulfill our responsibilities to this avid motorist, says Mr. Humphreys, we shall have safe expressways from coast to coast, making it more economical for a family to vacation in any part of the country. We shall bring savings to everyone through faster freight deliveries and less time-consuming business trips. We shall have more beautiful roadsides and clean, uncongested cities with easy shopping and convenient commuting. "Such a life would revolve around an even greater use of the motor vehicle."

We are struggling to fulfill Mr. Humphreys' dream. But alas, as House Roads Subcommittee Chairman John C. Kluczynski laments,

". . . no matter what we do, we are still fifteen years behind on our road system in the United States."

We are buying automobiles faster than roads can be built to accommodate them. Despite the $10 billion or so we are now spending annually on new highways, if our population is to double by the year 2000 and our automobile population is to triple, we haven't seen anything yet. As suburbs spread even further into the hinterlands and commuting trips lengthen, as the work week shrinks and the time for leisure travel increases, as the vigorous, resourceful and politically potent trucking industry shoulders a greater share of freight transportation, by the beginning of the next century passenger transportation demands will multiply five times and freight demands seven times. If we even make the attempt to satisfy this demand by movement of rubber-tired vehicles, vast sections of our nation will have to be cleared to make room for the highways that are needed. It is a very simple extrapolation.

But, according to the pavers, that is not necessarily bad. Many sections of our cities are cesspools of blight, and clearing them for highways is an excellent way to remove the blight. It is also an excellent way to take from people to give to the automobile, but that is the course to which we are committed. The highway builders sturdily maintain that the urban freeway, properly "integrated" with parking facilities, shops, offices, homes, and other parts of the city, can be completely compatible with other uses. Its design and construction, they say, "must involve the total environmental redevelopment of the area through which it passes." They envision the freeway as the primary urban structure, to which everything else is subsidiary. Freeways, according to this school of urban planning, should "take the lead in generating amenity in a city . . . by having parks and playgrounds pass under them, new structures built over them." In this way, one supposes, every building and every playground becomes instantly accessible to the motorist.

Those to whom the Ultimate City means islands of humanity separated by rivers of moving and stationary vehicles see the freeway, in the words of Baltimore urban expert James W. Rouse, "as one of the most important tools in breaking up the city into human-being sized communities that a man, his wife, and family can comprehend and be a part of." This is a most curious concept. Those who love the city as a place to live and work believe the urban community is best formed by the two or three fine-grained city blocks so well described by Jane Jacobs, which attains its sense of community and interdependence through the diversity of homes, shops, schools, and working places that form the neighborhood. It is difficult to see how the intrusion of streams of high-speed automobiles on eight-lane freeways can enhance the sense of community.

But the doctrine persists. The spokesman for the Automobile Manufacturers Association, Harry A. Williams, contends that the freeway is not only an excellent tool for creating neighborhoods out of urban chaos, it is the *only* tool. "These freeway networks," he insists, "are the only available method—let me repeat, the *only* available method —for redeveloping those parts of our central cities which have become blighted in coming years. Such freeways, coupled with major arterial routes feeding them, create neighbood cells within which the city planner can work with confidence in redeveloping neighborhoods that have become structurally or functionally obsolete." The word "cells" was, perhaps, ill-chosen, but, one believes, descriptive. If, as many believe, the automobile is responsible for a good part of the urban blight, the proposal to eradicate blight by building more freeways lacks logic.

One reason for hostility to urban freeways is that they are esthetically offensive. A freeway can never be as attractive to the eye as the park through which it runs. And even where it rips through blighted ghettos, the rotting tenements that it replaces might better be replaced with modern, attractive homes for the families who once lived there.

But the pavers argue that the freeway has a beauty of its own that makes it an asset to the urban scene. In the words of one city planner, ". . . the highway can contribute measurably to a higher order of beauty in metropolitan areas . . . and can serve the city's people in beauty as well as efficiency." Another says that of all the elements of our future transportation system, the freeway offers the "greatest potential for community improvement." It can not only serve our transportation needs, but it can also "guide and promote desirable development and create areas of beauty."

Rex M. Whitton, former federal highway administrator, admitted to a Congressional committee in 1966 that the expressway builders were meeting increasing resistance in a number of metropolitan areas all over the nation. One reason for this, he said, is that "some groups feel we are interfering or desecrating the cultural and historical and the esthetic values of the city. I do not have that feeling. I think that overall the highways are adding to the city's cultural value and esthetic value by making it possible for the people to see it." The argument that the beauties of our land are hidden from view, and that the highway makes it possible for the citizens to see and appreciate them, is frequently heard in connection with highway building in the National Parks and wilderness areas, with some justification. But the same argument applied to the city freeway appears to lack substance.

In a magazine article earlier that same year, Mr. Whitton went one step further: he stated that the highway designer attempts to provide a road that "enhances, where possible, established neighborhoods, school districts, church parishes, park and recreation areas, historical sites, wildlife habitats, and the landscape." It is difficult to conceive of the manner in which any highway, however cunningly designed, could possibly "enhance" any of these things—it is especially difficult to see how a highway can "enhance" a park, a historical site, or a wildlife habitat. As Mr. Whitton himself concluded, it is "a very large order."

This concern for esthetic values displayed by Mr. Whitton has been thrust upon the highway engineer by the heat and scope of the nationwide uprising engendered by his destructive march across the land. The engineer's attitude is customarily shaped by the physical parameters of the job to be done and the materials and money required to do it. It is typified in a paper published in a 1957 engineering journal describing how the civil engineer locates a new highway. This paper was published just as the Interstate Highway program was beginning, and before the national outcry had developed. In it, the author states that "freeways should be located to best serve traffic demands. . . . Where two or more routes are feasible within a general location, determination of the final line should be made upon the results of a road user benefit analysis." That is plain enough. The freeway is designed for the use of the motorist, and his needs are overriding. The author goes on to say that, wherever traffic demand between any two points is high enough to justify a freeway, it should be built. Finally, he says, if the community has a planning authority, the freeway development may be "dovetailed" into its future plans, but if no planning authority exists, the freeway will go in anyway, and "the freeway system will dictate, to a large extent, the future development of the area."

In the decade since that paper was published, the highway engineers have been moved slowly and grudgingly off that position. Community planners, architects, and incensed citizens' groups are chipping away at the dictatorial powers exercised by state highway departments in selecting highway routes. As a result, some proposed routes have been shifted about to reduce the damage in some communities, and construction has been delayed in others, but, with the possible single exception of San Francisco, no community has successfully thwarted the bulldozer completely.

The highway bulldozer is powered by an alliance of the federal and state governments, guided and stimulated by the lobbying activities of the beneficiary industries. For many years, the highway pork barrel has been nurtured and tended by a happy and compatible establishment comprising the Public Works committees of both houses of Congress, the Federal Highway Administration, the state highway officials, and the lobbyists for the many industries—automobiles, petroleum, construction materials, building contractors, auto clubs, and so on—that benefit from the huge amounts added every year to the barrel. There is considerable mutual back-scratching all along the line.

Cooperation between federal and state officials has always been very close. During the years when the Federal Highway Administration was part of the business-oriented Department of Commerce, the two federal highway administrators, Bertram Tallamy and Rex Whitton, both highway engineers, were past-presidents of the American Association of State Highway Officials. When the Department of Transportation was created in 1966, and the Federal Highway Administration was shifted there, a chink appeared in that relationship: neither the Secretary of Transportation, Alan Boyd, nor the new Highway Administrator, Lowell Bridwell, was a highway engineer,

Boyd having been a Florida lawyer and Bridwell an Ohio newspaper-man. Advocates of other forms of transportation can now get at least a hearing in the executive branch, but so far the money still goes to highways.

In the legislative branch, or, as former Senator Joseph Clark calls it, the "sapless branch," the devotion to the pavers appears to be un-dimmed. Billions of dollars each year are generated automatically in the Highway Trust Fund without the need for the Congress to lift a finger to tax anyone. It remains only to deal the money out to the states. The lobbyists for the various highway industries are in faithful, un-blinking attendance to ensure that no bottlenecks appear in the pipe-line. Members of Congress usually maintain a discreet silence about such things, but, in the fall of 1967, Representative Lionel Van Deer-lin, a Democrat from California, burst out in an unaccustomed fit of pique: "For far too long the automobile industry, swaggering through our House office buildings with high-handed lobbyists—some of them paid up to $100 an hour—has sought to impose auto management's selfish interests over the judgment of the American public." Mr. Deer-lin's ire had been aroused by the difficulty that Congress was experienc-ing in passing legislation to curb air pollution, but one feels confident that the same "high-handed lobbyists" are working just as hard to promote highway construction as they are to soften air-pollution con-trols.

The automotive industry is only the beginning. Every additional mile of highway means an additional 50,000 gallons of motor fuel consumed each year. We are adding pavement to the land at the rate of about 45,000 miles per year, which means an additional consump-tion of about 2¼ billion gallons of fuel each year. At 4 cents per gallon, that means an increase in the Highway Trust Fund of $90 million per year. In the face of this growth, the petroleum industry cannot be expected to maintain an attitude of cool detachment. Nor can the highway engineers. At least one of them has complained in writing about the proliferation of small foreign cars on our highways. Their fuel consumption is too low to support road-building at the proper rate.

About 90 per cent of the new pavement laid each year is topped with asphalt. Since the beginning of the Interstate Highway program, the capacity of the asphalt pavement industry has increased by 132 per cent—from 97 million to 225 million tons per year. There are 3,500 asphalt plants in the United States, distributed among 1,800 different companies. Asphalt production has set a new record every year since the Interstate program began, with the single exception of 1967.

The trucking industry also has an interest in better highways. There are now more than 15 million trucks on our roads, carrying 22 per cent of all our intercity freight, and carrying 90 per cent of our livestock and 63 per cent of our produce to market. Nearly ten million persons earn their living in the manufacture, distribution, maintenance, or commercial use of trucks.

The list goes on and on. The statistics are equally impressive for dozens of other industries dependent in one way or another on highway transportation. None of them is reluctant to communicate its faith in the importance of paving to our national economy, in the creed, as one of them puts it, that "as highway transportation grows so grows the nation."

H. E. Humphreys, Jr., says flatly that if "any impediment" is put in the way of the natural growth of highway transport, no city, no farm, no business, no family, no individual will be exempt from the destructive consequences. "The shuttle that weaves the web of our national life," he says, "is automobility." The engineering director of the Keystone Auto Club has wondered out loud how any opposition to highway building could possibly develop in a land where "the automobile has been so long a symbol of our high standard of living."

A recent full-page advertisement in *The Wall Street Journal*, "One of a series presented by Ford Motor Company on behalf of the American Trucking industry to help keep America moving ahead," helped to spread the gospel:

"You find congestion wherever you find people. Always have, even in the horse-and-buggy days.

"Automobiles broke the turn-of-the-century traffic jam. Downtown traffic moved faster, more freely. And because people became mobile they could spread out from the city's heart.

"Now the plot (and the traffic) thickens again. What's the answer? Keep private vehicles out of the central city entirely, as some planners advocate?

"Hardly. Keep cars away and you keep people away. That's how Americans are today.

"Modern highways don't cause congestion, they relieve it. You may complain about expressway traffic in New York or Detroit or Los Angeles. But you get in and out in about two-thirds the time you could a decade ago. And twice as safely.

"We need improved public transportation in many cities, certainly. (Interestingly, more than three-fourths of all transit passengers ride buses using the same highways and streets as passenger cars.)

"But this is even more certain: we also need to complete—and to supplement—our urban highway system so that cars, trucks, and buses can serve the American people more efficiently."

The Ford Motor Company has a message—simple, hard-hitting, appealing—and it has the resources to promote that message. It is unfortunate that nowhere does there exist an equally potent power center that can give equal time to the exploration of such postulates as:

1. The swift, efficient movement of automobiles is not necessarily the highest function of civilized man.

2. Spreading out from the city's heart may not be the most desirable demographic trend. If freeways were not turning our cities into such horrors, it might not even *be* the trend.

3. Just because Americans are wedded to their cars, we need not assume they cannot be divorced.

4. The reason why such a high proportion of transit riders move on rubber tires along highways may be that too few communities have had the foresight to build subways and support commuter railroads.

The Asphalt Institute, the trade association of the asphalt industry, sees a hard-headed need to encourage people with cars to keep on the move so that more gasoline will be burned, pouring more tax money into the highway construction pot. "It is the purpose of travel development to encourage motorists to take more pleasure and vacation trips and drive longer distances," says the Institute. "If the campaign is successful, it will automatically effect a rise in annual fuel consumption per vehicle and thus make more revenue available for road construction." Highway officials should recognize they are really the managers of vast "revenue-producing transportation systems nourished and extended by taxes on gasoline and other road-user commodities. Thus the more motorists travel, the more funds for road construction are produced, enabling highway departments to build and improve still more mileage as needed." It almost begins to sound like an argument for road-building as an end in itself. "We have a self-perpetuating cycle," the Institute goes on, "the key element of which is new paved roads. The 45,000 new miles added to the road and street network each year accommodate automotive travel, generate fuel consumption, produce road-building revenue. Scratch the new roads and the cycle ceases to function. . . . Paved roads produce revenue so highway departments can maintain existing mileage and build more roads."

A minor but significant triumph was recorded in the July, 1967, issue of the Institute's publication *Asphalt*. "No one broke a bottle of champagne," the article begins, "or threw a party, or snipped a ribbon, or wrote a story. But for the Connecticut Highway Department it was an event worth recording. One hot, cloudless afternoon last summer an asphalt paving machine covered up the very last mile of unpaved road on the state road system."

This event took place in the village of Woodstock, on State Route 197. The writer of the article describes Woodstock as "tucked quietly away in the northeast corner of the Nutmeg State," with big old comfortable homes standing among the ancient elms and maples that line the broad main street. It sounds like a Huck Finn kind of town. "Tranquility, in 1967, is not easy to find, but it is found in Woodstock." But the main street, once a sea of mud in winter and a cloud of dust in summer, has changed. "Now it is fully paved, its asphalt surface dark and smooth and inviting."

One is tempted to guess that tranquillity is no longer found in Woodstock, either.

The third corner of the federal-industry-state troika is distributed among the capitals of the fifty states.

The Congressional delegation for each state is pleased to announce annually an increasing allocation of federal-aid highway money. The governor is pleased to welcome the money and the state highway department is pleased to spend it. Highway construction and maintenance is the largest single activity of the state; it accounts for 70 to 75 per cent of all capital expenditures. The remainder takes care of schools, hospitals, public buildings, natural resources, and other miscellaneous needs. The highway department is thus by far the largest distributor of largesse in the state. It wishes to remain so.

The regular, continuing federal-aid highway program provides that half the construction costs will be provided by the federal government. The 41,000-mile Interstate program provides 90 per cent federal money. In both of these programs, there is feverish competition among the states to qualify as many projects as possible for federal approval. Therefore, when a route is proposed, one finds its quick approval being urged by the highway department, the governor, the state legislators, and just about everyone else for whom the federal dollar means votes, or on whom a dollar can rub off.

One quirk of the federal highway law can result in the bulldozing of entirely new roads across the landscape, when the improvement of an older route might do the job as well. The 90-per-cent federal money in the Interstate program is available only for *new* routes. For improvement of older routes, only 50-per-cent federal money can be had. So, faced with a choice, local officials find it tempting to push through the new road.

Even where federal funds are involved, it is the state that has the primary responsibility to select the route for a new highway, design it, acquire the land for the right-of-way, let the contracts to the road builders, supervise the construction, and thereafter maintain the completed highway. If federal funds are involved, the Bureau of Public Roads must review and approve each step along the way, and the states must meet certain requirements of federal law. These requirements have been tightened several times since 1956, in response to anguished outcries from local communities throughout the country as the combination of heady power and huge influxes of Trust Fund money sent state highway bulldozers slashing indiscriminately across the countryside.

At the time the trust fund was set up and the Interstate system approved, Congress added the requirement that no project would be approved unless the state could show that a public hearing had been held in the community and that the *economic* effects of the proposed highway had been considered. In the debate on this provision, some Senators opposed it on the grounds that it was an intrusion on states' right. The intrusion is minimal, however, since there is no requirement that the state take any heed of what is said during the hearings. As a result, the usual gambit of the highway department has been to delay holding public hearings until the plans for the highway are so far along that any major change in the route would be economically unfeasible.

In July, 1957, just as the Interstate system was getting under way, *Better Roads* magazine asked a group of state highway engineers, "How much information about proposed highway routes should be given out before the location of a route is definitely determined?" In explaining the reason for the survey, the magazine stated that "The omnipresent 'operator' trying to make a few fast dollars, and the landowner who does not want his property cut up, have both made this problem acute, and just about every road department has had to decide for itself how much information it should give out."

Responses to the survey ranged from "tell them everything" to "tell them nothing." Examples of the latter response illustrate the attitudes of some highway engineers toward their communities:

Daniel K. Kelly, a county engineer in Mississippi, said that if he had the authority, he would establish several alternate routes, even though he knew which one he was going to use. This would keep anyone from getting inside information and taking advantage of it. "I would run several lines, and when I had decided which one I was going to use, I would prepare the condemnation papers very secretly. Then I would drop them in the file all at once so that no one would have any advance notice."

W. W. Seltzer, right-of-way engineer in Pennsylvania, replied: "When surveys are being made for studies of future highway locations, we have many inquiries from individuals and organizations. It is our policy, however, not to give out any information before the highway alignment has been definitely established and the property

has been condemned. In Pennsylvania, condemnation is effected by
the governor's approval of the right-of-way plan. Before the date
of approval, we give out just as little information as possible."

H. F. Hart, special right-of-way engineer for the state of Delaware,
said: "On all proposed relocations of our highways, except for the
interstate system, we do not publicize the proposed construction of
these highways unless we have a definite centerline established and
know the right-of-way requirements. We find it advantageous to wait
until the definite location has been established. For the interstate
system, of course, it is necessary to hold public hearings regarding
proposed locations."

The distinction drawn by Mr. Hart is worth further examination.
What he says is that, when federal funds are involved in a highway,
a public hearing is mandatory. When only state funds are involved,
there is no requirement for public hearings, and the highway department plays the game very close to the vest—giving information to
the public only after the "definite location has been established." This
procedure varies from state to state. In California, for example, a
1964 law suggests that public hearings be held before construction
to give the people an opportunity to express their views on the proposed route. The last section of this law says, however, that failure
of the highway commission to hold public hearings "shall not invali-
date any action of the commission as to the adoption of a routing
for any state highway, nor shall such failure be admissible evidence
in any litigation for the acquisition of rights of way or involving the
allocation of funds for the construction of the highway." In other
words, hearings are recommended, but if they are not held, the
decision of the highway commission is still valid.

Any state that desires a highway badly enough need only forgo
federal funds in order to avoid the requirement for public hearings.
This situation poses an interesting commentary on the popular con-
ception as to the relative sensitivity and responsiveness to local needs
of the federal government, as compared with the state government.
There is widespread belief that, the further the seat of government
is from the local problem, the less responsive it is to the needs of
the people. Thus we hear the cry for states' rights and warnings
against any movement of jurisdiction to Washington. In most of the

highway controversies around the country, citizens' groups opposing this or that route are finding that their greatest protection against the arbitrary exercise of power lies in Washington.

Richard Stoddart, a leader of the citizens' group fighting the construction of Interstate 290 through the Shaker Lakes area, tells where the pressures are to build and where the restraints arise. At the local level: "The Cleveland Chamber of Commerce, which is now the Greater Cleveland Growth Association, has never gotten into the sophisticated questions of routing. Its attitude, like that of all chambers of commerce, is 'freeways are progress. Build them. It doesn't matter too much where.' " At the county and state level: "Political party doesn't seem to mean much. The county engineer is a Democrat. The governor is a Republican. When it comes to highways there is very little divergence in thinking. They don't think politically. They want to build freeways. They want that federal money. The governor's position as a Republican governor in the Great Society is 'Get the dollar.' The pressure is on at the state level to build Interstate 290—there's probably between $70 million and $125 million riding on it." At the federal level: "We think that the advent of Boyd and Bridwell in Washington is one of the finest things that has ever happened. The difficulty is that the people on the local level, and in Columbus, disagree with what Boyd and Bridwell are doing."

The proposed Hudson River Expressway along the east shore of the Hudson River between Tarrytown and Ossining is opposed vigorously by a Citizens Committee for the Hudson Valley, most of whose members are stanch Republicans, and therefore should be advocates of local rule and states' rights. In their view, the state of New York is attempting to ram this expressway down their throats. The chairman of this committee observed not too long ago that the members "are so shocked by this state legislative action that they have renounced their normal objections to federal intervention and now seek federal law to protect the Hudson Valley." As a result of their experience with this expressway, many of these Westchester County Republicans now believe firmly that the responsiveness of government at the federal level is much greater than at the state level. They give four reasons for this: (1) Because of differences in salary, a much higher caliber official can be attracted to government at the federal

level. Local governments simply cannot afford to pay the salaries
to get top-notch talent. (2) Public servants at the local level are
much closer to, and therefore much more vulnerable to, pressures
from local special interests, such as, in the case of highways, local
chambers of commerce, real estate developers, building contractors.
(3) The average voter shows much less interest in the selection of
people for local government, and therefore he usually makes a poorer
choice. (4) The fragmentation of political boundaries at the local
level, and the resistance of local governments to relinquishing any
power to regional governments all but paralyze government at the
local level.

A public hearing, if held, is presided over by an official of the
state highway department, usually the district engineer. Testimony is
taken, put in a neat package, and submitted to the Bureau of Public
Roads together with the state proposal. This is all the state is legally
required to do. It is under no obligation to heed any complaints or
any requests for a change in plans. If any action is taken on citizen
complaints, it usually must stem from a refusal of the federal government to approve the route without heeding those complaints. But it
is extremely difficult for a local citizens' group to make a strong,
reasoned case for change. The state has probably spent hundreds of
thousands of dollars on many months of study by expert highway
consultants. It can easily make the case that the economic effects
have been considered, as required by federal law, and that they are
beneficial. Finally, the information presented by the state at the
public hearing may be the first hard data available to the public.
There will always be some complaints about a proposed highway
route, no matter where it is put. In view of all this, it becomes a
very difficult proposition, indeed, for any group of citizens, no matter
how well organized, to present a case for a change of route that has
a chance of standing up in the face of the overwhelming weight of
the case brought by the state.

The value of public hearings depends on how much information
the public can get before the hearings are held. Starting cold, a citizen
hoping to present a case must find what information is available,
where in the bureaucratic maze of the state offices it lies, and what
cooperation or opposition he is likely to encounter in digging it out.

The paperwork generated by a highway study is mountainous, and the uninitiated, even given free access by busy highway engineers, which is unlikely, is faced with a difficult job to make sense out of it. In contrast to this situation, it is more than likely that special interest groups who can be counted on to speak out in favor of the highway are well briefed in advance in preparation for the testimony they will offer at the hearings.

Unless there is an organized citizens' group in opposition to a proposed urban freeway, testimony at the hearings is usually predominantly pro-freeway. At the hearing for the Tacony Expressway in Philadelphia, for example, which was held February 27, 1968, in the auditorium of Olney High School, most of those who testified were representatives of civic associations, chambers of commerce, and individual business firms. Although each of them had some quarrel with one detail or other, to a man they supported the plan for the expressway. Its route will follow the course of the Frankford and Tacony creeks from the Delaware River into the heart of northeast Philadelphia, through industrial, commercial, and residential land, for a distance of 4.69 miles, with seven interchanges. The estimated cost is $78.9 million, or nearly $17 million per mile.

Comments of the witnesses at this hearing were typical of the local businessman's attitude: "It is necessary for the economy of this area." "It is an area of rapid growth, where the automobile population is exploding at a rate three times that of the human population." "The Tacony Expressway will help to revitalize this major industrial area of Philadelphia." "A modern highway system is the key to Philadelphia's growth and progress." Some of those who testified took the opportunity to condemn the announcement by President Johnson, just one month before, that he was withholding $600 million in highway funds to combat inflation. One irate businessman stated that "the withholding of highway funds to inhibit inflation is ridiculous." Another complained that "the recent cutback in funds will again delay vital, long overdue highway programs. Keystone [Automobile Club] condemns this as arbitrary and completely unjustifiable."

Even the transit company voted Yes. Its representative at the hearing stated that "Philadelphia Transportation Company endorses the

construction of the Tacony Expressway. In its daily operations near
the proposed limited-access highway, it is confronted with continu-
ously increasing traffic congestion, to the detriment of the transit-
riding public as well as the motorist, and caused by the critical shortage of highway capacity in the area. We believe that this expressway
will substantially reduce this undercapacity, with resulting generally
improved economic attractiveness for all elements of the community
nearby."

One lone citizen, who had sat with growing impatience through
the lengthy opening remarks of members of the highway department,
then the weary parade of business boosters and their unanimous
urging to build highways, finally got the floor and vented his spleen:
"I think it's a farce to ask people to come and to have to listen to
the city officials, the state officials, the chamber of commerce, and
many of the other people downtown who have had the 'in,' present
their statements, when I think their concern should be to hear what
the citizens, the residents of this area are concerned about. I think
the procedure should be reversed. Let the residents of the area make
their presentation first, and let the city officials, let the chamber of
commerce sit and listen and find out what are the concerns of the
people."

This kind of testimony, although clearly sincere and passionate,
is hardly likely to persuade an official in Washington, reviewing the
transcript of the hearings, that the federal government should disapprove the highway plan because of local opposition.

Walter C. Frame, vice-president of the Conference of California
Historical Societies, bitterly condemned the pro-forma nature of
hearings on a proposed freeway through Sacramento. The fact that
the threatened area was a "treasure trove" of historical sites, he said,
"had no effect whatever upon either the engineers or the highway
commission. The meeting of the highway commission to consider the
effect upon history of the freeway construction in the spring of 1962
was a farce conducted in utter disregard of either decency or good
taste. . . . The meeting was held in a hearing room which would
not hold one quarter of the people who were called to the meeting.
The first two hours were devoted to witnesses in praise of the freeway. . . . Before the opposition speakers had finished their testimony,

various members of the commission left the room. The matter was taken under advisement and no public disclosure has ever been made of their findings, if any were made."

In general, a citizen whose property is condemned by the state for use by the highway department has recourse in the condemnation proceedings to arrive at a fair price for his property, and usually he does. But if he wishes to change the route of the highway and save his property, he has no avenue of appeal. Petitions and letters to government officials are of little avail. Testimony at public hearings can be recorded and then ignored. Presentation of an alternative route with any hope of acceptance is extremely difficult to accomplish because of lack of information and because of the high cost of a professional study. Finally, in most states, the courts have found themselves unable to intervene.

Typical is a ruling of a California court in 1950 stating that state highway legislation has given the highway commission power to determine when and where freeways will be constructed, and that this delegation of authority is right and proper. This was upheld by the California Supreme Court in a 1959 ruling stating that a decision of the California Highway Commission as to the location of a freeway is final and cannot be made an issue for the court to decide. This is true even though fraud, bad faith, or abuse of discretion on the part of the commission might be alleged by those opposing the route. The court further ruled that evidence of alternate routes or evidence as to the cost of acquisition of other land is not admissible.

Such decisions have been repeated in state after state. The Idaho Supreme Court, for example, has ruled that "the power to determine the location of highways is a legislative, not a judicial function," and thus there can be no judicial appeal from decisions of the State Highway Board on the routing of a new highway. The Colorado Supreme Court has held that the court cannot substitute its judgment for that of the State Highway Department in locating a highway.

In an effort to reduce the possibilities for arbitrary bulldozing by the state highway departments, the Federal Aid Highway Act of 1962 includes a section stipulating that the federal government shall not approve any program for projects in any urban area of more than 50,000 population unless it finds that such projects are based

on a "continuing comprehensive transportation planning process carried on cooperatively by States and local communities." The efficacy
of this move is questionable. Most communities have a planning
body of some kind or other. Who is to say what is "comprehensive"?
Further, if a continuing, comprehensive, cooperative plan in a given
area results in the recommendation that transportation needs can
be met only by building as many freeways as possible as quickly as
possible with all the federal money possible, who is to say it nay?

Such attempts to soften the impact of the highway on the city continue to proceed on the assumption that the highway should be built
—the problem being, where is the best place for it? There still remains the question, Should it be built at all? This question is being
asked, but not very loudly.

Taming the Wilderness

At Myers Flat, in Humboldt Redwoods State Park in northern California, there is a living redwood tree with a road built through its base. This triumph of engineering, which enables the tourist to drive his automobile through the heart of this forest monarch, might just be the most striking symbol in our nation, and possibly in the world, of man's subjugation of nature, as exemplified by the penetration of the highway into the wilderness.

This victory is not without its price. When a four-lane divided freeway was cut through Humboldt Park recently, thousands of trees were destroyed. To those who believe that one redwood is very much like another, this may be no great loss, but to those who believe that trees are more beautiful than asphalt, it was a disaster.

The pressure has been growing to extend this expressway in one continuous sweep through all the redwood groves of northern California. A bitter controversy over the proposed construction through Prairie Creek Park, to the north of Humboldt, ended recently in a temporary victory for the trees, but few of their protectors are so foolish as to believe that the battle is over, and pessimists among them see a future network of such highways, complete with plenty of "turnouts" where the traffic-stunned motorist can leave the roaring stream of cars and trucks for a moment to admire the view. In this way, the visitor can "see" many more trees per hour, without getting out of his car.

One businessman near Prairie Creek State Park, whose business would profit from increased traffic through the park, sees no reason why a few trees should stand in the way of better highways. Trees are no good unless people can see them. "What good is it," he asks, "to preserve to the point where a product, even though it be just esthetic, is available to only the few who have the time to stop off for an extended time and meander through the park?" Tourists travel in cars, the argument goes, so you have to provide for the movement of cars, not people.

In the same vein, a district highway engineer in California, arguing to build a highway along a beach, said, "I want to open up that beach for all the people, not just the few who will drive down an old gravel road or walk down there. You have to move with the times. People just don't walk any more. They drive cars."

If this argument is followed to its logical conclusion, the day will come when no spot in this land is out of sight of the highway. The wilderness, at last, will have been conquered. With the disappearance of the last trace of the American wilderness, a light will surely be extinguished in the American soul.

With the rise in the human population, the even faster rise in the automobile population, the increase in leisure time, and the seepage of affluence down through the middle class, the press of automobiles into recreation space is becoming critical. The response of governments, highway builders, and the tourist industry is to build more highways to accommodate the crowds, thus diminishing still further the remaining recreation space—unless, of course, one is willing to classify the high-speed movement of encapsulated humans along a strip of asphalt as "recreation." No less a body than the President's Council on Recreation and Natural Beauty has written that "driving for pleasure is the Nation's most important outdoor recreation activity," and perhaps it is so.

But the shrinking of the wild lands is a cause of deep concern to many. Former Senator Clinton P. Anderson has said that "wilderness is an anchor to windward. Knowing it is there, we can also know that we are still a rich nation, tending to our resources as we should— not a people in despair searching every last nook and cranny of our land for a board of lumber, a barrel of oil, a blade of grass, or a tank of water." But even beyond mere economic implications, urban man needs a place where he can go, if need be, beyond the sound of human voice, beyond the reach of highways and telephones. Once he knows that this is no longer possible, his despair will be complete.

Our National Park system was established more than a half-century ago, presumably to protect certain parcels of land from the "developer." But the legislation authorizing the system requires that its administrators adhere to two instructions which are apparently mutually contradictory. The purpose of the parks, says the law, is "to conserve the scenery and natural and historic objects and the wildlife therein and to provide for the enjoyment of the same in such manner and by such means as will leave them unimpaired for the enjoyment of future generations."

The part that says "conserve" and the part that says "leave them unimpaired" seem pretty clear. But how about "provide for the enjoyment of the same"? If people are to be able to "enjoy" parks, say the motel operators and the oil companies and the automobile manufacturers and the bulldozer operators and the asphalt crowd, they have to be able to get into them and move around. And that means automobiles, and that means roads. But how can building roads in a National Park be looked upon as obeying the admonition to "leave them unimpaired"? Thus the dilemma.

Most people who have never been there think of Yosemite Valley, in the heart of Yosemite National Park, as a place of unmatched grandeur, where the awesome silences and deep canyons are unspoiled by man's intrusion. But the valley contains seven gasoline stations. On a good summer weekend, 70,000 visitors crowd into the valley in their automobiles, giving it the appearance of a gigantic parking lot. On such days, a cloud of automobile exhaust smog hangs over the valley.

Ecologist Fraser Darling and geographer Noel Eichhorn recently appraised the condition of our National Parks for the Conservation Foundation. The parks, they report, now face "dangers from within," because of increasing numbers of people "bringing more of their automobiles and accompanying paraphernalia into the parks." They note, for example, that "the acceptance of the necessity of gas stations and restaurants in Yellowstone with its 250 miles of main roads is inevitable. . . ." The invasion of the automobile has turned the area around Fishing Bridge in Yosemite into a "slum." At Grant Village, many trees were cut down to make room for a trailer and automobile camp; now the remaining trees, deprived of the support and shelter of their fellows, are blowing down. Roads in and near National

Parks are "tongues of penetration," they say. "Yet in the eyes of many people, not least the local politicians and business communities, roads are of essence good and rewarding. This philosophy is constantly pressing on the National Park Service and is even accepted by some individuals in the Service."

In his book *Desert Solitaire,* Edward Abbey writes of the time ten years ago when he began work as a park ranger in Arches National Monument in the canyon country of southeastern Utah. At that time, the only way to reach the area was along a narrow, rocky dirt road that simply lay along the land. Then the road was improved and paved. "Where once a few adventurous people came on weekends to camp for a night or two and enjoy a taste of the primitive and remote," writes Abbey, "you will now find serpentine streams of baroque automobiles pouring in and out, all through the spring and summer, in numbers that would have seemed fantastic when I worked there: from 3,000 to 30,000 per year, the 'visitation,' as they call it, mounts ever upward."

Abbey believes that "police administrators, paved highways, automobile nature trails, official scenic viewpoints, designated campgrounds, Laundromats, cafeterias, Coke machines, and flush toilets" are not the proper environment for the enjoyment of nature's wonders. But when a new National Park is dedicated, the first question asked by the local chamber of commerce is, "When will the roads be built?" And all the rest follows.

In our effort to "provide for the enjoyment" of the parks, we destroy the very qualities that make them enjoyable. "Parks are for people," is the motto of the Park Service, but it behaves as though parks were for automobiles. It is not the 50,000 people visiting a park in one day who cause the noise, the distraction, and the crowding that ruin the experience for all; it is the automobiles in which they ride. Yosemite National Park contains 758,000 acres. When 50,000 people cruise about that space in automobiles, they crowd it; those same 50,000 people on bicycles, on horseback, and on foot would be easily assimilated. The simple arithmetic of speed and space shows quite clearly that highways shrink space. If our national parks are to be left "unimpaired for the enjoyment of future generations," as Congress has directed, we must stop building highways in them, and we must stop permitting automobiles in them.

Is there hope for the future? Probably not, say pessimists who point to the outcome of the controversy over an access road into the Mineral King Valley in the Sierra Nevada of California. This wild, rather narrow alpine valley lies within the Sequoia National Forest and thus is under the jurisdiction of the National Forest Service, a part of the Department of Agriculture. Several years ago, Agriculture Secretary Orville L. Freeman approved a proposal by WED Enterprises, Inc., one of the late Walt Disney's organizations, to build a $35 million resort in Mineral King, to include ski lodges and lifts, parking areas, and other facilities for the year-round enjoyment of an estimated 2.5 million annual visitors by 1975.

Very few questioned the desirability of such a magnificent resort, but there was one hitch. Mineral King is surrounded on three sides by the lands of the Sequoia National Park, and the only access to it is a primitive road, partly dirt, that runs for six miles across park land. This road is closed in winter by snow. The state of California, WED Enterprises, and Secretary Freeman wanted to build an improved, all-weather access road to Mineral King. But Interior Secretary Stewart L. Udall balked at the idea of a new road through one of the choicest areas of the National Park, and it could not be built without his permission. The result was a head-on clash between these two Cabinet officers.

"The experience of the postwar years tells us that the combustion automobile, with its fumes, noises, and accompanying clutter, is a paramount blighting influence within national parks," said Udall. "I am honestly worried by the thought that we will not be honored 25 years from now if we make a decision to violate this valley by a road."

Freeman replied that the proposal "simply calls for replacing the existing long-established seasonal road with a standard two-lane road usable" in all seasons. "I cannot construe this plan, or even understand it in the terms and context of 'violation' that you use."

Mr. Udall made it plain, however, that his chief concern was the degradation of the valley by mass automobile invasion, not the immediate effects of the road on the corridor through the park. "Many people seriously doubt," he said, "that it is humanly possible to crowd 20,000 people and parking lots containing 8600 autos into this narrow valley without serious damage. . . ." The breath-taking splendor of Mineral King Valley should be developed for the enjoyment

of people, not for the movement and storage of automobiles. "The
best way to make Mineral King the finest outdoor recreation area in
the West is through the exclusion of automobiles," he said. Access
could be provided by a monorail, or a small, modern electric railway. "Perhaps," Udall proposed, "we might even break new ground
by insisting that the California Legislature pass a law authorizing
the use of these specific highway funds for a different transportation
solution." He recommended a study of the situation.

A study was out of the question, replied Freeman. "There have
been long months of indecision and delay already. This Administration, through my personal action, is committed to the development
of Mineral King. . . . You, and your department people concerned,
are clearly attempting to limit our activities and block national forest
development in ways that are not justified."

In the end, Udall was forced to yield. Money simply is not available for building monorails or even conventional railroads, but it
is there in abundance for building highways. Therefore, to argue
against the highway in favor of a rail line is tantamount to an attempt
to "block national forest development," as Secretary Freeman
charged. A great deal of money will result from the commercial
development of Mineral King, and since the gold flow depends upon
the free flow of automobiles into the valley, the highway will be built.

Public transportation has also been suggested for moving people
in the National Parks, by naturalist Michael Frome, who says that
automobiles should be used "for arriving, not exploring." He envisions a rail line, or possibly a bus, traveling a loop route through
the park, stopping at camp grounds, picnic areas, scenic areas, hiking
trails. People can dismount where they wish and stay as long as they
wish. The alternative is the scene he describes in his recent book,
Strangers in High Places: "On almost any given weekend from late
spring through fall, or any day during the summer season, visitors
[to the Great Smoky Mountain National Park] hoping for a glimpse
of mountain majesty find themselves embroiled in bumper-to-bumper
traffic on the transmountain highway. Though coming to the Smokies
for a respite from the mechanized intensity of our age, they must
contend with the same racing motors, exhaust fumes, tension, and
traffic jams from which they fled in their home cities. The parking

areas are congested, the campgrounds overloaded night after night. The picnic areas are trampled. The scenic overlook at Newfound Gap is so completely swarming with people and littered with trash (despite all efforts at cleanup) that the thrill of the scene is often destroyed."

Only one road cuts across the Great Smoky Mountains National Park. Many persons insist that the way to alleviate congestion is to build another. In 1968, the construction of a second transmountain road through the park was narrowly averted, again through the intervention of Secretary Udall. But the battle was tough, and it could go the other way the next time. Few doubt there will be a next time.

The half-million acres of the Great Smokies include one of the few remaining remnants of the primeval forest that once blanketed the eastern half of the United States. Straddling the border between Tennessee and North Carolina, this park also includes the highest mountain range east of the Black Hills. "No road on earth," says one resident in the area, "is important enough to destroy the values inherent in these mountains." But the governors of Tennessee and North Carolina, congressmen from the mountain districts, local politicians and business groups, and all the proponents of mechanized tourism clamored for the new highway. The best way for the public to see this park, they said, is to drive through it.

Private citizens from all the surrounding communities opposed the highway. More than 6,000 letters poured into the Department of the Interior, arguing 4 to 1 against it. Conservationist groups pleaded to avert the "needless sacrifice of thousands of acres of priceless wilderness and miles of unspoiled mountain streams." On October 23, 1966, 234 people took part in a Save Our Smokies Wilderness Hike for 17 miles down the Appalachian Trail to the spot where the proposed highway would cross it. The hikers ranged in age from five to eighty-one, and they came from twenty-two states, from France, Canada, and Japan. Their purpose, they said, was to show that the people want the National Park Service "to leave the wilderness of the Great Smokies Park and that of all our other primeval national parks strictly alone."

On December 10, 1967, Secretary Udall announced that he would not approve construction of the transmountain highway. As a compromise, however, he gave the go-ahead for completion of a 14-mile road from Bryson City, North Carolina, to a spot on the north shore of Fontana Lake, where the Park Service plans to build a marina and campground. Thus the principle of private automobile transportation within the park won its victory.

But the pressure continues. Three months after Udall announced his decision, a delegation from the two affected states, including all four United States senators, requested a meeting with him to discuss plans for another road in or around the Great Smoky Mountains National Park. Another vocal advocate was former Senator Herbert S. Walters, chairman of an organization called the Tennesssee Smoky Mountains National Park Commission. How long can a Secretary of the Interior resist such pressure? And what will happen when the office of Secretary of the Interior is occupied by a man with less spine than Mr. Udall?

The mass violation of the primeval forest that Udall was fighting to prevent was taking place just a few miles to the east, where Interstate 40 was slashing its way across the mountains. This new superroad runs for about 20 miles along the banks of the Pigeon River bordering the eastern rim of the Park. Whole mountainsides had to be sliced away to make room for the four-lane roadbed. On the uphill side of the highway, the raw cuts into the mountain slopes tower as high as a forty-story building. The fills on the river side are equally awesome, plunging from the highway 350 feet down to the river's edge. An aerial view of what one starry-eyed travel writer calls this "spectacular new showpiece" affords a breathtaking view of what man can do to the wilderness if he just puts his mind to it.

Nearly all road controversies end with the roar of the bulldozers. The strenuous efforts of a citizens' group in Oregon seem unlikely to prevent construction of a proposed highway along an "undeveloped" stretch of beach. Beaches are likely targets for highway builders, especially if they are wild, relatively inaccessible, and on public land.

The beach-highway controversy in Oregon centers about Nestucca Bay and the town of Pacific City, about seventy miles southwest of Portland. U. S. Route 101 runs along the west coast of the United States from border to border, at times right along the shoreline, and at times swinging further inland. South of Pacific City the highway hugs the coastline, but as it approaches Pacific City from the south it begins to turn inland to pass around Nestucca Bay and east of Pacific City, then back to the coastline several miles to the north.

In 1966, the Oregon Highway Commission announced its intention to relocate Route 101 westward, along the coastline. The proposed route would run along the Nestucca Sandspit, a 3.7-mile-long undeveloped peninsula of beach between Nestucca River and the Pacific Ocean. It would also run between the ocean and Pacific City, on the eastern side of the river.

Opposition to the highway on the beach quickly formed behind the leadership of State Treasurer Robert W. Straub, and support for the relocation was led by Oregon Secretary of State Tom McCall. Straub, a Democrat, and McCall, a Republican, were the opponents in the Oregon gubernatorial contest. On Mother's Day, 1966, Straub led a march of 200 persons along the sand dunes to demonstrate opposition to the highway.

In the November election, McCall defeated Straub by 72,000 votes, but Straub continued his fight against the beach highway. Since it now had the support of the governor, the State Highway Commission, and the Federal Bureau of Public Roads, Straub's only hope seemed to be the Department of Transportation in Washington. But his appeal to Secretary Boyd brought the reply that the highway engineers, both state and federal, had appraised the location, held a public hearing, studied various alternatives, and done everything they could to select the route which would best serve the public need. "The route location," wrote Boyd, "has been selected in such a way that it will not destroy the beaches, but will enhance their value and make them more readily available for additional public use."

Two 40-acre sections of the land on the sandspit over which the proposed highway would run had been granted by the federal government to the state of Oregon to be used solely for recreational purposes. This offered another avenue of hope to Straub, who turned to Secretary Udall. "I am enclosing two pictures I took last year," he wrote Udall, "which I hope will persuade you more than words could do of the quiet, undisturbed beauty of this magnificent beach area. This is what the Bureau of Public Roads would destroy by bisecting this beach with an interstate highway.

"This spit, through the wise, far-sighted action of the State High-

way Commission, was acquired several years ago to be developed
as a state park. What a priceless, quiet, undisturbed park this can
be, consisting of approximately five hundred acres. Highway 101, if
built where planned by the Bureau of Public Roads, would slash
across this park, cutting off the majority of the park land from
the ocean."

Udall was at first unwilling to get involved, as long as there appeared to be any chance of settling the matter at the state level.
Straub then appealed to the highway commission to hold another
public hearing. When he was refused, he organized his own hearing
and collected 700 signatures on a save-the-beach petition. Straub
then went to Washington to talk with Udall, who agreed to support
his cause.

Nine days after Straub's visit, Udall wrote to Governor McCall.
"In all candor," he said, "I must report that my key conservation
advisors unanimously oppose the beach route proposed by your
highway department. Our experience in outdoor recreation land use
planning tells us emphatically that any major highway is totally incompatible with the wise preservation of small parks and beaches.

"The record in this case shows that there are viable alternatives
to the proposed relocation of Highway 101, and that at least one
such alternative route was studied by your highway department in
1965. The old argument by highway engineers that it is 'cheaper'
to route a road through a beach or public park was always out-
rageous from a conservation standpoint.

"Consequently, I have no alternative but to instruct the Director
of the Bureau of Land Management to disapprove the application
of your State Highway Engineer for a variance in the patent to permit highway construction on this land granted to the State of Oregon
exclusively for outdoor recreation purposes."

And that seemed to be the end of the controversy. McCall replied
to Udall four days later, saying, "I accept your mandate for the
relocation of the relocation in good grace." To newspaper reporters,
the Governor said, "If I ever catch a highway engineer looking even
cross-eyed at a sandspit, there will be the devil to pay." The beach
highway, he said, was a "closed issue."

But less than a month later, in September, 1967, McCall announced that he was reopening the issue. He called for public hearings on several alternative routes for the relocation, one of which would be along the Nestucca sandspit but aligned to avoid the federal-grant acreage. Asked about Straub's continued opposition, the Governor replied testily, "I'm beginning to wonder who won the election. It seems he is running the beaches and the highway department."

Straub's newly formed Committee to Save the Beaches hired a professional pollster to survey public sentiment. Among those who expressed an opinion, the vote was more than 6 to 1 in favor of the inland route. The beach relocation, said *The Portland Oregonian,* was rapidly becoming "one of the hottest highway arguments in Oregon's history." Highway commissioners were hanged in effigy. Governor McCall dubbed the beach route opponents "Oregon's noisiest minority" and accused them of resorting to "simplistic emotional attacks" in order to block the road and thus deny citizens access to their beaches. "Never," he intoned, "have so few kept so much from so many."

Proponents of the beach route had long used the argument that it was the only way to open up the area for use by the people. A reporter for *The Oregon Journal* visited the scene and wrote: "The Nestucca sandspit and its Kiwanda Beach area are not locked up from the public. At present it is possible to drive directly to the state-owned park lands . . . on a hard-surface, black-topped road. . . . Down the length of the spit itself, however, there is no road. . . . This lack of roadway is a mixed blessing. While it precludes campers and others, except those who don't mind walking, the lack of roadway has also preserved the Nestucca spit as an amazingly clean, unspoiled area. To see it and to walk on the spit is to be charmed by its beauty. No beer bottles, empty cans or broken glass mar the beach sands. The Marram dune grass waves in the ocean breeze unchoked by bits of paper or litter. The roar of autos does not drown out the roar of the breakers on the beach, or the cries of the sea birds."

Many, however, felt that a walk of a half-mile is not proper access.

Said a Tillamook County deputy sheriff, "People don't want to hike across a goddam sandspit. They want to drive as close to a spot as they can get, unload their beer, and get the kids off their backs."

According to *Oregon Journal* writer James Long, the highway department, "which is not run by social workers but by engineer-economists, couldn't agree more" with that attitude. The average motorist, wrote Long, "is not predominantly interested in the fine points of nature, but is willing to endure almost anything so long as he can drive to it." Further, the primary concern of the highway department in relocating Route 101 "is not whether it would preserve peace and quiet, or benefit anyone's ephemeral grandchildren, but whether it would be efficient in generating wealth."

At ten o'clock on the morning of November 29, a crowd of 300 angry persons jammed into the Elks Hall in Tillamook, Oregon, to witness the public hearing on the Route 101 relocation. The hearing lasted more than ten hours and heard some sixty speakers. The first two hours were dominated by highway department representatives, businessmen, and local politicians, who spoke, to a man, in favor of the beach highway.

Opening the hearing for the highway department was engineer Fred Klaboe, who testified that for many years the department had attempted to locate coastal highways "in close proximity to the beaches in order to open them up, to give access to them, so people can use them and preserve them for many years in the future. Often this has subsidiary, but substantial benefits in that we can build them at a cheaper cost and maintain them at a cheaper cost."

The State Parks Superintendent reminded those at the hearing that along with the highway on the sandspit would come a fine new park, including a bathhouse, picnic facilities, grass and landscaping, and hiking trails. Although the elevated highway would cut sections of the park off from the ocean, and fences along the highway would prevent anyone from crossing it, "four underpasses are planned at key locations to allow for safe pedestrian circulation to and from recreational facilities and attractions."

One housewife waxed sarcastic about the argument that the highway would provide better access to the beach. "You're camping on the river side," she hypothesized for the audience. "There are no campsites on the beach side. The kids want to go to the beach, so you walk to an underpass. That could be from one half to three quarters of a mile away. . . . Maybe sometime when you aren't looking, Johnny will climb this fence to get to the ocean quicker. Johnny was a nice kid. Do you call this better access to the beach?"

Robert Straub wondered whether the state planned to go ahead with the park, even though the beach route for the highway was defeated. At one point in the hearings, he directed this question to Victor Wolfe, the hearing chairman and a highway department official. Mr. Wolfe replied that it was "obvious" that if the coastal route was not constructed the park was out of the question.

Straub could not understand this reasoning. He pointed out that the right-of-way for the highway would consume 109 acres of beach and recreation land, and that an additional strip perhaps a hundred feet wide on either side of the highway would be unfit for recreational use. "This makes a total loss of a minimum of 320 acres of among the finest sections of beach and ocean view property that is left in Oregon," he said. A much better way to provide "access" to these lands, he said, would be to build the high-speed highway further inland and provide small access roads from it down to the beach area.

During the course of the hearing, it became clear that a majority of the ordinary citizens of the area preferred the inland route, but the beach route was nearly the unanimous choice of county commissioners, city officials, chambers of commerce, and business groups, who saw the highway along the ocean as an attraction for increased tourist trade. The only dissident voice in this commercial array was the chamber of commerce of Pacific City, which would be cut off from the ocean by the beach highway.

One businessman who stated the case for commerce quite clearly was Carl B. Koke, manager of the 20 Miracle Mile Chamber of Commerce in Lincoln City, about ten miles south of Pacific City. Said he: "The business community of the Oregon coast is very much concerned that we have a highway that will get as much access to the beach as possible. . . . All our promotions and advertising are designed to bring visitors to our area . . . and when I speak of visitors I speak of the kids, because along with the kids come mom and

dad and the rest of the family, and these are the people that we
want to visit us in our beautiful coastal area and we want them to
enjoy the wilderness area which we have heard spoken of today and
we want them readily accessible."

Local real estate interests pointed out that the highway on the
beach would use public lands, which were yielding no tax revenue
anyway; but the proposed inland route would take some private
property and thus reduce the tax base of the area. Said M. L.
Schmidt, "I represent the Real Estate Boards of Tillamook County,
and we have no special interest. . . . We think the highway engineer's
routing called the coastal route is the one to take. . . . God bless the
Highway Department for their logic, their insight, and their judgment
to protect the assets and the future of the tax base of the people of
Tillamook County by using the State-owned property at the present
time and make a highway that anyone can enjoy along the coastal
route."

The fate of the Nestucca Sandspit is undecided at this writing,
but recent events suggest the beach may be opened to the destructive
intrusion of the highway. The Committee to Save the Beaches, now re-
constituted as Beaches Forever, Inc., collected 70,000 signatures on a
petition to put on the November, 1968, ballot an amendment to the
state constitution stating that beaches should be kept for public use
and enjoyment and prohibiting the construction of main highways
on beaches or publicly owned sandspits. In a nice stroke of irony,
the amendment provided for a $30 million bond issue to allow for
the state to acquire additional beach lands for public use, the bond
issue to be retired with the help of a four-year, one-cent addition to
the gasoline tax. Thus would the automobile have been used to save,
rather than desecrate, the beaches of Oregon.

During the final weeks before the election, the highway lobby, with
the help of $90,000 collected from the major oil companies in Cali-
fornia, advertised heavily to defeat the proposed amendment. Their
campaign paid off. The amendment was voted down by a 6 to 4
margin, thus removing a roadblock in the way of the highway on the
sandspit.

A more hopeful development was the passage of the Wilderness
Act in 1964. This law provides a means whereby the remnants of

land still unspoiled by "development" can be preserved from that fate for the future well-being of our nation, in a National Wilderness Preservation System. Eligible for inclusion in the system is any federal land "where the earth and its community of life are untrammeled by man."

The Act set aside 9 million acres of land as the first "deposit" into this land-savings account. By 1974, the Secretary of the Interior must survey all additional eligible land and recommend to Congress the lands to be added to the system. He is directed to consider "every roadless area of 5,000 contiguous acres or more." An Act of Congress is then required to bring additional land into the system. Once in, the Wilderness Act stipulates that "there shall be no commercial enterprise and no permanent road within any wilderness area designated by this Act, and, except as necessary to meet minimum requirements for the administration of the area for the purpose of this Act . . . there shall be no temporary road, no use of motor vehicles, motorized equipment or motor boats, no landing of aircraft, no other form of mechanical transport, and no structure or installation within any such area."

Interior Secretary Udall had long urged the establishment of a wilderness system. In his book *The Quiet Crisis,* he wrote that such a system "will offer man what many consider the supreme human experience. It will also provide watershed protection, a near-perfect wildlife habitat, and an unmatched science laboratory where we can measure the world in its natural balance against the world in its manmade imbalance." In our increasingly commercial civilization, he wrote, "there must be natural sanctuaries where commercialism is barred, where factories, subdivisions, billboards, power plants, dams, and all forms of economic use are completely and permanently prohibited, where every man may enjoy the spiritual exhilaration of the wilderness."

During his eight years as Secretary of the Interior, Udall had often aligned himself with the birdwatchers and petunia planters in their confrontations with the road gang. When President-elect Nixon announced Udall's replacement, a stir of anxiety swept through the ranks of the conservationists. Before his election as Governor of Alaska, Walter J. Hickel had made his fortune as a builder and land developer,

which hardly seemed the kind of background that would prepare one
to qualify as the nation's first defender of our natural resources against
the ravages of commercial exploitation.

Anxiety was heightened by Hickel's performance in his first news
conference in December. "I think we have had a policy of conservation for conservation's sake," he told the newsmen. "Just to withdraw
a large area for conservation purposes and lock it up for no reason
doesn't have any merit, in my opinion."

No reason? Those who subscribed to Mr. Udall's words could only
pray that Mr. Hickel did not mean what he said. This was the talk
of a man who regards wild lands as useless and whose hands itch to
"develop" it for human uses. Such a man, far from barring highways
from the wilderness, seems more likely to promote their construction
to bring in the automobiles.

The urge to build highways into scenic areas to "open them up"
for viewing from the seat of an automobile is not the only source of
difficulty. Many problems arise when such an area has the bad
fortune to be on the "desire line" of a proposed highway. The list
of scenic areas, recreation areas, and wildlife refuges thus threatened
during the past several years is long and includes such places as
Gore Range-Eagle's Nest Primitive Area in Colorado, Jonathan
Dickinson State Park and Audubon Island in Florida, the North
Cascades Range in Washington, Long Trail on the ridgetops of the
Green Mountains in Vermont, Spruce Knob-Seneca Rocks National
Recreation Area in West Virginia, Franconia Notch in New Hamp-
shire, Cumberland Gap between Virginia and Kentucky, a greenbelt
of parks and woods in the middle of Staten Island, Butler County
Wildlife Management Area and Wheeler National Wildlife Refuge
in Alabama, Oliver Wildlife Refuge in Oklahoma, Everglades National Park in Florida, the western shore of Lake Tahoe in California, the famous Beaver Kill and Willowemoc trout streams in the
Catskills in New York, Butler and Westmoreland Wildlife Sanctuaries in New York—and on and on. A list of city parks would
be at least as long. Not all of these irreplaceable resources are lost
to the bulldozer: some have succumbed, some will be saved, and
others are still the subject of controversy.

Many new highways also add to the slaughter of game animals and the decimation of trout and other fish populations in hundreds of streams. In the western states, particularly, the wider fenced-in rights-of-way and higher speeds on the newer highways take a heavy toll of migrating animals. Deer and other big-game animals roam the high mountain ranges in summer and migrate to the foothills in winter. But the major highways often run along the base of the mountains, directly across the migration routes. The deer often attempt to leap the fences erected to keep them off the highways; some become entangled in the fences and die there; others make it across the first fence into the highway, then become confused by the onrushing automobiles and dash about frantically until they are hit. During one year in Michigan alone, 6,052 white-tailed deer were killed on the highways. There were 438 deer-automobile collisions in Wisconsin in 1951; by 1966, the count had risen to 11,662.

In hilly or mountainous country, often a streambed offers the most efficient route for a highway; the grades are gentle, and often the stream bottom provides gravel for the road construction. But the stream usually meanders back and forth aimlessly, and the highway builder straightens it out in a new, man-made channel to avoid constructing expensive bridges. This means death for the trout. It takes nature thousands of years to produce the set of conditions necessary for trout to thrive: cool water shaded by vegetation along the banks; deep, quiet pools for rest and protection; gravel bottom for spawning and production of good insects. Rechanneling the streams destroys this environment, and the fish die. Even nearby highway construction can remove the vegetation or produce erosion that fills the stream with silt that smothers the spawning areas. Gravel dredged from the stream bottom destroys both spawning and food-producing areas.

A typical fisherman's lament appeared in the April 14, 1962, issue of *The Baltimore Sun,* the opening day of trout season: "Alas, the area for trout fishing undergoes another constriction this year. Most popular hereabouts was the mile or so of Jones Falls . . . taken over for a vast interchange between the new Jones Falls Expressway and the beltway. Throughout most of its length the stream has been scooped out, diverted, and generally manhandled, and the wilderness along its borders which provided much of its charm scraped off by bulldozers, the banks are bare, the stream itself a river of mud."

In Montana, twenty-four streams were surveyed in 1961, and 78 miles of their original channel were found to have been lost, almost all of it to highway construction. There were once 1,200 miles of trout streams in the Black Hills of South Dakota; there are now only 160 miles. Most of this loss was caused by highway construction.

Until recently, the attitude of the highway builders was typified by the federal official who scoffed at pleas to preserve the Beaver Kill from damage: "What makes you believe that a river is more important than a concrete highway?" Former Federal Highway Administrator Rex M. Whitton saw no reason not to route Interstate 65 through Wheeler National Wildlife Refuge in Alabama. "Here, again," he said, "the issue is wildlife versus people. . . . The conservation groups have opposed any crossing of the area and have suggested that we adopt an indirect routing which would increase costs by several millions of dollars and travel distance by several miles. . . . I cannot believe that the welfare of wildlife should be given a priority over that of our citizenry."

Senator Lee Metcalf of Montana has been working for many years to reduce the destruction of fish and wildlife caused by highway construction. He first became interested in the problem while on a vacation in Yellowstone National Park. One day he was driving along the famous fishing stream, the Gallatin, while the road along the stream was being rebuilt. "They were taking sand and gravel out of the streambed," he says, "when they could have gone 50 yards or so to the side of the mountain to obtain the gravel; and they were dumping fill down below. I protested to the highway commission and was informed that it was not any of my business what they did, that their concern was to build roads as cheaply as possible."

The senator thereupon made it his business. In 1962, he introduced legislation that would require any federal-aid highway plans to be reviewed by the Secretary of the Interior to determine whether the plans "are satisfactory in the interest of conserving fish and wildlife and recreation resources." Congress has never passed Metcalf's legislation, the so-called "Save-Our-Streams" bill, but the Senator's continuous hammering at the theme has persuaded the Administration to take other measures.

The following year, the Bureau of Public Roads ordered all state highway departments to coordinate highway plans with state fish and game agencies. As a result of this directive, state highway departments are now consulting with fish and game departments to a greater or less extent. But there is some question as to the benefits accruing to the fish. In testimony to the Senate Public Roads Subcommittee two years later, Richard H. Stroud of the Sport Fishing Institute declared that the agreements between the state agencies "vary greatly in form, are generally without force, and generally lack significant degrees of effectiveness."

Other critics of the highway-wildlife cooperation program point out the immense discrepancy in political muscle between the highway department, which spends millions every year, and the fish and game department, which operates on nickels and dimes. In any confrontation, there is no contest. One highway commissioner, indeed, spurned the fish and game commissioner as an incompetent "who cannot even read a blueprint."

In 1965, the Fish and Wildlife Service of the Interior Department surveyed state fish and game officials to see how the program of cooperation was working out. Nearly all said they were satisfied with the program. However, when asked whether they could cite a "noteworthy example" of an effort to lessen damage to fish and wildlife, thirty-three of the states replied they could not. The report called this result "somewhat disappointing." Further, most of the "noteworthy examples" that *were* cited merely were efforts to provide access routes for hunters and fishermen cut off by the new highways, rather than efforts to preserve the fish and wildlife resources.

Despite the cooperative programs between the state agencies, the survey showed that "the encroachment of highways upon streams is a serious problem. The actual destruction of bank cover, stream bottom cover, and fish food organisms through profile alteration and channelization, and the ensuing sedimentation and erosion, frequently occur. Once destroyed, stream habitat can seldom recover to its previous condition." Further, the loss of living space for wildlife "is viewed as unavoidable but serious by many states." The problem posed by highway fencing to migrating big-game animals "stands without easy solution."

Fish and game departments simply don't have enough people to

do the job. Anthony S. Taormina, a regional supervisor in the New
York State Conservation Department, says that the cooperative program "is all fine on paper; the problem is to make sure the contractor
in establishing the project uses good judgment and doesn't foul the
whole thing up." Mr. Taormina's region covers all five boroughs of
New York City, including Staten Island, plus all of Long Island, which
is well over a hundred miles long and heavily laced with highways.
"Our fisheries manager," says Mr. Taormina, "is the only professional
we have in the fresh water program on the island." The highway
coordination work "is only one of the many jobs he has to do. We
can barely keep up with what comes in, let alone check things out.
Conservation is still getting the short end of the stick. We are never
overstaffed in this business. When money is to be made from exploit-
ing land, people resent conservationists. We interfere with progress."

To the entrepreneur, progress means growth—more people in
more automobiles with more money to spend. The resulting pressure
on our remaining open spaces is epitomized in a 1967 proposal of
the U. S. Department of Commerce to create a national system of
scenic roads and parkways. "Driving for pleasure," says the proposal
in the now familiar refrain, "is the nation's most important outdoor
recreation activity. . . . If Americans want to drive for pleasure, we
must meet their demand through a national program of scenic roads
and parkways."

The apparent goal of this program is to make every spot of any
scenic value in the nation available from an asphalt-paved "scenic
overlook." A "minimum" and a "maximum" program are described,
the maximum program calling for an expenditure of $8 billion over
a ten-year period to create 96,967 miles of scenic roads. Of this total,
26,146 miles would be new routes through scenic areas as yet untouched by asphalt, and the remainder, 70,821 miles, would be improvement of existing routes. Such improvement presumably would
include some widening and straightening of narrow, twisting country
roads so that drivers hungry for scenery can hurry to it and past it
more rapidly.

The program calls for 92 per cent of the total mileage to be open
to all kinds of traffic, so that most of the scenic corridors would be
filled with the roar and fumes of heavy diesel trucks as well as those

for whom, in the words of the Department of Commerce report, "the Sunday drive through the countryside is one of the great experiences that families share."

Some time before the release of this report, President Johnson set the mood in his remarks to the National Conference on Beauty in America. "More than any country," he said, "ours is an automobile society. For most Americans, the automobile is a principal instrument of transportation, work, daily activity, recreation, and pleasure. By making our roads highways to the enjoyment of nature and beauty, we can greatly enrich the lives of nearly all our people in city and countryside alike."

The sentiment is not unanimous. Carl W. Buchheister, president of the National Audubon Society, says the program would mean "utter disaster." If this network of nearly 100,000 miles of scenic roads should come to pass, he says, "it could destroy the few remaining places in America where a person may retreat from the incessant roar of internal combustion engines and escape the stench and litter created by automobiles." Lawrence S. Hall, chairman of the English Department of Bowdoin College, calls the program a "multi-billion-dollar War on Privacy" resulting from the mistaken idea that "leaving unused land just lying around in a state of nature is wasteful, shiftless, unprogressive, and not at all in the Public interest."

Foot-draggers like Buchheister and Hall were probably in the mind of the editorial writer for *Engineering News-Record* who protested that "it's time for the lovers of natural beauty, the Helen Hokinsons [*sic*] of the garden clubs, the wildlife enthusiasts, bird watchers, and conservationists of every stripe to get off the backs of the road builders." "Roads don't destroy beauty; they take us to it—even *create* it," the editorial argued. "Highway officials and engineers are not the despoilers of natural beauty and the great outdoors that they are so often accused of being by the irresponsible or the uninformed. Instead, properly designed and located highways are making natural beauty and outdoor recreation accessible to millions of people who otherwise would never be able to enjoy them. Highways are often enhancing natural beauty, complementing and strengthening conservation efforts."

In its proposal for the new highway network, the Department of

Commerce does not fail to enumerate the resulting commercial benefits. Cash returns from two dozen tourists per day, says the report,
benefit a community as much as a factory with an annual payroll
of $100,000. If this fails to stimulate grass-roots support for the
program, there is the additional reminder that the construction of
these roads would increase "manyfold" consumer expenditures for
such things as fishing and hunting equipment, camping gear, boats,
automobiles, gasoline, tires, motel services, and "other goods and
services too numerous to mention."

The report even makes the point that the proposed highway construction is the best way to preserve the land from encroachment by
less desirable uses. "Many recreation opportunities are lost," it says,
"as desirable land and water resources are increasingly being absorbed by the growing sprawl of urban development." True enough.
But, the report goes on, "the designation of scenic highway corridors
will reserve some of these resources indefinitely into the future." This
would seem to be a strange proposition—that the way to preserve
an area of natural beauty is to build a highway through it. One
would have thought the more straightforward course would be to
preserve it unchanged. The explanation, no doubt, is that $8 billion
can always be found for highways, but $8 billion for preservation of
the countryside in its natural state is more difficult to come by.

Fortunately, the fiscal strains of the Vietnam War intervened, and
the program for scenic roads and parkways now rests quietly in limbo.
But once the war ends, there remains the clear probability that this
proposal for desecration of our countryside will be dusted off and
shipped up the Hill to a willing Congress.

9

Your Highway Taxes at Work

Problems created by highways range from inconvenience to tragedy, and their locale ranges from the prairie to the big city.

Carl Kolpack's 163-acre farm near Springfield, Illinois, was in the path of Interstate 55. The state paid him well—$27,604 for the 16 acres the highway sliced out of his farm—but the land he has left is now in two pieces, separated by a barrier. The 28-acre piece on the west side of the highway contains all the buildings—farmhouse, machine shed, corn crib, barn. The 119 acres on the east side are fields and pasture. "My buildings are here, my pastures across the road," says the disgruntled farmer. "But it's four miles around by the nearest overpass. Every spring I'm forced to haul 2,500 bales of hay all the way around here to store it in the barn. Then I've got to haul it back for winter feed."

The Reuben Deyo Halfway House at Highland, New York, stood on the west bank of the Hudson River, halfway between Albany and New York City on Route 9W. The old stone house, built during the presidency of James Monroe, was classified by architects as "late Federal." For many years, it accommodated travelers in stagecoaches moving along the old Post Road. A gallows in an open drill field across the road gave Halfway House the unenviable tag among the locals of "Hangman's Inn," although none of them could recall seeing a body swing from it.

The coming of the railroads and steamboats drew passengers away from the stage line and cast a lengthening shadow of decay on Halfway House for some eighty years. Then around the turn of the century it was renovated and refurnished by Grace Van Braam Roberts, who operated its 60 acres of land as a dairy farm.

Miss Roberts continued to operate the farm successfully for many years, assisted by a close friend, Elizabeth Collier, a teacher at Hunter College in New York City. But when Miss Roberts died in 1956, the sharply rising costs of labor, feed, and maintenance were reducing the farm income to dangerously low levels. Miss Collier fought valiantly to save the farm, rising before daylight, attending to the animals, riding the train and subway to Hunter College in the city, teaching her classes, then taking the train back to the farm and working far into the night before starting the same cycle again the following day.

But, says historian Mabel Abbott, Miss Collier was fighting a losing battle. "Every cent she could earn or borrow went into the bottomless pit of expenses and increasing debts. Conditions became desperate; but she refused to give up, and lived on in the empty, indescribably uncared-for house, hobbling about with a cane, a small, emaciated, indomitable figure, fighting off lawyers and creditors and the bureaucracy with a shrewdness equal to their own."

But along came a force even stronger than the indomitable Miss Collier—the New York State Department of Public Works, with plans to put a new highway ramp right through Halfway House. A Committee for Preservation of Reuben Deyo Halfway House pleaded with the highway builders to shift the road 20 feet to save the house. But the Department of Public Works declared that the house wasn't historic enough to be worth saving. Mrs. S. Jeffrey Starin, chairman of the committee, purchased the house and announced her intention of moving it out of the path of the bulldozers in order to save it. But it was too late. On May 16, 1967, the Ulster County sheriff evicted Miss Collier, now a feeble eighty-three years old, from the house and deposited her in a small tenant house nearby.

Immediately, the bulldozers and power shovels began to smash the house into rubble. In the confusion of the move and the demolition, Miss Collier's cat disappeared. Except for the few belongings that Miss Collier managed to take with her, everything in the house was soon buried in a pile of smashed stone and splintered beams.*

---

* The cat never returned. Miss Collier died in a fire that destroyed the tenant house several months later.

Morristown, New Jersey, was a small, quiet community of about 18,000 persons some 28 miles due west of Manhattan as the crow flies, a little too far for easy commuting, but a little too close to escape the wide-ranging effects of the giant sprawl of the New York metropolitan area.

A town of broad, shaded streets, green lawns, and white, rambling clapboard houses, Morristown had its traffic problems, just like every other community. One of the attractions was the historic colonial mansion that served as headquarters for General George Washington during the Revolutionary War. Morris Avenue was the kind of tree-lined street that people photographed to illustrate everybody's idea of comfortable small-town America.

One day an engineer in the highway department drew a sweeping, curving line westward and northward around the densely settled supercity of Jersey City-Elizabeth-Newark-the Oranges-Paterson, defining a motorists' bypass to connect with the New York State Thruway. His line passed through Morristown, the seat of Morris County.

In 1960, the first and only public hearing was held to announce this event to the citizens of Morristown. One engineer said that the highway, now designated Interstate Route 287, should pass as close as possible to the center of Morristown so that automobiles could have easy access to the shops and the county offices. As a result, the new six-lane highway and two interchanges would usurp about 3 per cent of the land area in town, slice by a hospital, leap across a playground, plow under a hundred or so houses, some of them on the finest residential streets in town, and, at Morris Avenue, cut open a 250-foot-wide swath between an elementary school and the pride of Morristown, Washington's Headquarters. Those who knew about these things predicted that, by 1985, Morristown would be treated to the sight of 70,000 vehicles a day whizzing through town. The sleepy old small-town atmosphere would disappear in a cloud of exhaust fumes.

Some of the townfolk, however, liked the town just the way it was, and they began to complain. But here they encountered the "ping-pong" principle of highway planning: Appeals to the state highway department elicited the comment that the Bureau of Public Roads in Washington had final approval; appeals to Washington

were met with the comment that all initial planning and design was
done at the state level. Said the mayor of Morristown, caught in this
bewildering cross-current, "You could hear the music but you never
found out who you were dancing with."

The opponents of the highway were faced with the dilemma of not
knowing exactly where or what to attack. After the public hearing in
1960, the highway department clammed up. Requests for information were met with the standard comment that the experts were still
"studying" the proposal. One group of citizens went ahead anyway
and hired its own group of planners to map out an alternate route,
which would destroy only about thirty homes instead of the hundred
or so proposed by the state.

Finally, in 1963, the state suddenly announced that the original
route was approved, and that home-owners in its path had about
a year to settle up and get out. At this, the citizens' outcry burst out
anew. An Emergency Committee to Preserve Morristown organized
a march on the state capital at Trenton, which brought together in
common travail such unlikely allies as the Daughters of the American
Revolution and the Fourth Ward Democratic Club. In a poignantly
ironic twist, automobile bumper stickers appeared throughout the
town pleading "Keep 287 Out of Morristown." On Washington's
Birthday, the townfolk put on uniforms of Revolutionary War soldiers
and demonstrated on the green in front of Washington's Headquarters.
Governor Hughes finally instructed his telephone switchboard to stop
taking calls from Morristown, so heavy was the load of vituperation
from irate citizens. Even Lady Bird Johnson was bombarded with
letters pleading for help.

State legislators and members of the U. S. Congress gingerly
avoided the controversy. The politicians knew well that the first duty
of a politician—to get re-elected—demanded that they avoid earning
the enmity of the powerful state highway department, the governor,
and the commercial interests who advocated the "development" of
Morristown.

Highway engineers were minimally sympathetic. Said one: "We're
not damaging anything. This is going to be a good-looking road, and
if there's a little noise, we'll plant shrubs." Said another, philosoph-

ically, "Sure they've been yelling. We get yelled at everywhere. What's so special about Morristown?"

Since Washington's Headquarters was on federal ground, under the jurisdiction of the Department of the Interior, Secretary Udall tried to move the highway. In a letter to the mayor of Morristown, he expressed his concern about "the adverse effect this freeway would have on one of America's national historic treasures. Experts in the road planning field . . . have stated that the route chosen by the Highway Commission is, in its entirety, the most disruptive to existing land use patterns, and the neighborhoods through which it would pass, of all the routes studied. We believe the close proximity of the proposed freeway to this noted historic structure would be extremely harmful and would destroy the tranquil historic environment which is so necessary for a satisfying experience by the visitor. There would be objectionable sights and distracting traffic noises from a constant stream of trucks, buses, and passenger cars, which will appear in ever-increasing numbers, to say nothing of the noxious fumes and disturbing vibrations."

That letter was written in 1963. Two years later, just before construction was about to get under way, a member of Udall's staff repeated the note of dissent. "It's still an outrage," he said. "But we have no jurisdiction at all over roads. . . . Udall got turned down, that's all. We win some, and we lose a lot more."

A few months later the invading bulldozers appeared at the edge of town. In a final, desperate gesture of outrage, the women of the town marched into the streets and sat themselves upon the blades of the earth-moving machines. But, in the end, the women were forced to move, the engines roared, and the heavy steel blades bit deep into the soil of Morristown.

Glenfield, Pennsylvania, is a provincial little town of about 740 souls, nestled between two hills on the north shore of the Ohio River about 8 miles west of Pittsburgh. Running through the center of Glenfield, and following the course of the river, are the railroad tracks and the heavily traveled Ohio River Boulevard.

Glenfield is almost entirely a residential community of modest, individual homes mostly frame, mostly old, but in good repair. Many of the residents are old, too—there are quite a few pensioners in Glenfield. One of the newest buildings in town, built in 1954, is a tiny box which houses the post office and barber shop. There are only a dozen or so business establishments in the entire town. Except for the spots where the buildings sit, almost all the land is lushly green —Glenfield is a rural oasis between the bustling cities of Pittsburgh to the east and Sewickley to the west.

On the wall of the only tavern in town, someone has stapled a large map of the Interstate Highway System. Everybody in Glenfield has an intense interest in this system, because in 1966 they were told that Glenfield was to become part of it. At a public hearing in the borough building, which was attended by 150 residents, state highway officials announced that Interstate Route 279 would sweep down from the north, pass very close to Glenfield just to the west, soar across the railroad and the boulevard on towering concrete columns, then continue across the river and into West Virginia. The path of the highway would miss the main part of Glenfield, but, unfortunately, the interchange connecting the highway with the Ohio River Boulevard showed up on the highway engineers' maps right smack in the middle of town.

It looked as if about 100 of the 175 homes in Glenfield would have to go, as well as most of the business establishments. Also scheduled for demolition were the four-room elementary school, the town's two churches, post office, and firehouse. The right-of-way administrator for the state highway department was sympathetic. "The state feels bad about seeing you move," he told the assembled citizens, "but there's no use crying that you don't want to. You have to move. Glenfield will be one big interchange."

Glenfield Councilman Wendell M. Jordan, Sr., couldn't believe it. Didn't the highway people realize that this disaster could very easily destroy his town as a political entity? Taking land for the highway would reduce the valuation of taxable property from $593,000 to about $300,000, and lower the total tax revenue from $23,000 to about $11,500. At a meeting of officials from Glenfield, Allegheny County, Pennsylvania, and the U. S. Bureau of Public Roads, Mr. Jordan presented a three-point program to salvage something from the wreckage. He asked for outside help to prepare a study of the impact of the highway on his town. He asked that the state help to rebuild the town on a nearby hillside by providing an access road to the site and subsidizing water and sewage systems. Finally, he asked that the residents of Glenfield who were living on meager pensions be given relocation assistance over and above that provided by law. He emphasized that he was not fighting the highway, he was only asking justice: "We realize that we must not impede progress, but we are faced with a desolate and insurmountable task in survival. We believe in progress; all we are asking for is help from someone who can advise us on how to survive in the face of such progress."

The Allegheny County Planning Commission was sympathetic, but the state and the U. S. Bureau of Roads turned a deaf ear. Mr. Jordan's proposals would be prohibitively expensive, they said. The state would be unable to provide access to the hillside site. Mr. Jordan then appealed to Governor Raymond P. Shafer. "What are our rights?" he asked. With this highway threatening to "disembowel" the community, "who stands for our elderly retired, our minimal income group, and our home-owners with tiny properties and no chance to defend themselves individually?" But the governor simply referred Mr. Jordan's letter to the Department of Highways—the very agency whose action Mr. Jordan was appealing.

Mr. Jordan exhausted every avenue in his attempt to get a hearing. He wrote letters to his state senator, the Department of Highways, the governor, his U. S. congressman, and various other county, state, and federal officials. Replies were filled with brush-off phrases such as: "we are investigating the feasibility of," or "reviewing the possibility of," or "evaluating the merits of"; "this matter is now the subject of an intensive review"; "we are awaiting the receipt of certain decisions"; and "upon completion of our study you will be informed." Mr. Jordan's bitter comment was, "It's very difficult to get information from any of them. You get the buck passed continually."

Mr. Jordan was also subjected to the "ping-pong" treatment, which involves bouncing the subject back and forth between his state capital and Washington. A letter from his state senator, Robert D. Fleming, said: "This highway is being constructed with 90 per cent federal money, and all the plans are subject to the final approval of the Federal Road [*sic*] Administrator. His office has refused to consider

any other plan that has been offered except that which is under
planning at the present time. I have tried every way possible to see
if this could not be changed, but have run up against a stone wall.
As you know, I have contacted the District Engineer and the Secretary of Highways in an effort to have this changed, but they tell me
they are up against insurmountable barriers in the red tape of the
Federal Roads Administrator's office."

So the ball was in Washington. Mr. Jordan wrote to his U. S. congressman, Robert J. Corbett, who replied: "You did the right thing
writing directly to Governor Shafer, for the State of Pennsylvania has
the major say where this highway will be located. Federal funds are
allocated only after state approval of these projects. I certainly hope
something can be done in Harrisburg to prevent this destruction. . . ."

By now, Mr. Jordan was incensed. He began to write of the "cold,
crass attitude of the various agencies toward the destruction of a
legally constituted government. Beware the treading feet of the giant
in the name of progress! Move out of the way or be crushed! This is
one of the most cold-blooded acts ever performed by a large govern-
ing body against a defenseless child of its own making. If this damage
occurred from natural causes, the entire village would undoubtedly
be officially designated a disaster area, but there is no instrument
by which a community destroyed by an action such as this can col-
lect damages to allow for regrowth during and after the act of destruction.

"If this kind of thing is allowed to continue, it will mushroom to
horrendous proportions, and in the coming years nobody will be safe.
These great ribbons of concrete that we're laying down seem to take
precedence over everything, and humanity is becoming secondary to
the highway program."

The destruction of Glenfield was scheduled to begin in the spring
of 1968, but the partial freeze of federal highway funds announced
by President Johnson in January gave it a reprieve. Construction will
be delayed until the funds become available. Meanwhile, the residents of Glenfield live with the sword suspended above their heads. A
reporter visiting the town felt the tension in the atmosphere: "Children eye you suspiciously as they dart through interlacing midday
shadows along the narrow streets. Adult heads turn curiously as the

community's men and women trod a familiar path to and from its
tiny post office. They've seen the pencils, papers, and cameras before.
Some have watched engineers bore test holes in their lawns." A
seventy-two-year-old woman told the reporter that the thought of
moving was a constant source of despair: "Roads have to be built,
but why do they have to take the heart of a town? We go to bed at
night thinking about it and we wake up thinking about it."

A retired schoolteacher has determined never to leave her town.
"Most of us are living on pensions. We put our money in homes and
struggle to pay for them; then they say we have to get out. I'm going
to stay in Glenfield if I have to pitch a tent. I was born here and I'm
going to die here."

Another resident has visualized what it will be like to live in this
little backwater oasis after the interchange is superimposed on its
rural quiet. He has decided to move now, without waiting to see
whether he is one of the lucky ones to be spared. "They'd put you
in a hole anyway, with the highway running above. I'm getting out
of here whether they take the house or not."

A final irony capped Mr. Jordan's efforts to save the town. In preparing his presentation to high authorities asking for aid, he studied
the history of Glenfield, which was first settled by a German religious
sect at about the time of the Civil War. When he read the name these
settlers had given this site nestled between the hills along the Ohio
River, a wry grin darkened his face. The name? "Safe Harbor."

The farmer in Illinois, the historic old house in New York, the
small town in New Jersey, and the tiny village in Pennsylvania are
all part of a nationwide mosaic of contention and tragedy that has
developed in the past decade. During the early years of the Interstate
program, while most of the construction was taking place in the open
countryside and the smaller towns and villages, the furor was relatively low-key. Now, however, with most of the rural mileage completed, the new routes are beginning to thrust themselves into the
tissues of the cities, and the cries of anguish are more audible.

The antifreeway forces, in addition to those whose homes or businesses are destroyed, usually include architects, conservationists,
historians, curators of civic landmarks—people normally with very

low political horsepower. To these are often added civil rights groups, since, in the majority of the big cities, most of the displaced humanity consists of poor Negroes. The opposition of these groups is often deeply resented by the freeway establishment, who refer to the conservation-minded as "petunia planters, birdwatchers, and do-gooders." When the town of Pleasant Ridge, Michigan, attempted to block the intrusion of Interstate 696, *Newsweek* magazine quoted an irate highway official as saying, "Pleasant Ridge has a history of opposition. They ought to raze it, pave it, and turn it into a parking lot."

The American Automobile Association's Kermit B. Rykken says that "the whole approach to urban freeway development is being hampered and hamstrung by the peculiar preachments and doctrines of small but highly articulate minorities which, after searching in vain for a more euphemistic term, I must identify as the 'wrecking crew.' They use various arguments, most of them without the slightest foundation in fact, but all having one common objective—to postpone or halt freeway development in major American cities."

The real estate columnist for *The Philadelphia Bulletin,* Bernard C. Meltzer, distressed by the delays in completing Philadelphia's expressway network, writes that it will never be completed until "some method is found to overcome citizen and community obstructions." The "art of objection," he claims, "has become a science, and any well-organized vocal group can literally hold the entire community at ransom." The highway builders, he reasons, will be able to satisfy all objections "only if we substitute flying carpets for automobiles." Meanwhile, the result of citizen complaints is "to strangle desperately needed progress."

Mr. Meltzer is certainly right about one thing: the minorities are dissenting.

In Spokane, Washington, construction of Interstate 90 through the heart of the city was halted in 1964 by a suit brought by the Deaconess Hospital. This six-lane expressway will carry traffic high in the air, on a 100-foot-wide viaduct supported by 5-foot-diameter concrete columns. For a two-block stretch, traffic will roar by, directly outside the windows of the hospital. The hospital sued to stop the highway, claiming that the Interstate traffic would disturb its patients. After deliberation, a Spokane superior court judge saw it that way, too, and decided that the I-90 route through Spokane had been selected on a "fundamentally wrong basis" and was arbitrary and capricious. Work on the highway stopped.

The highway builders appealed. Sixteen months later, the Supreme Court of the state of Washington reversed the decision. It was impossible for the highway to be a nuisance, said the Supreme Court, because, according to an 1891 law, if the route was chosen by a duly constituted authority, then it was automatically the correct one for the community, and any subsequent judicial finding to the contrary was invalid. The bulldozers resumed their work.

The park lands along the lakefront in Milwaukee are soon to be invaded by a freeway, running north and south along the bluffs above the shore. Two interchanges, less than a mile apart, will also be constructed in the parks to connect the Lake Freeway with east-west freeways through the city itself. Called the largest single public works project ever undertaken in Milwaukee, this freeway was the center of civic debate and controversy for several years.

Citizens formed a Lake Front Preservation Committee and collected signatures on a petition for a referendum to "preserve exclusively for park purposes" all the park lands along the lakefront, which would have blocked construction of the freeway. In sixty days, 48,000 signatures were collected, more than enough to force the referendum.

The highway engineers wanted to build the freeway into the 60-foot-high bluff above the lakefront, the northbound three lanes at one level and the southbound at another, so that motorists traveling in either direction would have an unrestricted view of the lake. Concrete retaining walls would be installed to prevent erosion of the bluff. The county engineer stated that the freeway would "enhance the beauty of the lakefront" because it would "permit grading of the bluff to open a vista of the lakefront." Here, again, we witness the logic of the highway builder, which reasons that the beauty of a scene is enhanced by adding a highway to it so that motorists can gain "increased visual access."

On the contrary, said the Lake Front Preservation Committee. The six-lane freeway with wire mesh fences, overhead signs, directional signs, and ramps would "substantially destroy the beauty of the lake-

front. It would destroy a part of the bluff and replace it with concrete retaining walls. We find it impossible to believe that this tends
to beautify a park." The land traversed by the freeway would be
completely lost to human uses, but the damage would extend "to
those park lands not physically occupied by the concrete but affected
adversely by traffic, noise, dirt, and fumes. The effect will be to ruin
the quiet, serene atmosphere which makes a park a refuge."

The Lake Freeway was approved by the Common Council of
Milwaukee, the Expressway Commission, the County Board, the
State Highway Commission, the Milwaukee City Plan Commission,
and an impressive number of civic groups.

The referendum to deny use of park land for the freeway was held
on April 4, 1967. It was defeated by a vote of 69,971 to 35,828. To
some, it is significant that the citizens of Milwaukee had, by reject-
ing the referendum, approved the construction of the freeway by a
vote of nearly 2 to 1. To others, it is significant that one-third of the
voters disapproved the building of the freeway, even though it would
give them great new areas of concrete on which to move their automobiles, and even though it promised to improve "access" of the
motorist to downtown Milwaukee and thus be an economic boon to
all.

In a nice bit of symbolism, part of the freeway will be built over
the abandoned right-of-way of the Chicago and North Western Railway. The seventy-eight-year-old depot, with its 234-foot-high clock
tower, has long been a city landmark and once served as the proud
gateway to the city, handling as many as ninety-eight passenger
trains a day. A Metropolitan Folk Group recently attempted to raise
money to renovate the tower, but the drive met with little success.
The depot stands in the way of the freeway and will be demolished.
Meanwhile, in the words of *The Milwaukee Journal,* "it stands as a
vandalized, pigeon-stained, disconsolate monument to the history of
a city which does not care."

The story of the Lower Manhattan Expressway exemplifies the
power of federal money to get things done.

To the untutored eye, the last thing that Manhattan Island appears
to need is expressways to bring more rubber-tired vehicles into the
city. As originally conceived in the mid-fifties, the Lower Manhattan

Expressway would cut a 200-foot-wide swath right across the island, to connect the Hudson Tunnel on the west with the Williamsburg Bridge on the east. A spur would also connect with the Manhattan bridge just to the south of the Williamsburg Bridge. In the mode of the times, the expressway was designed to be carried high in the air on concrete stilts, and the approach ramps for the interchanges would coil and snake among the surviving buildings of the city like the tentacles of a conquering octopus.

You couldn't spit in lower Manhattan without inundating somebody's property; so clearing the right-of-way for a gigantic highway, ten lanes wide with a divider strip, would cause certain inconveniences. The experts calculated that the living quarters for some 2,300 families and the places of 800 businesses employing about 10,000 persons would have to be destroyed to make way for this 1.2-mile-long highway. Cost estimates came to about $115 million. On both counts, violent objections were soon heard.

Harold Harmatz, chairman of the East Side Chamber of Commerce, asked a congressional committee to "stop the expressway in order to prevent a small business disaster area from being created by constructing the wrong thing, in the wrong place, at the wrong time, by a gross misuse of public funds and a flouting of popular will that constitutes a mockery of democracy."

Leonard Farbstein, Congressman for the threatened district, told Congress that "as one who lived as a boy on the lower East Side, I know from personal experience how the 'el' shut out the sunlight, caused noise and dirt, and scarred the neighborhood. It should be obvious to the city planners that the Lower Manhattan Expressway will have an even worse effect, for the subway never emitted noxious fumes from automobile engines."

Representative Farbstein knew full well that the provisions of the highway laws that purported to compensate displaced persons were wholly inadequate, that severe injustice was frequently the result of a highway displacement. "I hope the Lower Manhattan Expressway is never built," he said. "But if it is, if the 800 businesses and 2300 families along its route are displaced, then I should like to see my constituents receive the aid they deserve." Property owners should get full compensation for their property. Renters should get "com-

pensation for the contract right which has been taken from them."
Businessmen should be compensated for the loss of business during
the move, the permanent loss of good will, the capital needed to set
up business in a new location, the full amount of moving expenses.
Persons who lose working time when a business moves, or who lose
their jobs when a business folds, should be compensated.

Even while the arguments went on, the proposed corridor of the
expressway began to deteriorate, because banks would not lend money
to residents to improve their property, and prospective new businesses were scared off by short-term leases. Since 1963, when the
route had been officially "mapped" by the city, no further work had
been done to any property along the proposed route, and decay was
taking over.

In response to vehement opposition from the residents of the
threatened area, Mayor Wagner finally halted the developmental
work on the expressway and asked for further studies. While the
studies were under way, John Lindsay took over as mayor and installed Arthur E. Palmer, Jr., as his transportation administrator.

In October, 1967, Mayor Lindsay announced new plans for the
Lower Manhattan Expressway. Instead of a highway on stilts, it
would be a highway in a trench. A short section leading to the
Holland Tunnel would be put underground, as would a section in the
approach to the Manhattan Bridge, in order to avoid the destruction
of the Sara Delano Roosevelt playground. The remainder of the highway would be in an open trench, although plans called for covering
over the trench in certain places to accommodate apartment and other
buildings and to provide open space for park land. Estimates of displacements were down to about 400 businesses and 1,350 families.
Estimates of cost were up to about $150 million.

Mr. Palmer suggested that the walls of the trench could be lined
with sound-absorbing material, and the exhaust fumes could be collected and controlled. "It can be done by a big stack," he said rather
vaguely.

The idea of using the air rights above the highway for buildings
and parks is the newest thing in highway construction. Its proponents
say that this is the way to "blend the highway in with the urban
environment." Mayor Lindsay called this "joint development" con-

cept "probably the most dramatic, dynamic breakthrough the nation has yet seen in the planning of highways through congested urban areas." The Bureau of Public Roads called it "an excellent example of planning."

New York residents who lived in the path of the joint development were still opposed to being uprooted. Louis DeSalvio, the assemblyman whose district would be sliced by the expressway, spoke for them all: "The underground idea is better than the elevated highway proposal, but we don't want to see any highway at all." The five-year fight by Mr. DeSalvio's constituents to kill the expressway ended in March, 1968, however, when the Board of Estimate approved the highway plan.

Three weeks later, remarks made to a committee of the City Council by City Planning Commissioner Donald H. Elliott raised a question in some minds as to just how eager the city officials were to slash across Manhattan with new expressways. Mr. Elliott pressed for prompt action to begin construction of the Lower Manhattan Expressway, but in the same breath he stated that the first transportation priority for the city should be "to provide improved transit service to serve 1.5 million daily commuters into Manhattan, as well as to discourage additional people from driving" downtown. As Mr. Elliott well knew, the Lower Manhattan Expressway, stabbing directly into the heart of the city, and described as having "adequate access to and from the street systems," will certainly not discourage people from driving their automobiles into Manhattan.

Why the contradiction? Why did Mr. Elliott ask that construction of the expressway begin without delay, and at the same time ask for improved transit to keep automobiles out of the city? In testimony before the Senate Subcommittee on Roads several months later, New York City transportation administrator Arthur E. Palmer, Jr., gave the probable reason. Neither highways nor transit systems can be provided without substantial federal money. But, said Mr. Palmer, while the 1962 Federal Aid Highway Act calls for a "continuing comprehensive transportation planning process" by metropolitan areas, it provides federal aid only for highways. Even though a city might plan for a balanced transportation system, with transit playing its full role, the federal dollar was not to be spent for transit, only for highways. Therefore, said Mr. Palmer, the fine phrases in the federal statutes calling for "balanced" transportation planning were empty ones. Washington must put its money where its mouth is if we ever hope "to provide the balanced transportation system so vital to the future of the city," concluded Mr. Palmer.

By now the three approaches to Manhattan that are to be connected by the Lower Manhattan Expressway—the Holland Tunnel, Williamsburg Bridge, and Manhattan Bridge—all have been designated Interstate routes, and they point at the lower end of the island like threatening fingers. The Lindsay administration, says Mr. Palmer, has been under urgent pressure to build the expressway to complete these Interstate routes—pressure "from the State Department of Public Works, and from the Federal Bureau of Roads and now the Department of Transportation." Further, the city has been warned that if it does not build this link through Manhattan, the federal government might withdraw the 90-per-cent federal money promised for it, and it might withdraw the Interstate designation from the three approaches to it, thus reducing federal aid for these already completed sections from 90 to 50 per cent. If this happens, says Mr. Palmer, the financial impact on the city would be "unbearable." This kind of pressure on a city, he says, constitutes "planning with a pistol at your temple."

Mr. Palmer charges that the Interstate Highway program, by bringing these six- and eight-lane superhighways up to the edges of the cities, has created major headaches for the communities that are supposed to be benefited. Some of the effects of the superhighways are:

They attract people from transit into their cars and thus "erode alternate transportation modes on which the city was historically grounded." In twenty years, daily riders on New York's commuter railroads have declined from 283,000 to 200,000. In the same period, riders on the rapid transit system have declined from 6,100,000 to 4,500,000 per day.

They vastly increase the city's maintenance and improvement expenses for its local streets.

They "increase traffic circulation to a point approaching glut. . . .

The advantage of the motor vehicle as a flexible and freely moving mode of transportation has been lost in its own uncontrolled and unprovided for abundance—like a herd of protected elk reduced to starvation by its own proliferation on a limited range."

They cause untold emotional distress and financial difficulties for the thousands of businesses and individuals who are displaced for their construction.

They impair the quality and safety of urban life, through "the blight created by hastily conceived freeways, massive interchanges, overpasses and access ramps which has not only buried thousands of acres of potentially valuable real estate under concrete but depressed the abutting land values; the unceasing roar of heavy traffic along these new superhighways which is comparable to that of the old Els long since discarded in the city's center as unsuited to conditions of urban living; and, last but not least, a threat to life itself which only now is being reckoned with—the matter of air pollution from exhaut fumes."

They force the middle-class and well-to-do citizens to abandon the scene of destruction, thus eroding the tax base and deepening the financial plight of the city.

These, says Mr. Palmer, are some of the consequences of a national policy to build an Interstate Highway system. The more successful this policy, the more terrible are the consequences for the city.

Mr. Palmer notes wryly that "in 1867, just 100 years ago, the *New York Times* observed: 'There is not enough room on the surface of the city to accommodate the traffic which its business requires.' And we are not able to take issue with this statement."

Residents of Cleveland point out that, if all planned freeways in the area are eventually built, the fifty square miles or so comprising the eastern suburbs of the city will be more heavily laced with freeways than any other area of comparative size in the nation.

Ringing the center of the city on the east is the Inner Belt Freeway, and striking off to the south from this is the Willow Freeway. Running north-and-south are, in order: the Bedford Freeway, the Lee Freeway, and the Outer Belt East Freeway. Running east-and-

west through the area are: the Lakeland Freeway, the Heights Freeway, the Central Freeway, the Clark Freeway, and finally the Outer
Belt South.

Except for the Clark Freeway, the routes for all these are firm,
and their construction is either completed, begun, or committed. The
Clark Freeway, which has the Interstate designation I-290, and
therefore will qualify for 90-per-cent federal money, is the only link
in Ohio's entire freeway network for which there is as yet no
definite route. It is surely no coincidence that the proposed route
for the Clark Freeway cuts through one of the nation's finest residential areas—Shaker Heights—and desecrates one of the nation's
finest urban park lands—the 275-acre Shaker Lakes Park. Indeed,
if the plans of the highway engineers come to fruition, the east-west
Clark Freeway and the north-south Lee Freeway will intersect at a
60-acre interchange right in the center of Horseshoe Lake, the east-
ernmost of the two large lakes that, together with wooded areas and
grassy slopes, comprise Shaker Lakes Park.

In the Euclid Arcade in the center of downtown Cleveland hangs
a 20-foot-long aerial photograph of the proposed corridor for the
Clark Freeway, with the eight-lane highway and all its interchanges
superimposed in white. The symbolism is valid; since 1963, when
the proposed corridor was first announced by the county engineer,
the Clark Freeway has been a center of controversy. It has been
the subject of at least three task-force studies, and it has aroused as
much vehement opposition as any urban freeway in the nation.

Shaker Heights is an affluent suburb of bank presidents, insurance
executives, attorneys, and similar executive and professional types.
It is an area of large homes and sweeping expanses of lawn—the
kind of place in which a certain air of detachment is possible. Indeed,
one resident, upon hearing about the proposed freeway, remarked,
"I hope they put a kink in the freeway; maybe it will just take the
tennis courts."

The reaction of the mayor of Shaker Heights, Paul K. Jones, was
Churchillian: "I do not propose to preside over the disfigurement
and dismemberment of this city," he said. "I am appointing a citizens' committee to spearhead our objections to this proposal, and
we will use our entire resources to combat what certainly would be

a desecration of our most beautiful home section and the resulting loss of taxable property."

In a talk to the Heights Rotary Club, county engineer Albert S. Porter asserted that taking land for a highway does not result in any tax loss. "When this argument is raised against freeways," he told his listeners, "people forget that when the land becomes a road, it no longer needs the tax-supported services of fire departments, police departments, garbage pickup." It is not recorded whether Mr. Porter went on to discuss the costs of maintenance and repair of the completed highway, of plowing and sanding in the winter, providing traffic regulation and policing, cleaning up litter and smashed automobiles, and so on. The implication seems clear, however, that automotive needs are more easily provided for than human needs.

Park lands are a natural target for freeway builders, because the land is usually very inexpensive, and dislocation of people is minimized. But the nation has recently begun to realize that green spaces in metropolitan areas are very precious, all but irreplaceable. The proposal to cut a freeway through Shaker Lakes Park aroused the ire of Cleveland's Park Conservation Committee, which declared: "To exchange this park of irreplaceable beauty for a mass of concrete roadways would be an unthinkable act of vandalism." In an act of defiance, the Shaker Lakes Garden Club in 1966 spent $400 of its funds to plant flowering trees around threatened Horseshoe Lake.

Deputy County Engineer Robert Vannice is less enthusiastic about the beauties of the lakes and the surrounding park land. "You should go out there in the summer when the water is about six inches deep," he says. "The septic effluent is stinking. We should really take credit for that whole area being cleaned up, because, until the Clark Freeway report was released, they spent practically nothing on most of that area out there to keep it cleaned up. There was trash and brush and everything all over the place. Within about three months after we put out that preliminary report, both the city of Shaker Heights and the city of Cleveland Heights had their crews out going through the park, cutting down dead trees, sawing up old dead logs, and cleaning it out. One citizen told me that the group in his neighborhood had been trying for eight years to get the city of Cleveland Heights to clean up this area of so-called park out there, it was an utter disgrace.

"That area of the Shaker Lakes belongs to the city of Cleveland. Shaker Heights leases its part from the city for a dollar a year. Cleveland Heights wouldn't even pay Cleveland a dollar a year and wouldn't even go near it and didn't go near it until this Clark Freeway thing came up, and all of a sudden Cleveland Heights discovered they had a great thing going down there."

Much of the pressure to build the Clark Freeway is generated by suburbanites who wish to drive to their jobs in Cleveland. This very common demand usually results in the construction of a freeway through the black ghetto to accommodate white commuters, but in Cleveland the situation is somewhat unusual. Shaker Heights is quite close to the city—the lakes are only about seven miles from the center of Cleveland—and many commuters living in more distant suburbs wish to drive their cars through Shaker Heights on their daily run to the city. Residents of Shaker Heights take the attitude, however, that their community should not be required to sacrifice its amenities in order to provide a transportation corridor for the suburbanite to the east, who must, they maintain, "accept the liabilities as well as the advantages of living at great distances from his place of employment." The freeway pattern for the area, they say, should not "permit the inner rings of the suburbs to be used as mere steppingstones by residents of the more distant suburbs." An excellent rapid transit system serves the eastern suburbs of Cleveland. Shaker Heights residents argue that this system, which is used well under capacity, should be expanded to handle the growing traffic demand from the outer suburbs.

Unfortunately for the advocates of rapid transit, the county engineer, Albert Porter, believes that the rubber-tired vehicle is the way to move people, not "Toonerville Trolleys." The fact that Mr. Porter happens also to be the Democratic Party chairman in a Democratic county adds weight to his argument. According to Richard Stoddart, chairman of the Cleveland Heights Transportation Advisory Committee, in Porter's mind, "highways are the only answer—transit is out. Slowly and surely, inroads are being made in that position, but the guy has a phobia about freeways."

Porter's deputy, Robert Vannice, explains very clearly the argument of the highway engineers: "What we're saying is that there are a sufficient number of cars desirous of moving east-west through the Clark Freeway corridor to require an eight-lane freeway. We approach it, not on the basis of what municipality is hit, or anything like that. We approach it on the basis of: 'Here is a traffic demand. What is the best way to handle the traffic demand? The best way to handle the traffic demand is a facility in this area.' In this particular area, it is a corridor that goes through Shaker Heights.

"The opponents of these freeways," Mr. Vannice goes on, "as in most cases of this sort, are really a small minority. But this small minority is very loud and they are willing to throw their money around. They come out with what they claim to be statements of fact, but they have no background for them, no basis for a lot of the so-called data that they come up with."

Mr. Vannice gives every indication of being a very competent highway engineer who, for many years, has faithfully built good roads for his state and who suddenly is faced with a vociferous element in his community that not only fails to appreciate his professional competence, but has developed a positive enmity toward it. "On this freeway system," he says, "we had an advisory committee; we utilized the services of the regional planning commission; we had the mayor's and manager's association; we had the chamber of commerce; we had all kinds of civic organizations in an advisory committee. And yet you hear these people say today that 'this man Porter just sat down and started drawing lines.'"

But Richard Stoddart disagrees: "This whole plan was developed without ever conulting the municipalities that it cut through. This whole network was conceived in a vacuum. No municipality was ever asked, 'Is there a place in your city that we might use as a freeway corridor?' No one was ever consulted. These are arbitrary lines drawn by engineers, using so-called desire lines. It was merely a matter of running a desire line until it got dark enough, then you have a corridor. Then you look in the corridor to avoid a cemetery, a school, a church—and that's how the lines were drawn."

What Mr. Stoddart and other opponents of the Clark Freeway
fail to understand, according to Mr. Vannice, is that this road is
part of a complete system, and "if you take one link out of a system,
you change the balance of flow in the rest of the system."
    Mr. Stoddart and the other opponents of the corridor chosen for
the Clark Freeway realize that it is part of a system which, unfortunately, is otherwise all committed. Some provision, they know,
will have to be made for the traffic that the rest of the system will
generate. "For a long time," says Stoddart, "we have said we didn't
want it built there, and we didn't want it put in anyone else's back
yard. We have now been forced to come off that position to some
extent and attempt to look at alternatives. But if we can't get agreement among the communities as to where it is going to go, we'll
stand and hold hands and say 'No.' But we're willing to make an
effort to find a home for it."
    Mr. Vannice has evidence to support his claim that the freeway
opponents are in the minority. For several months after the first
announcement of the Clark proposal, he spoke at meetings "at least
once a week" in the affected communities, describing the plans of
the highway department. "I spoke in Shaker Heights one night to
a crowd of 650 people," he recalls. "That's all they would allow into
the auditorium. After the meeting, a crowd of people headed down
for the stage, and I thought they were about ready to lynch me.
But instead, they were congratulating me and expressing their support of the setup. They seemed to appreciate that we were trying
to provide a facility to relieve the congestion in the area and give
the streets back to the people in the area."
    Further evidence, says Mr. Vannice, is a county election held
less than a year after the announcement of the Clark Freeway proposal. Albert Porter was running for county engineer, and on the
same ballot was a $500 million state bond issue for building high-
ways. Both Mr. Porter and the bond issue gained a plurality in
Shaker Heights. In another election in 1967, says Mr. Vannice, "we
had a $10 million highway bond issue on the ballot. We need a
55 per cent plurality in this state to pass a bond issue. We got 54.7
per cent. In the city of Shaker Heights it was something like
64 per cent."

Albert Porter accuses the freeway opponents of hypocrisy. Nearly everyone, he says, is in favor of freeways. The typical citizen wants them so that he can drive where he wishes, and he votes for them until one threatens his own back yard. "Then you scream, howl, run to your councilman, mayor, congressman. You write to newspapers. You bad-mouth the man who proposed the freeway as a heel, a bum, an arrogant bureaucrat, when all he is doing is a job required by law."

But Mr. Stoddart and his associates are plainly concerned about the effect of the freeway network on the quality of their community. "All the figures that I have been able to find," says Mr. Stoddart, "presuppose that everybody is going to be able to drive anywhere they want to in 1990. It seems to me that this is foolhardy. Nevertheless, nobody has had the guts to take the bull by the horns and say, 'this is the way the metropolitan region should look in 1990.' They can't do it; it would be suicide."

"Our best ally is time," he says. "The federal picture has changed so tremendously—the thinking, the allocations of funds, the ability to pull funds out, the ability to tell states 'no, you can't do it that way, you can't have them there.' The planning people, the real planning people, have taken over at the federal level from the old highway engineers. This is the most significant thing that has happened. This, I think, is a fantastic development for us in the cities."

But time, according to Mr. Vannice, is a luxury the community cannot afford; the demand for movement of traffic is now. The whole policy of the freeway opponents, he says, "has been to wait in the hopes that the problem will go away, or that people will take to the rails, or that some rail transit system will be developed that will be a panacea. When you get right down to it, this is what these people are looking for. Their attitude is 'don't do anything now, because somebody might come up with a solution.' Well, we sit back, we who are responsible for providing transportation, for providing for the movement of people and goods in this area, and we see nothing coming out of industry or development of any kind, which is going to take the place, in the reasonably foreseeable future, of the automobile. They offer the grand solution, which is to build rail rapid transit lines, and everybody is going to flock to them, and they're going to go where the rail rapid transit line wants them to go. Well, the American people are not like that."

The opponents of the freeway builders gained a valuable and powerful ally when Carl Stokes became mayor of Cleveland. In January, 1968, shortly after he took office, Mayor Stokes wrote to Governor Rhodes that he was "unalterably opposed" to the network of freeways proposed for the eastern suburbs. He said that he planned to call together officials from the eastern suburbs to "evaluate community planning and mass transit concepts" in an effort to find the best routing for Interstate Route 290, the Clark Freeway. "I am, as you know, convinced that there must be a balanced approach to transportation problems. Such planning must incorporate solutions to other urban problems: mass transit, use of railroad rights of way, use of natural geographic lines of demarcation, and use of air rights."

This letter, according to Richard Stoddart, "hit like a bombshell in the highway department and in the county engineers' office. Of course, from the political standpoint, this is fascinating, because the county engineer is also the county chairman of the Democratic Party, which supported Carl Stokes in the election, but not in the primary. That may have something to do with his opposition to this freeway network, although he does feel very strongly, I think, that this configuration with all these routes into the central business district just doesn't make any sense. We can't handle all those automobiles in 1990 unless we're going to devote a hell of a lot of downtown to parking."

The Stokes study group was the third to enter the field. A regional planning group was working on the problem, and Governor Rhodes had appointed his own study group several months earlier. The governor, exasperated by the delay and the proliferation of study groups, according to one observer, "pounded the arms of his chair" at a highway conference and declared, "I'm going to speak for the motorists. I think motorists think they are being paralyzed by being analyzed." The governor, fearful lest the delay result in the withdrawal of federal funds for the freeway system, warned, "What Congress gives, Congress can take away."

After five years of battle, Richard Stoddart and his associates were

also showing the strain. At one point, perhaps wistfully, Mr. Stoddart recalled the days when the laws of the state of Ohio stipulated
that a highway could not be built through a municipality without
its consent. In 1963, that consent ordinance was removed from the
books because a town in the southern part of the state refused to
accept a highway within its borders, and the engineers had to route
it around the town. "The governor then convinced the legislature
that was a hell of a way to build roads," Mr. Stoddart recalls, "and
so it was removed."

Mr. Stoddart makes his living as an attorney, but for the past
few years, he has devoted more and more of his time to the citizens'
effort to find an acceptable alternative to the Clark Freeway. But
he may be running out of gas. "After what I've been through," he
says wearily, "I really understand why people in most cities say,
'You can't fight City Hall—let 'em build the damn thing.' "

10

A Road for Rocky

The battle over the Hudson River Expressway includes just about all the elements of similar battles across the nation, plus a few that are unique. The proposed route along the east bank of the Hudson River is being pushed vigorously by a Republican state administration; it is violently opposed by nearly all the affected communities; and it is viewed with unconcealed distaste by the federal authorities in Washington. It promises to enhance or to despoil an area of great natural beauty, depending upon whose testimony is being heard. The threat of wholesale displacement of people, mostly Negro, in one community gives substance to charges of white racism. A proposed interchange threatens to destroy what is left of the once quiet charm of a riverside suburban village.

A citizens' group organized to fight the expressway is made up of predominantly upper-middle-class Republicans, the party that traditionally opposes centralized authority in Washington. Yet this group of Republicans found itself turning to a Democratic Administration in Washington for help in fighting the Republicans in the State House. Finally, there are the ugly charges that a patrician governor is twisting arms to build this expressway because it promises to increase the value of the lands in his private estate adjoining the proposed route.

In May, 1965, a bill was introduced in the Rules Committees of the New York State Senate and State Assembly providing for construction of a highway. "Beginning at a point on interstate route 503 in the vicinity of Beacon or in the vicinity of Wiccopee, to be determined by the superintendent of public works, thence in a generally

158

southerly direction to the vicinity of Ossining and then continuing
southerly, west of U. S. route nine, along or near the Hudson river
to the north city line of New York, thence generally southerly and
easterly to a connection with interstate route connection 512 in the
city of New York, to be determined by the superintendent of public
works."

In the controversy that developed over this proposed highway, its
opponents charged that this bill was unique in several respects. First,
its title was vague and nondescriptive, stating merely that this was a
bill "to amend the highway law, in relation to state expressways on
the state highway system," without stating the location of the proposed highway. Second, no sponsor for the bill appeared on the
document; usually the New York State Department of Public Works
is identified as the sponsor. Third, in violation of customary practice, no preliminary plan was announced and no public hearings held
before the legislation was introduced. Fourth, the route numbers
used in the description of the highway are the route numbers used
by the Department of Public Works on its own internal maps; they
are not the numbers found on any public maps, and therefore they
are not likely to be meaningful to the casual observer. Fifth, a bill
such as this is customarily accompanied by a supporting memorandum explaining the need for the legislation. No such memorandum
was sent to the legislature until after the bill had passed.

Finally, the bill shot through the legislative mills with record-
breaking speed. It emerged from the Rules Committee of the Senate
and was passed on May 24. On the following day it reached the
floor of the Assembly. Despite its vague title, Assemblyman Lawrence A. Cabot noted that the expressway would run through his
district. He left the floor of the Assembly and called the district
office of the Department of Public Works in Poughkeepsie, but was
told the department knew nothing about the expressway or the
legislation. He then called the department headquarters in Albany
and was told that the bill had been "requested" by the localities along
its route. Knowing that this was untrue, he hurried back to the
floor in time to vote against the measure, but in vain.

Sensing a "railroad," Cabot asked Speaker Anthony Travia to
recall the bill, but Travia said that a special courier was rushing it

to Governor Rockefeller for his signature. The governor signed the bill on May 28, the same day that the supporting memorandum from the Department of Public Works reached the legislature. The memorandum was dated May 14.

So poorly identified was the bill that at least two state senators later admitted they voted for it in error, believing it was just a routine highway study bill. Said one of them, "I have been deluded. I am ashamed."

A companion bill that received the same priority treatment provided for a 3.5-mile east-west spur expressway to connect the Hudson River Expressway with Route 9A about three miles to the east. This spur would run roughly along the northern edge of the Rockefeller family estate, and its ostensible purpose would be to remove traffic from Route 117, a winding, two-lane country road which cuts through the heart of the estate where the Rockefeller mansions are located. The spur has thus become known as the "relocated route 117."

Only two assemblymen voted against the highway legislation: Mr. Cabot, a Democrat, and Richard A. Cerosky, a Republican. The proposed Hudson River Expressway would run through their districts. After passage of the bill, Mr. Cabot had several private conferences with Governor Rockefeller, asking him to support repeal of the legislation or to modify the proposed route. The governor refused. Mr. Cabot also asked the governor for factual evidence supporting the need for the expressway, but Rockefeller replied that no traffic studies had been made.

The mayors of the towns strung along the east bank of the Hudson River in the path of the expressway unanimously condemned it. Shortly after the passage of the legislation, the mayors of Ossining, Briarcliff, Irvington, Tarrytown, Dobbs Ferry, North Tarrytown, and Hastings sent telegrams to their state legislators asking them to repeal the expressway act and chastising those who had voted for it: "Your vote in favor of this bill without consulting local communities and without considering possible effects of the route chosen is frightening."

The failure to consult with those affected was deeply resented. Said Assemblyman Cabot, "What irks me most is that the Department of Public Works introduced legislation affecting particular areas without any prior knowledge on the part of the legislators who are to vote on it." U. S. Representative Richard L. Ottinger, the young freshman congressman who gave strong leadership to the expressway opponents, complained, "No hearings of any kind were held. No notice was given to the public. The mayors of the villages to be affected were ignored in spite of promises by the governor that they would be consulted." Ossining Mayor Richard E. Purdue accused Governor Rockefeller of "bad faith, bad judgment, and bad public policy" in pursuing his "juggernaut tactics."

The citizens of the affected towns were equally outraged. Assemblyman Cabot reported that he and his fellow legislators received more mail on this issue than the combined mail on the sales tax, capital punishment, and birth control.

Rockefeller's state officials stood foursquare behind his decision. Westchester County Planning Commissioner S. J. Schulman declared that the expressway "will result in cleaning up the shoreline of the Hudson, and it ties in with the new federal highway program for beautiful highways and the state plan to clean up the waterways." Charles E. Pound, commissioner of parks, recreation, and conservation for Westchester County, also saw the expressway as an opportunity to "clean up the riverfront and provide a magnificent scenic drive." The opposition charged that Schulman and Pound were confusing beautiful highways with highways through beautiful areas, and that there were more effective ways to "clean up" a waterfront than to build expressways along it.

Schulman and Pound, however, were joined by all the state, county, and local politicians who owed their jobs to Rockefeller patronage or who simply were awed by the Rockefeller name. Strong support also came from the Westchester County Association, representing some 550 business organizations.

The newspaper nearest the center of the storm, *The Tarrytown Daily News,* enthusiastically supported the expressway from the outset, pointing out that it could "add millions to area wealth." With its eye firmly on commercial gain, the newspaper urged its readers to "face up to facts. The expressway will be built. . . . Let's forget politics. Let's thank the governor for inking legislation that gives the project daylight. . . . Let's concentrate on building the project along the shoreline of the Hudson where it belongs."

During the gubernatorial campaign that fall, pressure on the governor reached such a pitch that he finally agreed to repeal the part of the highway act providing for the route *south* of Tarrytown. That part, he said, could be added later. True to his word, he did push the repeal, and it passed the following spring. The governor thereupon was accused by the communities *north* of Tarrytown of using divide-and-conquer tactics, since the opposition of the re-prieved towns south of Tarrytown would now be difficult to maintain at fever pitch. The only remaining bone of contention was the 10-mile portion of the Hudson Expressway between Tarrytown and Ossining, plus the relocated Route 117 spur along the Rockefeller estate.

Tarrytown, population about 12,000, and North Tarrytown, popu-lation about 9,000, lie along the eastern shoreline of the Hudson roughly 20 miles north of Manhattan's Central Park. The two towns, and their bedroom suburbs of Philipse Manor and Sleep Hollow Manor, house a number of upper-middle-class citizens who commute to the city on the Hudson branch of the Penn Central railroad, whose tracks run right along the river's edge. The 3-mile-long Tappan Zee bridge brings the six-lane New York State Thruway across the Hud-son just at the southern edge of Tarrytown, from which point it swings southward toward the city of New York.

Ossining, about 10 miles north of Tarrytown, has a lower percent-age of affluent commuters; therefore a higher percentage of its pop-ulation of 22,000 depends for its livelihood on local industry. Roughly 12 per cent of the population of Ossining is Negro. Dominating the town at its southern edge is the great, gray rock of Sing Sing Prison.

Just north and east of the Tarrytowns, at the heart of Washing-ton Irving's beautiful and historic Sleepy Hollow country, is the 3,500-acre Rockefeller estate, which centers on the Pocantico Hills and stretches from the Saw Mill River Parkway all the way to the Hudson River in a narrow corridor north of Tarrytown. The man-sions on the estate include homes for John, David, Laurance, and Nelson Rockefeller.

At one time, no doubt, Tarrytown was a lovely, quiet village nestled along the banks of the Hudson, with a splendid view of the majestic river rolling along at its feet. But the sleepy-village atmosphere was dispelled when the town permitted construction of a giant $100-million General Motors assembly plant on the banks of the river. Assembled Chevrolets pour out of this plant in an unceasing stream, some on the tracks of the Penn Central, which run right through the plant, and others on truck vans, which thunder along U. S. 9 through the center of Tarrytown. A clot of traffic chokes the streets of Tarrytown during shift change at the plant; but the pounding of the heavy automobile vans through the streets is incessant.

From the opposite shore, the banks of the Hudson at this point and north toward Ossining invite the eye. The wooded land rises rather steeply from the water's edge, and the roofs of the villages interrupt the foliage in a pleasing pattern. A closer inspection, however, reveals no evidence that the river affords pleasure to the community. Its waters are heavily polluted, and the railroad tracks along its edge isolate it from the villagers. Its cluttered shoreline portrays the blight of neglect and careless waste disposal typical of so many American riverbanks.

At Tarrytown itself, the enormous gray complex of the General Motors plant completely destroys any scenic value that this section of the shoreline might once have had. Thus Tarrytown finds itself of two minds with regard to the proposed Hudson River Expressway. On the one hand, a planned interchange ramp going right down into the parking lot of the General Motors plant should siphon off plant traffic that now clogs the village streets. On the other hand, if the expressway is built, the town will all but disappear in the snarl of interchange ramps connecting the Hudson River expressway with the eastern terminus of the Tappan Zee bridge and the New York State Thruway. What is left of the town, once nestled securely in the scenic bosom of the Hudson, will be caught in the tentacles of two superhighways, with approach lanes and ramps running freely through its vitals.

A few weeks after the legislation for the Hudson River Expressway and the Route 117 relocation passed, a group of aroused residents formed a Citizens' Committee for the Hudson Valley and proclaimed that they were "unequivocally" opposed to the routes and prepared

"to fight these proposed highways and any other future scarifying
encroachments of the Hudson's remaining natural beauty, by publicity, by organization of community protests, and, where feasible, by
legal action." The committee added that "urban sprawl, expressways,
industrial ugliness are not needed in the Hudson Valley. This legislation is an act of madness. Our government has become the foe instead of the friend of the people." The first chairman of the committee, William Rodgers, declared that the proposed expressway would
engulf a beautiful and priceless heritage in "automobile fumes, commercial ugliness, and technological progress."

Opposition to the expressway grew. In June, angry officials of
the towns and villages along the route charged that the expressway
would destroy the "quiet charm" of their communities, "slash real
estate values, wipe out years of town planning, and burden their
downtown areas with the roar and stench of heavy truck traffic." A
representative of the town of Mount Pleasant said his first choice
for the route would be "a half mile off shore and ten feet under
water."

Support came from Washington. Interior Secretary Udall stated
that such an expressway would seriously impair the highly scenic
and historic values in the corridor. The Federal Bureau of Outdoor
Recreation urged that the expressway be killed. "The construction
of such a highway," it said, "serving commercial and industrial traffic as well as private automobile traffic, would seriously impair and
destroy prime recreation values. It would destroy public access
routes to the river necessary to scenic and recreation enjoyment."

On the contrary, said *The Tarrytown Daily News*: "We, too,
believe in scenic conservation, but we also hold that . . . there
should be roads—such as the expressway—that make it possible
for the masses to enjoy this scenery."

The Hudson River Valley Commission, a regional planning group
headed by Laurance Rockefeller, reported that the expressway
would be an excellent means of providing much better "visual access"
to the river for motorists. The Citizens' Committee thereupon asked
angrily what kind of visual access it would be "when you are thundering along at 60 miles per hour between two high speed trucks?"

In reply to an anxious inquiry from Senator Jacob Javits, Governor Rockefeller counterattacked. Charges that the expressway would impair the beauty of the valley, he said, were "most idiotic" and most "viciously false." The governor promised that the highway builders would work closely with the Hudson River Valley Commission, "recently created on my recommendation," to "enhance" and "restore" the scenic beauty of the Hudson. "Some uninformed or deliberately misleading critics have characterized the proposed road as a 'truck expressway' and have conjured up the specter of a noxious, noisy 'gasoline alley' along the riverfront," Rockefeller fumed. "According to the studies of the Department of Public Works, the traffic on the proposed road would consist of more than 95 per cent passenger cars and less than 5 per cent trucks."

Editorial writers for *The Tarrytown Daily News* unswervingly touted the governor's expressway. One editorial warned: "Hysteria blocks progress and the rights of the majority. Its to be regretted that minorities nurse imaginary wounds. . . . We think thanks should be showered on the governor for planning now and not waiting until the area is more choked with traffic." Another said that "interference" from Washington would be overcome. "This is a sovereign state, and it is its right to build the expressway the way it will benefit all. If Washington will not contribute towards it, the state will finance the job itself."

As spokesman for the "hysterical minorities," William Rodgers condemned the newspaper for supporting a highway that would destroy community and esthetic values along the eastern shore of the Hudson. "We shall fight you," he wrote the editor, with sweeping Churchillian defiance, "in the legislature, over the telephone, in small meetings, in the streets, and along the beaches of the polluted Hudson until the end—or until there is no fight left in us."

Destruction of scenic values along the Hudson was only one of many arguments leveled at the expressway. But specific complaints about dislocation of people and businesses could not be formulated until the state released information about the exact route. So far, only the corridor had been defined in general terms. Not until June, 1967, more than two years after passage of the legislation, did the state publicly reveal detailed plans for the expressway. The Citizens' Committee later charged that the behavior of state officials during those years—statements issued and later denied, maps released and later disavowed—was purposefully designed to confuse and confound the opposition.

Many nasty accusations flew about during the long fight over the expressway, and the ugliest of all was the charge that Governor Rockefeller's desire to move in the bulldozers was born of a wish to increase the value of the land in his Pocantico Hills estate. The proposed relocation of Route 117 (also called the Pocantico Expressway) would run along the northern edge of the estate, through relatively inaccessible land. Over the years, the Rockefellers had obtained zoning changes in the northern parts of the estate, with the apparent intention of developing it with apartments, shopping centers, and office buildings. A relocated Route 117 would not only divert traffic from the areas near the family mansions, but it would send traffic into the areas marked for development. Some estimated that construction of the Pocantico Expressway would quadruple the value of the 3,000 acres in the northern part of the Rockefeller estate, which is some distance from the barbed-wire-enclosed family enclave in the south.

In addition to this, the intersection of the Hudson River and Pocantico expressways along the shore of the river would create a region of incalculable commercial value. The land to the north of this intersection belongs to the Rockefeller family.

Tarrytown Mayor Anthony Veteran has called the expressway plan a "crass abuse of gubernatorial power by Mr. Rockefeller, whose own lands stand to increase in value by millions of dollars while Hudson River communities are cut to pieces, while taxable properties are wiped out and all life irreparably disrupted. . . . This expressway is for the benefit only of the Rockefellers paid for by public expense. It's a fraud from start to finish." William Rodgers, the first chairman of the Citizens' Committee, states bluntly that "the story behind this scandal is a singular demonstration of the avarice of the very rich."

The governor has repeatedly denied that his interest in the expressways is in any way connected with personal financial gain. He has denied, in fact, that the relocation of Route 117 would improve his family's property. And in a cynical attempt to avoid responsibility for a proposal that he all too obviously initiated, the governor told the press that he had "no choice" but to support the recommendation of the State Department of Public Works. As Mr. Rodgers notes, the mind boggles at the picture of the billionaire governor of the Empire State knuckling under to a decision by his own highway department affecting the welfare of his own baronial estate.

Although the rest of the Rockefeller family has not commented publicly, there are reports that other members of the family are opposed to the Route 117 relocation. According to one member of the Citizens' Committee, the governor has said ruefully, "My brother John isn't even speaking to me" on the question.

State employees are unanimously loyal to the governor, as one might expect. In a press interview in January, 1966, Joseph P. Ronan, administrative deputy in the Department of Public Works, admitted that there were "political" overtones in the whole subject. "They all think Rockefeller is pushing this 117 thing for personal reasons, but it just isn't so. There has been no pressure from the governor on this matter. None."

The innuendos continue, however. Ossining's Mayor Purdue stated baldly: "The proposed road is more than just another state highway. It is an outright investment in the North Tarrytown property of Governor Rockefeller." *The New York Times* noted that "the old two-lane road winds close to the homes of three of the Rockefeller brothers—the governor and Laurance and David Rockefeller—and a replacement for it has been sought by some members of the family since 1932." An irate member of the Tarrytown Board stated publicly that the benefits that would accrue to the property owner at the junction of the two proposed expressways would "make Senator Dodd look like a kid stealing green apples."

Representative Ottinger wonders why the "unnecessary and extravagantly wasteful expressway has been pressed with such unseemly haste and cloaked in such strange secrecy?" "What is it for?" he asked in a public meeting, "Whose interests will it serve?" He promised that, before any construction could proceed, federally sponsored hearings would have to be held. Then, he went on, "the question of who benefits from this road—and how—will be fully and publicly explored."

The Taxpayers Association of the Town of Mount Pleasant, in

which the bulk of the Rockefeller estate is located, is also highly critical of the governor's part in the Route 117 relocation fight: "It is well known to many persons in Mount Pleasant that the Rockefellers have been trying since 1932 to have Route 117 relocated. They want truck and automobile traffic through residential park and the hamlet of Pocantico Hills, which they own, reduced as much as possible.

"One look at a map of the proposed relocation indicates it has been designed to cross the estate where it will do the least amount of damage and will be far removed from all Rockefeller homes. . . . When the Governor commented that the revised alignment of the road would result in less cutting-up of properties, he was entirely right. It would—his family's. He failed to mention that the hiking and equestrian trails he said would be protected are wholly within the Rockefeller preserve.

"Also omitted from the Governor's remarks was reference to the commercial zoning the Rockefellers sought and obtained now in the vicinity of the new expressway. . . . This zoning was revoked by the Mount Pleasant Town Board last January as being inconsistent with the semi-rural atmosphere of adjoining areas. At the hearings, a spokesman for the Governor's family said the Rockefellers did not object to the rezoning, but 'they do think, however, that rezoning should be deferred until the route of the spur [Route 117] is determined.' Does this signify the disinterest or displeasure the Governor would like the public to believe his family has in the 117 relocation?

"The Mount Pleasant Taxpayers Association objects to the Governor's repeated assertions that opposition to the relocation is politically motivated. Mount Pleasant citizens of all political persuasions, like the preponderance of citizens everywhere, aware of the facts, are shocked by the ruthless manner in which the 117 relocation and Hudson River Expressway were rammed through the Legislature . . . and are aghast at the questionable way in which these roads are being given top construction priority."

At the public hearings on the Hudson River Expressway held in February, 1968, an opponent of the highway stood up in the rear of the packed Ossining High School auditorium, and, with the aid of a bullhorn, shouted to District Engineer M. Nicholas Sinacori, who was presiding, that, in view of the fact that Mr. Sinacori worked for Mr. Rockefeller, whose private real estate interests were involved in the decision, Mr. Sinacori should disqualify himself to chair the hearing. An aide to Mr. Sinacori left the stage, walked up the aisle, and gently quieted the obstreperous citizen.

In the spring of 1966, a carrot was added to the stick behind the Hudson River Expressway. The state announced plans to build a 4-mile-long riverfront park between the expressway and the river, complete with sand beaches, marinas, bicycle and hiking paths, fishing piers, and plenty of parking space for automobiles. The opponents of the expressway were inclined to agree with *The New York Times* editorial stating that this plan sounded like "elaborate window dressing" designed to make the expressway more palatable to the residents. Of course, the park was a fine idea, and would be a big step forward in the badly needed rehabilitation of the banks of the Hudson, said the editorial. But this should be done without building an expressway; the two were entirely separate questions.

At the February, 1968, hearings in Ossining, detailed plans for the park development were unveiled. Artists' breathtaking renderings showed vast green areas containing badminton and tennis courts, swimming pools, fishing piers, a marina for 400 boats, picnicking areas, a restaurant, a golf course, hiking trails, and, of course, parking space for 2,000 automobiles. When the full sweep of the scene was uncovered for the thousand residents jamming the school auditorium, many of them laughed cynically. "It's great," shouted one, "but where are all the ferris wheels?" Another citizen asked, "Why can't waterfront parks be built along the Hudson *without* an expressway?" The school building rang with applause.

In his testimony at the Ossining hearings, John G. Mitchell, chairman of the Staten Island Greenbelt Natural Areas League, questioned the "sincerity of the state in its proposal to combine this truck route with a waterfront park—built, incidentally, on fill into the river in total disregard of the river's delicate ecology. The paradox of picnic tables and passing trucks is all too familiar to us. The state recreation planners also envisioned such incompatible uses for the Staten Island greenbelt—a hiking trail, if you will, 70 feet from a 55-mile-per-hour parkway!"

Another speaker suggested that the riverfront park could easily be built without the highway. He turned to District Engineer Sinacori during the hearing and told him that, as a gesture of good faith, the state of New York should publicly declare its intention to build the park, even though the expressway should be defeated. The state, he argued, should not hold out the park "as some kind of lure, or prize." The boisterous applause drowned any reply that the engineer may have wished to offer.

In the late summer of 1966, the Citizens' Committee uncovered a report by the State Department of Public Works issued four years earlier over the signatures of Superintendent J. Burch McMorran and District Engineer M. Nicholas Sinacori, in which the Hudson River route for an expressway was rejected as unsound. The report argued that the river route "would confine costly facilities to a narrow corridor without provision for the greatest traffic needs of the region."

If the expressway was such a bad idea in 1962, the committee asked, why was it suddenly the solution to the region's traffic problems in 1966? The committee implied that the Department of Public Works, against its better judgment, was knuckling under to pressure from the governor. During the remaining years of the controversy, the committee returned again and again to this question, but heard no satisfactory answer.

In June, 1967, more than two years after passage of the enabling legislation, state officials sponsored the first public "information meeting" on the expressway. According to one witness, the meeting was "jammed to the rafters with more than a thousand people." The opening presentation by highway officials was interrupted with "some applause, jeering, yelling and laughter." The hero of the hour was Representative Ottinger, whose long, impassioned condemnation of the proposed highway route was greeted with enthusiastic applause at every other sentence and a standing ovation at the end.

The legislation for this highway, said Ottinger, had been rushed through the legislature in an "extremely unusual—not to say irregular fashion." Since that time, plans for the highway had been "shrouded in mystery." Ottinger had repeatedly asked the governor and his representatives to explain the need for the expressway. The answers, he said, ranged from the "unresponsive to the ridiculous."

Ottinger heaped derision on the argument that the highway would benefit the region by making available filled land in the river for recreation purposes. This justification, he said, was spurious, ridiculous, and self-contradictory. Can't they think of cheaper and more effective ways to provide parks and recreation lands, he asked, than to build a six-lane commercial expressway? The claim that the expressway would enhance the scenic resources of the river valley, he said, was a "desperate and dishonest effort to justify the project after the fact."

The congressman noted that the state was just then in the process of going to the voters for approval of a $2½ billion bond issue for transportation, most of it to be spent on highways. This money, he said, could be used by the state to build highways without recourse to federal aid and thus without the need to comply with federal requirements. If the state was planning to use that means of ramming through the Hudson River Expressway, said Ottinger, it would fail, because the approval of two federal agencies would still be required. The expressway was to be built for about half its length on fill in the river, and the law clearly stated that this required approval of the U. S. Army Corps of Engineers. Also, a bill sponsored by Ottinger and passed by the Congress the previous fall required that any decision by any federal agency (the U. S. Army included) affecting the Hudson River Valley had to be reviewed by the Secretary of the Interior, who was already on record in opposition to the Hudson River Expressway.

Ottinger called for curbs on the unlimited state powers of eminent domain. "The state," he said, "cannot be permitted to just crash around the countryside, dividing villages, destroying homes, wiping out whole sections of towns, desecrating natural resources, without any effective check."

At the June meeting, James C. Harding, commissioner of public works for Westchester County, presented forecasts of traffic demands to justify the need for the Hudson River Expressway. He also defended the "cloak of secrecy" in which the state and county agencies had wrapped their plans for the highway. It was a very difficult thing, he said, for engineers to take the public into their confidence during preliminary design stages. The minute anything is announced, the engineers are "deluged with requests for information as to just where it is going to be located. This, they, of course, do not know, until preliminary investigations, designs, etc., have been completed." It is impossible to present a highway project to the public without drawing criticism from "some group or other."

As for Secretary Udall's statement that the Hudson River Expressway would impair the natural beauty of the valley and destroy public access routes to the river necessary to scenic and recreation enjoyment, Mr. Harding replied that "this is ridiculous. Where is there any adequate public access to the river now between Ossining and North Tarrytown? Where are there any recreation areas? How can any public access or recreation areas be provided except by means of a road similar to that proposed?"

Community leaders in Ossining and the Tarrytowns had been arguing for years that the traffic problems existed *in* the towns, not along the entire 10-mile route *between* the towns. They had long ago prepared an alternate plan which included construction of bypass routes around the towns, connected by an inland route using an abandoned roadbed of the New York Central, bordering the eastern edge of the Rockefeller estate. This plan, the mayors claimed, would be far less disruptive of existing property and would cost less than half the estimated $115 million for the expressway. State officials unswervingly treated this proposal with disdain.

Eight months after the June meeting, the state held the first official public hearings to unveil detailed plans for the Hudson River Expressway. During the twelve hours of hearings, which heard testimony from some seventy persons, only three spoke in favor of the proposed highway. These February hearings clearly delineated the destructive route of the bulldozer. Of the 9,000 residents of North Tarrytown, 853 would lose their homes—nearly 10 per cent of the population. Also in the path of the highway were thirteen businesses and a 2½-acre park including a children's playground. The tax-assessment value of the property scheduled for demolition exceeded half a million dollars.

Altogether, it looked as if Tarrytown would lose $2 million in assessed valuation, including public and private waterfront property, an insurance company, many homes, a firehouse, a recreation facility, the state police barracks, parts of two schools, Washington Irving and Tarrytown Board Clubs, the village's Losee Park, a commuter parking area, and several additional business sites. This was an impressive list for a village having a population of only about 12,000 persons.

A clergyman testified that most of the displaced persons in the Tarrytowns were low-income families. Those who owned their homes lacked the means to buy new ones. Many, however, were tenants who would be forced to find new homes to rent. These did not exist. After four years of operation, a full-time urban renewal director with a staff in North Tarrytown had been able to place five or six families. "How are they going to find places for 900 people," the clergyman asked, "when a full-time urban renewal director has been able to find only five or six?"

The expressway threatened to plow through the Negro section of Ossining, displacing a quarter to a third of the entire Negro population of the town. Of the thousand or so persons threatened with displacement, about 90 per cent were Negro. The ugly accusation was that Ossining Mayor John Donzella looked with favor on the expressway for this very reason—that it would wipe out a large section of the Negro community. "Wipe out" would be accurate, since Ossining, with a population of some 22,000, has no low-cost housing program. As one witness said, "The consequences of these displacements can not be other than a forced departure from the village of Ossining."

The first night of the hearings, the Ossining NAACP distributed handbills designed to look like circus posters. In big, black Barnum-and-Bailey type, they shouted: "Welcome to Rocky's Magic Road Show Featuring The Hon. J. Donzella. Guaranteed to be the Greatest Sleight of Hand Show on Earth. See Gov. Rockefeller & Mayor Donzella MAKE 1,000 BLACK PEOPLE DISAPPEAR. See Gov. Rockefeller's Concern for Ossining's Black Residents EVAPORATE INTO THIN AIR! See Ossining Mayor John Donzella's Relocation Housing Program VANISH BEFORE YOUR VERY EYES!!!"

William B. Rascoe, president of the Ossining NAACP, charged that the officials of the village had repeatedly refused to entertain

any proposals for relocation housing. The expressway, he said, would
"slash into the very heart of the community, destroying the homes
of hundreds of Negro families. To all intents and purposes, these
are plans for Negro removal." The village government, said Rascoe,
sees the expressway as "an opportunity to get rid of hundreds of its
Negro residents."

One Negro resident deplored the "total disregard for human lives
that has been displayed by the governor, the State Department of
Transportation, and, last but certainly not least, the village government of Ossining." At the conclusion of his testimony, he read a
statement prepared by his wife:

"The outlook of over 200 families in the village of Ossining is one
of bleak despair, a despair compounded with frustration at the injustice this road would bring to most of those families, who are
Negroes. The history of the Negro people in the United States has
been one of bitter rejection, of a continuing struggle up the economic
and social ladder of this land to achieve some degree of self-respect
and sense of accomplishment. Some have succeeded in overcoming
the barriers thrown up in their paths, and through almost super-
human effort have managed to take a place in the mainstream of
American life.

"This is what many of the 200 families have done. Homes obtained after many years of privation and self-denial are being threatened by this proposed highway. According to this plan, the road
would cut through the area where the majority of the Negroes in
this village have purchased homes. These are families who have
achieved stability through prudent use of their meager resources—
families who wanted to assume full citizenship, its rights and responsibilities. A number of the people threatened are elderly, retired
people, who cannot hope to purchase again to replace those homes
acquired while actively employed.

"These people lend dignity and worth to any community, and if
they are forced to leave their homes, Ossining will be poorer spiritu-
ally and morally for their departure. The proposed highway would
wipe out much of the stable Negro community while retaining
blighted slum areas. Such action would only add discontent and
anger among those residents who could lose what incentive they have
for forging ahead.

"It is not our desire to stand in the way of 'progress,' but is progress to be measured only by the number of motor vehicles that thunder along a six-lane highway at 60 miles per hour? We love the Hudson and are moved by its grandeur and beauty. What mechanized juggernaut roaring along its banks can appreciate the river? Is not the human element worthy of consideration? Cannot New York State truly be the Empire State and concern itself with social justice as well as superhighways? This great state must surely put man before motor."

It may be more than just coincidence that, during the tumultuous days following the assassination of Dr. Martin Luther King, Jr., racial tensions reached near the explosion point in Ossining. Students left their classes in the high school and ran through the corridors. Several hundred of them massed in Main Street, blocking traffic for three hours. But property damage was held to several broken windows, and there were just a few injuries to Negro youths. Only quick action by a Negro neighborhood youth corps director and officials of the Ossining Interfaith Council for Action and the Afro-American Teens took the steam out of the impending disaster.

Negroes weren't the only minority group threatened by the expressway. The lines drawn by the highway engineers passed right through Sing Sing Prison. One citizen commented wryly: "Now that I see that the expressway is going to pass through Sing Sing Prison, I hereby resolve to make an extra effort never to be found guilty of a felony in New York State, and I hope that the State Department of Transportation will show the same resolve."

As the second night of the hearings came to a close well after midnight in the Sleepy Hollow High School in North Tarrytown, and the echoes of the jeers and hisses died, all possible debate and dialogue seemed exhausted, But the big questions still remained. Would the state of New York use part of its $2.5-billion transportation bond issue to build this expressway wholly with state funds and thus avoid a possible federal veto? Would the Hudson River Valley Commission, the regional planning group created by the governor (and now headed by Alexander Aldrich, the governor's cousin) approve the plan for the expressway? Would Interior Secretary Stewart Udall weaken in his opposition to the expressway, as Representative Ottinger had warned? Would the nearly unanimous hostility displayed at the pub-

lic hearings persuade the governor to change his plans for the expressway?

Several months later, in July, 1968, one of these questions was
answered, and a hint was dropped about another. The Hudson River
Valley Commission unanimously approved the plan for the expressway, a decision that was a surprise to no one. Also predictable was
the reaction of Representative Ottinger, who protested that the decision made a "complete sham" of the Commission's assignment "to
encourage the preservation, enhancement, and development of the
scenic, historic, recreational and natural resources" of the valley. The
Commission, he said, had "allied itself with the violators of the river."

The hint was dropped by a New York state official who declared
that the expressway would be financed from state funds.

By the end of the year, yet another question was answered: Stewart
Udall's opposition collapsed. Further studies by his Bureau of Outdoor Recreation, he said, had concluded that the Hudson River Expressway would not "unfavorably affect the scenic, historic, or recreational values" of the Hudson Valley. In a letter to the Corps of
Engineers, Udall wrote that the Department of the Interior would
not stand in the way of the necessary dredging and filling along the
river's edge. He did ask, however, that the work be done carefully
to prevent "undue siltation and turbidity in the Hudson River."

Udall's about-face, one of his last official acts as Secretary of the
Interior, comprised what *The New York Times* called a "victory for
Governor Rockefeller but a defeat for the public." Representative
Ottinger was incensed. "I just don't believe that any self-respecting
Secretary of the Interior could impartially conclude that a six-lane
highway is an advantageous use of the resources of the Hudson River,"
he fumed. Udall, he went on, must have "succumbed to pressure grow-
ing out of his long-time close relationship with the Rockefeller family."

The Citizens' Committee for the Hudson Valley, which had worked
for so many years to thwart the governor, joined forces with the
Sierra Club and the NAACP to decide whether a court action offered
any hope as a last-ditch measure. At the time of this writing, that
decision had not been made.

White Roads through
Black Bedrooms

The ugly element of racial discrimination that hung over the express-way fight in Ossining, New York, is common to many, if not most, of the citizen outcries against proposed urban highways. First choice of highway planners for their inner loops, outer loops, radials, spurs, and links is park lands and creek beds, since the land is cheap and the flak comes from politically impotent birdwatchers and petunia planters. Second choice is slum areas, which usually means Negro ghettos, since the land is relatively cheap, and the flak comes from politically weak black residents.

In city after city, the completed expressways run through the ghettos. But recently, as the anger of the black community began to find expression in physical violence, the hand of the establishment has been delayed, if not deterred.

In the midst of recent hearings on the proposed freeway system for Washington, D. C., a black militant ran to the microphone and shouted his defiance. "This will stop the freeways," he said, holding up a book of matches for all to see. Several weeks later, large sections of the city were in flames.

In Baltimore, black residents of the West Side ghetto formed a Relocation Action Movement to fight eviction and—if necessary—take its fight into the streets. Only when their leaders threatened to block the streets with black bodies during the Friday evening rush hour did city officials begin to listen. It is too late to change the route, but the Negro's cry for fair compensation and open housing is at least being heard.

In Philadelphia, the Crosstown Expressway was drawn on the map

177

running from river to river through the heart of the city, along a line separating a black ghetto from the downtown district and its adjoining white town houses and expensive apartments. Opponents castigate this proposed block-wide ditch as a Mason-Dixon Line, an asphalt barrier between white and black people. In the heat of his 1967 campaign for re-election, Mayor James Tate was finally persuaded by the picketing and the incessant cries of outrage to delay construction until adequate provision for relocation housing is available for the 6,500 persons that would be dispossessed. If he keeps his word, construction will be delayed for some time, since a study by urban expert Charles Abrams reveals a shortage in Philadelphia of 50,000 low-income housing units.

In city after city, the black community is making it somewhat more difficult for the white man to build his roads. In Nashville, Tennessee, the fight went all the way to the U. S. Supreme Court before the highway builders got their way.

In 1956, the year the Interstate system was born, the engineering firm of Clarke and Rapuano laid out a freeway system for the city of Nashville, which included, in common with most such plans, an "inner loop" surrounding the central business district and radial highways coming in to join the loop. One of the radials shown on the Clarke and Rapuano plan was Interstate Route 40 coming in from the west on a direct line to join with the inner loop near the center of town. For almost half its course through the city, I-40 would run through or over railroad tracks and yards. Nearer to the center of town, a few white-owned retail businesses were in the path, but damage to property was otherwise held to a minimum.

During the following months—in a series of meetings among state highway engineers, city planners, and other local officials—all the routes in the Clarke and Rapuano plan were approved except one. The exception was the 2½-mile section of I-40 connecting with the inner loop, the section that would wipe out several white-owned businesses. Out of these meetings came an alternate plan, which was adopted: the link, instead of coming straight into the city, would swing north on a wide loop through the center of the Negro community in North Nashville, where it would wipe out Negro homes and churches, slice through a Negro college complex, and run along the main business street for sixteen blocks, wiping out all the Negro-owned businesses on one side of the street and isolating those on the other side from their customers. Some 650 homes, 27 apartment buildings, and several churches would be pounded into rubble. Isolation of the ghetto would be increased by the creation of fifty dead-end streets along the course of the expressway.

The original plan of Clarke and Rapuano was never discussed publicly—in fact, it did not come to light until ten years later, during a court hearing on the racial aspects of I-40. Instead, in May, 1957, a mysterious "public hearing" was held on the route through the black community in order to comply with federal requirements. No announcement of the hearing appeared in the press; the only public announcement consisted of notices placed on the bulletin boards of eight branch post offices, not one of which was in the North Nashville area. The hearing date on the notices was May 14, but the hearing was held on May 15. No explanation was ever offered for the change of date. The transcript of the hearing records only the statements of highway officials and their answers to questions from the floor. The questions are not recorded, nor are the names of the questioners. The transcript contains no reference to Interstate Route 40.

By 1967, ten years later, the 2½-mile section of I-40 was still not built, and residents of the Negro community of North Nashville had brought suit charging that the shifting of the route into their neighborhoods was an act of racial discrimination. They testified that they had never known of the hearing in 1957. Three newspaper reporters who covered highway matters, one of whom later became city editor of *The Nashville Tennessean,* swore that they knew nothing about the hearing, nor had they written anything about it. Negro Councilman Harold Love stated angrily that "we can't find a person in this community who remembers the so-called 'public hearing' the state said was held in 1957 for this project. Well, when this is over, they're not going to be able to say they didn't know what effect I-40 would have on the people of North Nashville. They will know because we intend to inform them."

During the ten years between the public hearing and the court suit, speculation about the proposed highway began to appear in the newspapers, but residents of the threatened area who appealed to officials for information were put off with evasive replies. The plans were still "preliminary" and "subject to change." At least seven witnesses testified to this treatment during the 1967 trial: two city councilmen, three leaders of civic organizations, a businessman, and a university faculty member. But some people apparently knew the route. A number of residents of North Nashville testified that real estate men had come to their homes during those years and told them they would have to sell because the highway was coming through. So they sold their homes to the real estate operators. One witness testified that these operators had made big profits "buying up shanties" from the black residents to sell to the state.

Federal approval of the route was granted in 1958, the year following the obscure public hearing. For some unexplained reason, the state waited seven more years, until 1965, before it began to acquire property for the right-of-way. But it was not until two years after that, in the fall of 1967, that the state made public the exact route of the highway when it asked for bids from contractors. At this point, a citizens' group calling itself the "I-40 Steering Committee" was organized to prevent the destruction of the Negro community. It included businessmen, teachers, ministers, civic and professional leaders, and black and white residents of North Nashville.

The committee immediately appealed to the mayor of Nashville, the governor of Tennessee, the Tennessee Congressional delegation, the federal highway administrator, and the Secretary of the U. S. Department of Transportation to delay letting contracts so that the route could be studied. All such petitions were denied.

The committee then petitioned the U. S. District Court for an injuction to halt construction. Pointing out that the highway plan was very careful to minimize damage in areas of "higher socio-economic level," but that it cut ruthlessly through the Negro community, the petition charged that the I-40 plan was "arbitrary and based on race." It violated the rights guaranteed to citizens under the Fourteenth Amendment, which requires equal protection of the laws for all citizens.

In a nation where increasing numbers of black citizens were despairing of lawful means of redress and taking their case to the streets, Nashville City Councilman Harold Love said pointedly that the petition for an injunction would show "whether responsible citizens can protest in a sensible, peaceful way, or whether people have to burn down the town to get something done."

District Judge Frank Gray, Jr., quickly scheduled hearings on the petition. A city planning consultant testified that there were 234 Negro-owned businesses in the area with a total value of about $4.5 million. Interstate 40 would disrupt 80 per cent of them. It would destroy one-third of the park facilities. It would slash right through a cluster of three small Negro colleges, cutting off one from the other two. It would "increase ghettoization" of the entire community by weakening the middle-class structure, undermining the economic base of the business community, decreasing employment opportunities, cutting residents off from readily accessible goods and services, and destroying many small businesses. It would disrupt community patterns of school and church attendance, recreation, employment, transportation, and programs of public health and housing. In short, it would destroy or disrupt all the values, activities, and ties that make a community.

During the court hearings, the Tennessee highway commissioner was questioned about the original Clarke and Rapuano route, which had been abandoned in 1957 for the route through the ghetto. At first he denied any knowledge of the earlier route. When he was confronted with minutes of a meeting held in 1956, at which he was present, and during which the Clarke and Rapuano route was discussed *and approved,* he replied weakly that if the minutes showed he was there, he must have been there, but he had no recollection either of the meeting or of the earlier plan.

Negroes whose homes were taken for the highway swore that they had received no help from the state or the city in finding a place to live. Black businessmen told the court that they were finding it impossible to relocate their stores—there was not enough commercially zoned land left in the ghetto, and they were barred from relocating in white areas. To add to their troubles, a new white-owned shopping center to the north of the ghetto promised to absorb all the business they were losing.

But approval of I-40 by the federal government as an Interstate route would bring 90 per cent of the total cost of perhaps $20 mil-

lion into the state from Washington. The highway commission, the
mayor, the governor, and the Nashville Area Chamber of Commerce
were putting all their weight behind this construction. More than a
thousand properties had already been acquired, at a cost of $9.5
million, and the state had already spent a million dollars for engineering studies. Despite court suits, human adversity, and community
damage, this kind of economic stake had a momentum all its own.

On November 1, 1967, Judge Gray gave his decision. He had
"grave doubts" about the wisdom of the route selected for I-40, but
he could find no "adequate basis" for granting an injunction on the
grounds of racial discrimination. He agreed with most of the charges
brought by the I-40 Steering Committee—the highway, would, indeed, have an adverse effect on the residents, the businesses, and the
colleges in North Nashville. However, said the judge, none of this
proved "deliberate purpose to discriminate against the residents of
North Nashville on the basis of race or socio-economic conditions."
The route chosen for I-40 might be unwise, but it was perfectly legal.
The highway would be built.

A week later, the NAACP Legal Defense and Educational Fund
joined the fight and appealed the case.

Because of the "great public interest in the case," the U. S. Court
of Appeals made room on an already full docket and heard the case
at once. Its decision on December 18 gave another green light to the
bulldozers. True enough, said the court, the complaints of the highway opponents were valid. The notice of the 1957 hearings had been
"unsatisfactory," and the transcript of those hearings left "much to
be desired." But a hearing, after all, *had* been held, and that is all
the federal law requires. True enough, consideration of the damage
that would result to the Negro community was "inadequate," residents and businesses would be "gravely affected," a public park used
predominantly by Negroes would be "destroyed," and many Negro-
owned businesses would have to be "relocated or closed." But none
of this showed "any intent or purpose of racial discrimination," and
therefore no one could claim that he had been deprived of his rights.

The court reminded the community that "the routing of highways
is the prerogative of the executive department of government, not the
judiciary." No matter where you put a highway, someone will be
hurt. But the "minimizing of hardships and adverse economic effects

is a problem addressing itself to engineers, not judges." The Court of Appeals had "no choice" but to agree with Judge Gray's opinion that no injunction to halt construction could be issued.

The highway route had been shifted from a white to a black area with no apparent reason except to move the scene of destruction. As one city planner said, the proposed route "literally goes out of its way to devastate the Black business community, uproot Black homes and churches, and restrict the growth, operation, and interaction of three major Black institutions of higher learning." The courts were willing to grant all this. Yet, they said, unless actual *intent* to exercise racial discrimination could be proved, the courts were powerless.

The suppliants exhausted their last legal recourse in a petition to the U. S. Supreme Court, which refused to review the case.

After a trip to Nashville to confer with local officials and members of the I-40 Steering Committee, Federal Highway Administrator Bridwell affirmed federal approval of the route, with five modifications to soften the blow. These included three additional underpasses to reduce the barrier effect of the highway. Bridwell also urged city officials to press for zoning changes that would make it possible for the displaced Negro businessmen to relocate. "We are convinced," he said, "that the steering committee had an essentially accurate description of the difficulties faced by North Nashville businessmen in finding suitable locations at reasonable prices in order to continue operations." Privately, Bridwell admitted his proposals were "just a patch job." The design of I-40, he said, was "atrocious." The bulldozers began to move within hours of his announcement.

The I-40 Steering Committee met once again and vowed to continue the fight in the courts. But from this point on, it would be a fight only for principle. According to an NAACP lawyer, "Practically speaking, we have lost, as the case would only come to trial after the highway has been built."

Other voices were urging that the fight be taken to the streets. The steering committee meeting echoed with threats to block the bulldozers with the bodies of Negroes, to disrupt the community with massive demonstrations, to welcome "supportive actions from any outside agency." But outside the meeting room could be heard the growl of the bulldozer.

A Nation Derailed

Anyone suggesting a slowdown in highway building must offer an alternative to travel by automobile. The alternative that is evolving for interurban travel is the airplane, but airports are already overburdened, air traffic near big cities is already dangerously dense, and open land for building new airports is rapidly disappearing.

In the summer of 1968, in fact, our complete dependence on airplanes and automobiles finally caught up with us. At Kennedy International Airport in New York, Sunday afternoon traffic jams produced lines of cars two miles long waiting to enter parking lots already choked with automobiles. Out on the taxi strips, airplanes queued up thirty and forty in line waiting their turn to take off into the overcrowded air. Incoming planes circled overhead for hours waiting their turn to land. At airports all over the country, flights to New York were canceled because there was no way to get in.

Schedules fell so far behind that flights were canceled by the dozens. Some giant jets circling endlessly over New York finally were forced to land elsewhere because their fuel was running low. One pilot leaving Bermuda bound for New York told his passengers he had a three-hour flight plan: "Two to get there and one to circle." In the so-called golden triangle formed by New York, Washington, and Chicago, delays were costing the airlines a million dollars a day. New Jersey Congressman Cornelius Gallagher, introducing a measure to give federal agencies dictatorial powers over airport usage, warned that the system was approaching "complete and catastrophic breakdown."

In all the hand-wringing over the air jam, the talk is of more airports, more air controllers, more sophisticated equipment to speed the process of landing and departure. What is plainly needed is a sweeping renaissance of the railroad.

In the face of this desperate need, railroads are killing off passenger travel as rapidly as the federal government will permit. The passenger train may soon follow the passenger pigeon into extinction. In the past forty years, the number of intercity passenger trains has shrunk from 20,000 to 600. During the past decade thirteen of our nation's railroads have eliminated all passenger service. In just six months of 1967, seventy-five passenger trains were abandoned, and at the beginning of 1968, applications were pending with the Interstate Commerce Commission for abandoning 108 more.

In October, 1967, the Atchison, Topeka and Santa Fe Railway Company announced plans to eliminate thirty-three of its passenger trains, including the famous "Santa Fe Chief" and the "Grand Canyon," traditional luxury trains between Chicago and Los Angeles. The future of the remaining trains, said Santa Fe President John S. Reed, "will depend on continued patronage." The railroad, he said, is suffering "staggering" losses from its passenger operations. But "Santa Fe did not abandon the traveling public; travelers showed an increasing preference to drive or fly."

In November, the New York Central reduced the number of trains traveling between New York, Albany, and Buffalo. In December, New York Central's "Twentieth Century Limited," for sixty-five years one of the nation's most famous trains, made its last run from New York to Chicago. One week later, the Pennsylvania's "Broadway Limited," also on the New York-Chicago run, made its last trip.

On December 20, the Pennsylvania Railroad asked permission to reduce from four to two the number of trains running between New York and St. Louis. One of the trains scheduled for extinction was the westbound "Spirit of St. Louis," which had made its first run in 1927, the year Charles Lindbergh flew his Ryan monoplane of the same name from New York to Paris.

In January, 1968, the Southern Pacific applied to the Interstate Commerce Commission for permission to stop running the "City of San Francisco" between Ogden, Utah, and Oakland, California, with stops at Reno and Sacramento. This would leave Reno without any passenger-train service whatever, and it would leave Sacramento with only one train to Oakland, the Western Pacific's "California Zephyr." But the Western Pacific had already announced plans to drop the "California Zephyr."

In the same month, the Union Pacific asked for permission to drop the "Portland Rose," running from Kansas City through Denver, Cheyenne, and Boise, to Portland, Oregon.

Also in January, the Missouri Pacific's "Colorado Eagle" stopped making its daily round trip between Kansas City and Pueblo, Colorado.

In March, the newly merged Penn Central Railroad applied for permission to discontinue the "Admiral" between New York and Chicago and the "Fort Pitt" between Chicago and Pittsburgh. In its petition to the ICC, the railroad said, "It is now possible to drive from Chicago to New York without encountering a single traffic signal. With these highways available most travelers give little thought to public transportation—least of all rail service."

In April, the Norfolk & Western announced plans to drop the "Arrow," between Norfolk and Cincinnati. On April 7, the Southern Pacific's "Lark" made its last run between Los Angeles and San Francisco.

In May, the Penn Central asked permission to stop running the "Juniata" between Philadelphia and Pittsburgh.

One by one, the great passenger trains, once the symbol of opulent travel, are disappearing from the land. Mere nostalgia for the lost splendor of a more leisurely past is hardly reason enough to wish for their survival, but a desire to save the land from further ravages of unfettered asphalting is something else again.

The trains are no longer running because people are no longer using them. Santa Fe President Reed is right: travelers are showing an increasing preference to drive or fly. While the annual intercity passenger-miles traveled by automobile is now more than double what it was in 1950, and the number traveled by air is up sevenfold, the number traveled by railroad is less than half the 1950 total.

The last trip of the "Broadway Limited" in December, 1967, carried only twenty-nine passengers. Santa Fe passenger revenues fell 17.3 per cent in the first eight months of 1967. A New York Central spokesman said that sometimes more railroad employees were needed to operate the "Twentieth Century Limited" than there were passengers. The "City of San Francisco" averaged only 145 passengers per trip in 1967. The "Wabash Cannonball," once a famous crack train between St. Louis and Detroit, can handle its payload now with a baggage car, one coach, and a snack car. A sixty-day survey of the "Powhatan Arrow" by the Norfolk & Western showed an average of thirty-eight passengers westbound from Norfolk to Cincinnati and fifty-six eastbound. The great city terminals that once buzzed incessantly with thousand-footed arrivals and departures and whose vaulted rooms echoed the hiss and clang of giant engines, now sit deserted in a rank miasma of neglect and stale washroom deodorant.

Of the passenger trains that remain, the railroads lose money on every trip. The losses, depending upon whose system of bookkeeping you accept, are staggering, or merely serious. Using the accounting procedures of the Interstate Commerce Commission, which allocate a proportional part of all expenditures to passenger service, the railroads claim a loss of $410 million on their 1964 passenger operations. Yet this figure is no measure whatever of the savings that would result if passenger service were abandoned altogether. For example, under the ICC formula, as a Santa Fe official has pointed out, several hundred thousand dollars was charged to bridge maintenance, yet "there isn't a bridge that could be done away with if we had no passenger trains." Transportation expert Stanley Berge suggests that the realistic way to measure the "profitability" of passenger operations is to compare passenger revenue with the expenses that could actually be eliminated by dropping all passenger trains. Using this scheme, the loss in 1964 comes out at $19 million rather than $410 million.

But the fact remains that passenger service loses money, and freight service makes money, and so railroad men would be only too happy to get rid of passenger service entirely. Most of them, in fact, are shedding passenger service as rapidly as they can obtain approval from the Interstate Commerce Commission. In the meantime, to strengthen their case with the ICC, they are doing everything they can to make travel by train a nightmare so as to deplete the ranks of the remaining faithful. Peter Lyon, whose book *To Hell in a Day*

Coach chronicles the decline of the American railroad, attributes
the primitive conditions on the modern passenger train to "the im-
placable hatred that most railroad executives have for their passengers." Whether from hatred, or from a fundamental desire to rid
themselves of a losing venture, the railroad executives are clearly
making things as difficult as possible for the few diehards who insist
on buying railroad tickets to transport their bodies from one city
to another.

In the days when it brought in nearly $10 million per year, the
"Twentieth Century Limited" pampered its passengers in the style
of a luxury hotel, carrying barbers, manicurists, valets, bath atten-
dants, and leading chefs—and serving champagne on its snowy dinner tables. The passenger list regularly included the names of the
wealthy and famous, and it was a mark of distinction to be included.

One British Prime Minister reportedly referred to the train as "my
gentlemen's club when I am in the United States." On its last run in
December, 1967, the "Limited" reached Chicago nine hours late.

The journey on the Union Pacific train No. 6 from Los Angeles to
Omaha has been described by one paying subject as a "nightmare."
The 1,660-mile trip takes forty-three hours, for an average of thirty-
nine miles per hour. There is no sleeping car, but you can rent a
pillow for thirty-five cents. There is no dining car, not even a snack
car, so the train must stop along the way to give passengers a chance
to dash into the station for a quick bite. You get twenty-five minutes
in Las Vegas for breakfast, fifteen minutes in Milford, Utah, for
lunch, and a generous thirty-five minutes in Ogden, Utah, for dinner.

A recent *Wall Street Journal* story reports that a passenger on the
New York Central's "Wolverine," from Detroit to Chicago, couldn't
see out of the windows because the mud was too thick. The bread
in the dining car was moldy, and the litter of beer cans and bottles
in one of the coaches "looked as if there had been a party and nobody had cleaned up afterwards." According to the newspaper, the
railroads "are touchy about gripes that they discourage passenger
travel with deliberate inconvenience, dirt, discomfort and discour-
tesy." In the same story, the mayor of Pittsburg, Kansas, described
his most recent attempt to ride a train: "With others, I went to the
depot at 4 A.M. to ride the 4:10 A.M. train. We were told it would be

late, so we went out for breakfast and came back only to be told it wouldn't arrive before 7 or 8. So we got a car and drove to Kansas City."

One train crewman for the Southern Pacific reportedly blamed the railroad managers for the deteriorating service. "They've downgraded this train by taking off dome cars and Pullmans, making it late on purpose and telling people there's no space available to the point that today it's just uncomfortable to ride it. Call up the Ogden ticket office and they'll tell you there's no space on the train."

Testimony given in a recent hearing on the application of Southern Pacific to discontinue two trains between Phoenix, Arizona, and Tucumcari, New Mexico, forced the ICC to the conclusion that "Southern Pacific has continued to discourage use of these trains by passengers. In fact, it has intensified its efforts in that direction." This, said the Commission, is dirty pool. "The adverse conditions surrounding intercity trains in the past ten years do not justify attempts by some railroads to downgrade service deliberately in an attempt to prove particular trains are an undue burden."

This, however, is the pattern.

The "Wabash Cannonball," with its single coach, snack bar, and baggage car, now takes 10½ hours to cover 489 miles between Detroit and St. Louis.

The afternoon "Burlington Zephyr," the fastest train in the United States, averages only 67.4 miles per hour, counting stops, between Chicago and St. Paul. The trip takes twenty minutes longer than it did twenty years ago.

The only train between Memphis and Birmingham, a trip of 253 miles, is a night train with no sleeping cars.

Between Cleveland and Detroit there is only one train per day, and the trip of 165 miles take 5½ hours, including a wait of nearly two hours in Toledo for a connection.

If you live in Philadelphia and wish to get to Washington for a 10 A.M. appointment, you take a train that leaves at 7:10 A.M. and arrives at 9:45 A.M., a total of 2 hours and 35 minutes to go 135 miles, or an average of 52 miles per hour. The train has no diner. Is it any wonder that, for the 227-mile trip from New York to Washington, twice as many people fly as go by train?

There is no question that rising costs and taxes, stifling union work rules, government subsidies for the railroad's competitors, and the spreading network of Interstate highways have all played their part in putting the passenger train at a disadvantage and luring the traveler into the airplane and the automobile. But the blame must be shared by short-sighted unimaginative railroad management, which has thrown up its hands in the face of difficulties. "The only answer, as we see it, is abandonment of over-the-road passenger trains," says Penn Central executive Arthur E. Baylis. "The reasons lie in the improving technology in the building of highways; the fact that you now can go almost across the country without seeing a traffic light; the great popularity of moving families together, and the economy of the private automobile, and no red-tape regulations. The common carrier by rail, as a result, does not even consider competing."

A 1968 report of the Engineers Joint Council notes the "near absence of significant technological improvement in intercity rail passenger service" and attributes this to "shortage of new ideas" in the railway industry. The report also concludes that no one seems to care: "There has been no popular consensus that preservation of intercity rail passenger transportation is important." Most people are buzzing around happily on the shiny new expressways, or taking to the air, and mentally equating the passenger train to the dodo.

For their part, the railroads are exerting every effort to alienate the affections of those who wish to see passenger service continue. Three times—in 1954, 1960, and 1961—the Pennsylvania Railroad and the Pennsylvania-Reading Seashore Lines attempted to curtail passenger service to the seashore areas in southern New Jersey, but each time the railroads were denied permission to do so. During hearings held to consider a fourth application, in 1967, commuters charged that the railroads were retaliating by making things miserable for them. One commuter testified that, after the railroads were denied permission to curtail service in 1961, they "took the offensive." In only three months there were 136 delays in arrivals and departures of trains between Philadelphia and Atlantic City. Of these delays, fifty-nine were directly connected with engine breakdowns. Some of the delays were as long as two hours, during which "wives were unable to get the station on the telephone to find out what happened to their husbands."

When the trains did run, the commuters charged, they were "too hot in the summer, too cold in the winter, dirty, and without water for the passengers." The hapless train riders organized an Atlantic City Commuter Club to protect themselves from inhumane treatment.

Other commuters vented their spleen in one of the few ways still open to their downtrodden breed—letters to the editor. Wrote Theodore Hunsbedt, of Briarcliff, New York: "As a half-frozen, harried commuter, on the Hudson Division of the New York Central, let me say that I do not believe my train was on time more than once or twice between the first of December and the middle of January. I wish that the executives [of the railroad] would join hands with me and freeze their knees on the shores of the Tappan Zee (there isn't room in the station) for an hour or so after train time on a frosty morning." John L. Komives, of Kalamazoo, Michigan, complained of "the filth, the surly attitude of so many passenger-train employees (from ticket agents to dining-car waiters), the non-functioning of schedules, and the unwillingness of management to work with local and state communities to improve this mess."

For a short time following the 1968 merger of the New York Central and the Pennsylvania Railroad, some were so foolish as to hope that improved passenger service might result. An editorial in *The Philadelphia Inquirer* said hopefully: "Coming at a time when highways are increasingly congested with auto and truck traffic, and there is a rising national awareness of the need for greater emphasis on mass transit development, the consolidation of the Pennsy and New York Central lines may well give impetus to a trend away from endless expressway proliferation and toward a rejuvenation of rail transportation."

But the management of the new Penn Central quickly disabused the public of such notions. During a press conference in February, Stuart T. Saunders, chairman of the Penn Central, told reporters that rail passenger service on trips of more than 400 miles was "dead" and that "in several years there will be very little, if any, long-line service." Such service by the merged railroad would be abandoned "in due time" unless the "states involved want to make up the loss." Even shorter runs in densely populated areas, he added, could be sustained only with "appropriate government help." He insisted, however, that the Penn Central "does not have a negative attitude toward passenger service."

The president of the new line, Alfred E. Perlman, agreed. When asked whether he thought the merger might produce some improvements in passenger service, he replied that any improvements would come "less as a result of the merger but more as a result of the new policies of the state and federal government." Private enterprise was ducking out.

With other mergers being proposed among the nation's railroads, New Jersey's Senator Harrison Williams, Jr., began to wonder whether merger plans included any hope for the commuter. Noting that this question had "not been discussed or even raised," Senator Williams sponsored hearings to explore it, noting, "It's important that the commuter's voice be heard before it is drowned out by the rumble of freight cars."

At the opening day of the three-day hearings, Transportation Secretary Alan Boyd told the members of Senator Williams' Urban Affairs Subcommittee that railroad mergers were "unlikely" to yield any significant improvement in conditions for the commuter. If the railroads save money through increased efficiency from their mergers, said Mr. Boyd, they will invest those savings in improved freight operations, where their profits are. "It is unrealistic to think that railroad management will divert a large portion of these savings to commuter operations."

Paul J. Tierney, chairman of the Interstate Commerce Commission, agreed with Secretary Boyd. Further, he said, it would be unreasonable to require that the benefits of mergers be used to absorb "undue losses from commuter operations." Mr. Tierney, Secretary Boyd, and New York Senator Jacob K. Javits all stated that improved railroad passenger service could be achieved only with greatly increased public support and government financial aid.

In the spring of 1968, ICC examiner John S. Messer tried another scheme for saving railroad passenger service. In an unprecedented move, he recommended that the federal government prescribe minimum standards of humane treatment for railroad passengers, in the hope that warmth in winter, air conditioning in summer, hot meals, and other amenities might attract more passengers back to the railroads and thus stem the tide of extinction. In all its eighty-one years of existence, the Interstate Commerce Commission had never before dared to presume to tell management how to run a railroad.

The states of California, Arizona, New Mexico, Texas, and Louisiana, through which the Southern Pacific's "Sunset Limited" runs from Los Angeles to New Orleans, had complained to the ICC that the railroad had deliberately downgraded service to discourage passengers. The time for the 2,000-mile trip on the "Sunset" had been increased by four hours, and sleeping cars and diners had been eliminated. During the 45-hour trip, passengers wishing to sleep could doze in their seats, and hungry ones could eat at a snack bar.

In a 49-page report on the situation, Mr. Messer recommended that the federal government require the railroads to provide meal service on all trips of 250 miles or more; provide sleeping cars on all overnight trips; install heating, lighting, air conditioning, rest rooms, and drinking-water facilities; keep passenger cars clean; and schedule passenger trains to run at least as fast as the fastest freight train. He also recommended that local governments be required to buy and maintain their railroad stations, that labor contracts be renegotiated to relieve the railroads of some of the burdens of medieval work rules, that ICC accounting procedures be changed to show more realistically the cost of providing passenger service, and that the railroads be permitted to deduct passenger deficits from their federal income taxes.

Mr. Messer's recommendations were widely applauded by millions of long-suffering riders of the nation's cattle cars. Even if the ICC does issue such regulations, however, the railroads may be expected to challenge them in the courts.

In June, 1968, the ICC asked Congress for a federal study to decide whether railroad passenger service should be saved from extinction. The Commission told Congress that the present service cannot be maintained intact "without a change in Federal policy." The present policy "merely offers the guidelines for eliminating service." In subsequent hearings on a bill to implement such a study, Professor George W. Hilton of the University of California testified that the passenger train "is absolutely hopeless, has been for some years, and should be allowed to pass out of existence unimpeded."

European railroads, which are commonly supported by government subsidies, apparently believe otherwise. The "Trans Europe Express" carries its passengers in luxury at speeds up to 100 miles per hour through Austria, Switzerland, and the six countries of the Common Market. Trains are not being dropped from the schedule, they are being added. Passengers recline in individual, foam-rubber seats and watch the scenery through vast expanses of clean glass. For the businessman, stenographic and telephone service is available. Meals are served to passengers at their seats. On trips up to 250 miles, the pampered train passenger often arrives before the jet passenger.

Recent increases in train speeds have reduced the time from Hamburg to Zurich by a half-hour, from Bremen to Mannheim by twenty minutes, from Paris to Le Havre by a half-hour, from Oslo to Trondheim by two hours and fifteen minutes, from Paris to Copenhagen by forty-five minutes. The newest crack train between Paris and Toulouse, the "Capitole," runs at 124 miles per hour over part of its route. During the first few months of operation, its patronage increased 37 per cent.

In Japan, where, admittedly, the roads are poor and only 1 family in 15 owns a car, the railroads are showing what can be done. The "Tokaido" linking Tokyo, Nagoya, and Osaka makes its 320-mile trip in just three hours and ten minutes. At 130 miles per hour, the surface of the tea in your cup, served to you in your seat, barely quivers. Seats are comfortable, the car is clean—and full. Profit on the "Tokaido," climbing every year, hit $60 million in 1968. Air travel along the route of the "Tokaido" has fallen by 33 per cent since 1964, when the trains began to run. The Japanese government, which operates the railroads, plans to extend this service to connect most of the major cities in the country. It is now spending $470 million on a line from Osaka to Okayama.

In view of the U. S. railroads' earnest desire to shed all responsibility for moving people from place to place, it is plain that if passenger rail service is to survive, the federal government must save it. So far, there has been much talk and very little action in

Washington. In 1965, Congress authorized $90 million to be spent over three years for research and development in high-speed ground transportation. When it got around to appropriating the money, however, Congress doled out $18.5 million for fiscal year 1966, $22 million for 1967, and $10.3 million for 1968, a total of only $50.8 million. When he learned of the slash in his budget for 1968, Robert A. Nelson, director of the Office of High Speed Ground Transportation, said sadly, "I feel badly shaken and quite bloodied."

The cause of adequate transportation in this country will be even more shaken and bloodied unless Congress can be persuaded to get into the railroad business in a big way, because obviously the railroads have no intention of going it alone. As Penn Central President Perlman says all too plainly, "If there is a public need for this service, and it must be operated at a loss, this is the problem that faces the free enterprise system, because the shippers of freight are not willing to subsidize that loss. . . . So the national transportation policy will have a big part to play."

As though to underline Perlman's words, in February, 1968, Penn Central Chairman Saunders observed that most of the commuter cars in the Philadelphia area are "worn out and should have been replaced years ago." Penn Central, he said, could not improve commuter service until its "entire fleet of cars is replaced with modern equipment. And this equipment cannot be purchased until the public funds are made available." Two months later, Mr. Saunders reiterated his plea for large infusions of government money to subsidize railroad passenger service. "A tax dollar," he pointed out, "can buy up to 20 times as much rail transportation as it can when it is spent on urban highways." This is good economy for the governments involved, he said. And this doesn't even take into account the questions of air pollution or tax losses on property taken for highways. But, says Mr. Saunders, "The U. S. government is spending virtually nothing to assist 73 million people to get to and from their jobs, while putting up $25 billion to send three men to the moon."

If there is one place in the United States where passenger train service should be able to pay its own way, it is in the densely populated corridor from Washington to Boston, which is peopled by

40 million souls, or 20 per cent of the U. S. population, and in which the traffic jams on expressways and at airport terminals, both in the sky and on the ground, are legendary. The Washington-to-New York run is one of the few railroad passenger routes that still shows a profit. For this reason, the Penn Central Railroad has put up $44 million of its own money, to match $11 million from the federal government, to finance a "demonstration" project on which the future of rail transportation in this country could stand or fall.

Sleek new "Metroliners" will speed between the two cities at speeds up to 110 miles per hour—eventually, it is hoped, up to 150 miles per hour, which would make travel times competitive with those of jet airplanes. Train crews will take special instruction to learn how to be courteous to passengers. Hot meals will be served to passengers at their reclining swivel chairs. Cars will be roomy, comfortable, air-conditioned. Trains will run every hour, making the 226-mile run from New York to Washington in less than three hours at the 110-mph speed, and in only two hours and eighteen minutes at the 150-mph speed.

But the technology that can send men into space and build supersonic bombers had some difficulty meeting the specifications. The new service, scheduled to begin in the fall of 1967, was postponed to the spring of 1968 because of difficulties with the equipment. Trouble with brakes, electrical components, and control systems was blamed for the delay. One unforeseen difficulty was discovered during early test runs in New Jersey, when air pressure from the high-speed cars whipping by pulled windows out of old wood-sash commuter cars on adjacent tracks.

Explaining these technical difficulties to a Congressional committee, Penn Central Vice-President R. W. Minor blamed the national policy "which has to date provided over $260 billion of public funds for air, water, and highway transportation and nothing for railroads until this demonstration project." The result, he said, is a "deficiency in engineers, manufacturing facilities, and product development" for improving railroad service. "We are a profit-making organization and we will not undertake a line of business that has no future."

In the spring of 1968, another delay was announced by a Penn

Central spokesman. When pressed by newsmen for a new start-up date for the high-speed service, he replied somewhat testily, "I don't know, and nobody knows when they will be running." We hope, he said, "sometime this year." *The Wall Street Journal* reported that most railroad executives were labeling the project a "publicity stunt." According to another reporter, "railroad executives around the country think the Pennsy is just plain crazy to spend $44 million on the passenger business."

It is unfortunate that railroad executives take that attitude. Instead, they should be vigorously pressing to speed up and improve passenger service all over the country. One study shows that increase of speed to 125 miles per hour between all major cities up to 500 miles from each other would halve the running time between those cities, which would put the passenger train well ahead of the automobile and in direct competition with the airplane, considering airport check-in times, ground travel from city to airport, weather delays, and so on.

Such a program would require completely new trains. It would also require the railroads to improve their roadbeds, put in continuous welded rail, strengthen bridges, ease curves, eliminate grade crossings, and improve signal systems. The estimated cost for all this was about $15 billion in 1966 and would be somewhat higher now. A lot of money? It is just about the sum that is spent in this country to build and maintain streets and highways *in one year*. This is the kind of money we should be spending to bring our railroads into the twentieth century. It is fashionable now, even among the stanchest members of the highway establishment, to advocate a "balanced" transportation system for our nation. But it is empty talk. What's more, it is extremely doubtful that we will put our money where our mouth is before the hardening of our transportation arteries brings us to the brink of strangulation. Edmund K. Faltermayer, writing in *Fortune,* doubts that, even if passenger service could be shown to be profitable, the railroads would espouse it. Freight service will always be *more* profitable, therefore passenger service, he says, "is bound to be shortchanged of capital and managerial talent." The only solution may be "a new private or semi-public corporation with government financial backing to manage passenger services," using the railroads' facilities and reimbursing them for the use of their tracks and train crews.

Private enterprise has amply demonstrated that it cannot or will not provide passenger railroad service for this nation's travelers. Another way must be found to provide that service, and soon. We are a society becoming hardened to the word "crisis." Yet the word is not too strong to describe the state of our transportation system. A champion of high-speed rail transportation in the Senate, Claiborne Pell, attempted recently to warn his fellow Senators of its imminence. "Three years ago," he said, "the Congress was given abundant evidence of an impending crisis in passenger transportation, particularly in our congested and growing urban areas. The only change in the situation since that time is that the crisis is closer at hand." Too often, we fail to act until we are engulfed.

Toonerville Trolleys

If a rebirth of intercity railroad passenger service is needed to save our countryside, a rebirth of intracity mass-transit facilities is needed to save our cities. If we abandon the city to the automobile and the freeway, it will become a wasteland in which no one will wish to live, to work, or even to visit. Complete dependence on the automobile for urban transportation will destroy the city as surely as bombs.

In May, 1968, the Institute for Rapid Transit held its annual meeting in Atlanta. *The Atlanta Journal* looked forward to the conference. "A national conference on rapid transit will be held here later this month," the newspaper said. "The Institute for Rapid Transit is sponsoring the meeting. The idea is to emphasize the need for rapid transit in metropolitan planning. That ought to be easy. Put the delegates up at a motel on the outskirts and have them drive in on the expressway for an 8:30 meeting."

A demand for improved transit is widespread among city officials and planners. A recent report of the Delaware Valley Regional Planning Commission called the automobile the "major threat to the business community." Speaking of the problem in Philadelphia, the report said: "The increased use of the auto has brought mass transportation systems to the point of crisis, threatened to strangle the downtown street systems, and has thrown a huge parking burden not only upon business, but on government." The report said there are now 30,000 parking spaces in the center of Philadelphia, but at least 92,000 will be needed by 1985. "Improvement of mass transit appears to be the largest step in preventing further strangulation of the downtown area."

This is not a new thought. As far back as 1952, four years before the inception of the Interstate Highway system, *Public Management* magazine was saying that "the cities just cannot resign themselves to automobiles and let mass transportation slide to ruin and extinction. They must preserve mass transportation or stagnate."

Why have we been so slow to take this excellent advice? One reason is a widespread misconception of what is meant by mass transit. The freeway advocates would have us believe that rubber-tired buses on freeways and city streets comprise mass transit. This is not so. The term implies a transportation system using its own exclusive right-of-way, not sharing it with private automobiles. This usually means rails—subways and railroads. Buses in city streets or sharing congested freeways with private automobiles can never provide efficient mass transportation, simply because they must fight for space in competition with the automobile, the cause of the problem they are supposed to relieve.

Point-to-point travel by a bus sharing traffic jams with automobiles takes about twice as long as in the automobile. In the summer of 1967, a bus, a bicycle, an automobile, and a long-distance runner competed in a 12-mile race from Pearl Harbor to the Honolulu Zoo in Waikiki. The bicycle won. The automobile was second, the runner was third, the bus was last. The times were 35 minutes for the bicycle, 57 for the automobile, 77 for the runner, and 82 for the bus. One of the riders on the bus, a Honolulu city councilman, said that the bus had run 20 minutes ahead of schedule; it usually took an hour and forty minutes for the trip.

Another reason why mass transit languishes is that affluent Americans prefer to drive their cars; they regard mass transit as lower-class transportation for the unfortunates who cannot afford an automobile. Since it is only the poor who actually *need* mass transit, effective political pressure to salvage it has been lacking. In recent months, public awareness of this and other needs of the urban poor has been somewhat heightened as the flames of our burning cities shed new light on the situation.

The California Governor's Commission on the Los Angeles Riots concludes that the failure of the city to provide mass transit for its citizens is one reason why they rioted: "This lack of adequate transportation handicaps them in seeking and holding jobs, attending schools, shopping, and fulfilling other needs. It has had a major influence in creating a sense of isolation, with its resultant frustrations, among the residents of central Los Angeles, particularly the Watts area."

As industries move to the suburbs, and industrial parks spring up in outlying areas, city ghetto dwellers find themselves increasingly isolated from job opportunities in the absence of mass transit. For example, if you live in Watts, you can drive to a job at the Burbank plant of the Lockheed Aircraft Corporation in less than an hour, if you have a car. If not, you may have to take as many as four buses and as much as two hours.

Robert C. Wood, Under Secretary of Housing and Urban Development, says that mass transit is the "one tragically missing link" between ghetto dwellers and jobs in the suburbs. Mayor Joseph M. Barr of Pittsburgh agrees. "It doesn't make much sense," he says, "to give a man a new job and then make him spend half a day getting to it."

In a massive report on urban transportation completed in the summer of 1968, Stanford Research Institute concludes that half of all city dwellers have "inadequate mobility," and their plight is deepening. "We have generated an auto-dominated society," says the report, "which is causing serious problems of traffic congestion, environmental pollution, and freeway disruption. Meanwhile, many of our non-driving citizens are left relatively immobile." The recommended remedy is a sweeping commitment to provide modern public transportation.

The 1968 Report of the National Advisory Commission on Civil Disorders also indicts inadequate mass transit. Noting that most new jobs are being created in the suburbs, the report says that some way must be found to link the job with the central-city Negroes. Either industry must be persuaded to create new employment opportunities near the Negro homes, or the Negroes must be helped to find homes in the suburbs, or better transportation must be provided between the ghetto and the suburbs. The third alternative, says the report, has received little attention from city planners and municipal officials. A few demonstration projects show promise, but carrying

them out on a large scale will be "very costly." But perhaps not
as costly as rebuilding our cities from the ground up. It seems likely
that, once the Negro finds a job in the suburbs, he will eventually
find a home there, too, which seems the only adequate solution to
the problem of the Negro ghetto.

A third reason for our indifference toward mass transit is its
squalor. Subway cars are filthy, noisy, depressing. Stations are like
dungeons: dank, dark, dangerous. At rush hour, the crowds are
savage, crushing, cattle-like. Late at night, the subway platform is
deserted, menacing. One woman in Philadelphia complains that
passengers on the PTC are not treated like animals, they are treated
like ants. Another rider likens mass transit to a "pipeline of human
sludge." How much space, he asks, does it take for a man to sit
in dignity, cleanliness, with a decent view, not be shaken up, pushed,
or elbowed?

Shabby mass transit is a tradition in this country. In his delightful
history of mass transit in the United States, John Anderson Miller
quotes the newspapers of an earlier day on the accommodations
then available. An 1864 editorial in *The New York Herald* cele-
brated the horse-drawn omnibus:

"Modern martyrdom may be succinctly defined as riding in a
New York omnibus. The discomforts, inconveniences, and annoy-
ances of a trip on one of these vehicles are almost intolerable. From
the beginning to the end of the journey a constant quarrel is pro-
gressing. The driver quarrels with the passengers, and the passengers
quarrel with the driver. There are quarrels about getting out and
quarrels about getting in. There are quarrels about change and quarrels about the ticket swindle. The driver swears at the passengers
and the passengers harangue the driver through the strap hole—a
position in which even Demosthenes could not be eloquent. Respect-
able clergymen in white chokers are obliged to listen to loud oaths.
Ladies are disgusted, frightened, and insulted. Children are alarmed
and lift up their voices and weep. Indignant gentlemen rise to
remonstrate with the irate Jehu and are suddenly bumped back into
their seats, twice as indignant as before, besides being involved in
supplementary quarrels with those other passengers upon whose
corns they have accidentally trodden."

Neither the omnibus that ran on the street nor the car that ran on steel rails was fit for human occupancy. "The cars are quieter than the omnibuses," the editorial continued, "but much more crowded. People are packed into them like sardines in a box, with perspiration for oil. The seats being more than filled, the passengers are placed in rows down the middle, where they hang on by the straps, like smoked hams in a corner grocery."

Curiously, it appears that then, as now, civilizations of other lands were far ahead of the United States in the quality of their public transportation. An editorial in *The New York Tribune* complained that "the Broadway 'Bus is not a Thing of Beauty. It combines more ugliness and discomfort than were ever crowded together in one vehicle. During all the years it has lumbered and rumbled down Broadway it has elicited the liveliest expressions of amazement from strangers within our gates—amazement, for the most part, that so progressive and inventive a people should tolerate a mode of conveyance as far behind the ages as an old mail-coach is behind a Pullman drawing-room car. Of all kinds of public conveyances ever devised it is the most clumsy and inconvenient."

With conditions like these prevailing in our mass transit systems, we need not wonder why transit riders reacted to the automobile like a starving man in a supermarket. Here was comfort, convenience, privacy, independence. Surveys of commuters in cities across the land reveal the same reactions to transit riding: too slow, too crowded, too expensive, too inconvenient. Of a thousand households interviewed in Milwaukee, 34 per cent said they would use transit more often if service were more frequent; 38 per cent said they would use it more often if it were cheaper; 27 per cent said they would use it more often if the ride were faster. But a hard core of 56 per cent said they would commute to work in their automobiles no matter what improvements were made in mass transit.

The story of the decline of mass transit in the United States follows the dreary pattern set by the railroads. With exceptions in a handful of cities, little effort has been made to save the patient. And even where the effort is made, it usually lacks public support and adequate financing.

Since the end of World War II, Cleveland is the only city in the

United States to create a new rail transit system. In that same period, we have spent more than $150 billion on highways.

As riders deserted transit and took to their automobiles, income from the fare box slumped. As income fell and costs rose, the transit companies reduced their service and increased their fares, thus forcing more riders to desert them. At first, government was not sympathetic. Transit companies had long been profitable for their owners and a good source of tax money for local government. They paid corporate taxes, franchise taxes, vehicle license taxes, paving taxes. Some cities required them to share the costs of street maintenance; some required that public employees such as police and firemen ride free. Many required low fares for schoolchildren. In Washington, Congress extracted money from the transit company to pay policemen's salaries.

Heavily burdened by taxes and rising costs, deserted by their riders, scorned by an automobile-loving public and short-sighted city government, the transit companies began to fold. From 1954 to 1964, while the volume of transit riding was dropping by nearly 40 per cent, nearly 200 private transit companies went out of business, and 270 others were bought out by their municipal governments. In sixty-nine cities with a population of 25,000 or more, citizens found themselves with no public transportation system whatever. Those without automobiles were simply out of luck. As the transit companies disappeared, the need for additional highways increased.

Many city governments, faced with collapse of privately owned transit companies, buy them to avert disaster. But the city is able to do little more than simply sustain life. Services can rarely be improved, since local governments already have more demands on them than they can meet with their limited resources. Mass transit may very well be the key to restoring the quality of life in the cities, and some mayors and city planners may understand this, but the tax-paying citizen continues to press for more and more expressways. He feels that a transit company worth its salt should support itself out of the fare box. If it can't, it deserves to die. Certainly, he doesn't want any of his tax money poured down that particular rathole.

For sheer ability to move people from place to place, the automobile isn't in the same league with mass transit. One lane of expressway can carry about 2,200 persons per hour, and the car occupies 200 to 300 square feet of land for parking at each end of the trip. One line of rail transit, on the other hand, can carry about 50,000 persons per hour—the equivalent of more than twenty lanes of freeway—at a much lower cost. Leland Hazard, Pittsburgh industrialist and lecturer, said recently that the comparison in costs is "shocking." An eight-lane freeway can carry 9,000 persons per hour in each direction at a capital cost of $1,670 per person. A subway or elevated train can carry 50,000 per hour at a capital cost of $440 per person. Rapid transit does five times the work at one-fourth the cost. "What are we waiting for," said Hazard, "or should we have our civic heads examined?"

The freeway advocates (and thus, almost by definition, transit opponents) insist that efficiency and low cost should not be the overriding factors. The best transportation, they say, is whatever it takes to satisfy the desires of the individual citizen. Says the Automobile Manufacturers Association, for example: "In no case should the passenger-carrying capacity of a given mode of transportation be confused with *public demand* for that mode." (AMA's italics.) If we defer a decision to invest heavily in modern transit until we hear public demand from the automobile drivers of the nation, we will have waited too long; by then the land will be drowned in asphalt and used cars. The public demand, however, is loud and clear. We can hear it in the anguished cries of the conservationists, the sobs of the dispossessed, the warnings of city planners, and the angry curses of the ghettos.

Members of the highway establishment argue that a rail transit system is practical only in cities of very high population density—high enough so that potential riders live within walking distance of the station. They conclude that, at most, a dozen U. S. cities qualify. One of these persons, Eugene T. Canty of General Motors Corporation, has noted some "envy" among civic leaders in this country of the spanking-new subway systems in Toronto and Montreal. Don't be envious, he says. The population densities in those cities are more than 20,000 per square mile, roughly equal to that of

New York City. Subways, he implies, are impractical for most lower-density U. S. cities. "I would expect that most of the future activity in rail rapid transit should be in adaptive improvements to existing systems rather than wholly new systems."

Even city planner Victor Gruen seems to have been persuaded by this argument. In *The Heart of Our Cities,* he states that public transportation "cannot for practical reasons be introduced" in areas of urban sprawl, where population density is low. "Nowhere," he writes, "are there sufficiently large concentrations of people who would like to be transported together to specific destinations to make the planning or operating of public transportation possible."

At a population density of 20,000 per square mile, 20,000 people live within about a half-mile of a subway stop, which is easy walking distance. Even the highway establishment will grant that these conditions can justify a subway. At a much lower density of 1,500 per square mile, which is typical of the thin smear around Los Angeles, 20,000 people would live within only two miles of a subway station, which is a quick bus ride. Many experts see this as the ideal public transportation system for sprawling metropolitan areas: rail rapid transit, with short feeder bus lines to stations in areas of low population density. As the population thins out, of course, the stations are spaced further apart, thus speeding the ride between stations.

While our cities are wringing their hands about traffic congestion and besieging Washington for more freeway money to relieve it, Toronto and Montreal have built themselves modern subway systems. As with passenger railroads, many European cities are also decades, perhaps generations, ahead of us in mass transit. When the first U. S. subway was completed in Boston in 1897, there were already three in London, one in Glasgow, and one in Budapest. A. P. Robinson, who designed a subway for New York in 1864 but was never permitted to build it, argued for it as the perfect means of transportation for the city: "I can conceive of nothing so completely fulfilling in every respect the requirements of our population. . . . Passengers would not be obliged to go into the middle of the street to take a car. They would have simply to enter a station from the sidewalk and pass down a spacious and well-lighted staircase to a dry and roomy platform. . . . The passenger would be carried to his destination in one-third the time he could be carried by any other conveyance. These would be the advantages to those who ride, and for the other great public in the streets. . . . Everything would be out of sight and hearing, and nothing would indicate the great thoroughfare below." Further, added *The New York Times*, a subway would be "perfectly feasible; a similar road has been in successful operation in London for one year; it encroaches on no vested interest; takes no one's land or house; interferes with no traffic or thoroughfare; offers cheap, comfortable, and speedy transit from one end of the island to the other. . . ." But despite the enthusiasm of its proponents, the first New York subway train was not to run until forty years later.

In 1964, while arguing for the subway system for Washington, D. C., that had so long been denied, Representative Basil L. Whitener complained that "the capital city of every major European country has a subway system, while ours does not. And I wonder how we can talk about being far ahead of the Russians in all fields of endeavor when Moscow has one of the finest subway systems in the world while we are still talking about building one for Washington."

Subway construction in Washington has been blocked for years by highway buffs in Congress who refuse to approve mass transit until local authorities lift their opposition to expansion of the freeway network. While this political haggling wastes away the years, the citizens of Moscow are enjoying the beauty and efficiency of their world-famous subway system, with its spacious, well-lit, well-ventilated stations, some ornately decorated and hung with chandeliers between marble columns.

Cities throughout the world that have provided subway systems for their citizens number about thirty-five. Only five of these are in the United States. Our cities are equipped with automobiles; others prefer transportation.

In West Germany, subways are running in Berlin and Hamburg and under construction in Cologne, Frankfurt, and Munich. When these are completed, West Germany will have as many subways as there are in *all* of the United States. Anyone whose experience with subways is limited to the filthy wreckage in New York, however, might wonder whether we shouldn't be dynamiting our subways instead of building new ones.

As air pollution soars above the danger point in our cities and traffic jams approach the ridiculous, a handful of our larger cities are beginning to think about mass transit. Cleveland, as noted before, is the only city in the United States to build new rail transit since the end of World War II. It has just completed a 4-mile, $18-million line from the center of the city to Cleveland Hopkins airport, the only rail line on the continent of North America connecting a major city with its airport. Chicago has installed rapid transit along the median strips of its Kennedy and Dan Ryan expressways. In one of the most successful recent demonstrations that modern transit can lure the motorist from his beloved automobile, the city of Skokie, Illinois, about fourteen miles north of Chicago's Loop, took over the abandoned right-of-way of the Chicago North Shore & Milwaukee Railway for commuter transit service. The new transit authority fixed up the right-of-way, bought new high-speed cars, built new loading platforms with protection from the weather, installed a parking lot for 480 cars, and provided thirty "Kiss 'n Ride" spaces for wives to drop off their commuting husbands. Service was planned at ten-minute intervals, and the optimistic hoped for a thousand riders a day. On the first day, 4,000 showed up, and service was increased to provide trains every six minutes. Ridership has since increased to about 7,000 per day.

New York, Boston, and Philadelphia, which already have rail rapid transit, plan to extend and improve their systems. Atlanta has developed plans for a 40-mile system costing $750 million.* Washington's system has finally been approved. Feasibility studies are under way in perhaps a dozen other cities. But it is a long time from feasibility study to running trains, and there can be many a slip along the way. In February, 1968, voters in Seattle defeated a $385 million bond issue for rapid transit. At the same time, they approved $81.6 million for additional highways.

The most ambitious project, and the one that many other cities

---

* These plans were scrapped in November, 1968, when Atlanta voters rejected a bond issue to help finance them.

are watching with intense interest, is the Bay Area Rapid Transit System (BART) under construction to connect San Francisco to Oakland and thirteen other nearby towns in the Bay Area. This 75-mile system, the largest project of its kind in half a century, is living testimony to San Francisco's aversion to freeways, an aversion that was first expressed some years ago when irate citizens, horrified at the destruction being wrought to their waterfront, stopped construction of the elevated Embarcadero Freeway in midair. In 1962, the voters authorized a $792 million bond issue for BART, the total cost of which was then estimated at $923 million. Since then, cost estimates have risen to $1.2 billion, but BART officials have been refused help by the California legislature. Proposals to help with an additional bond issue, a ten-cent increase in the toll on the San Francisco-Oakland Bay Bridge, a gasoline sales tax, and an increase in the motor vehicle license tax all were defeated. With the BART project scrounging for money, and a planned opening date in 1970 drawing closer, BART is in trouble long before the first train runs. Some 400 miles to the south, where officials of the Southern California Rapid Transit District are talking about a $2 billion system for the sprawling Los Angeles metropolitan area, the birth pangs of BART are inducing sympathetic pains of indecision.

14

A Question of Balance

One of the more instructive statistics in the Bay Area Rapid Transit experience is the size of federal support. For a system now costing some $1.2 billion, the federal government has contributed $80 million, or about 7 per cent. Federal contribution to an Interstate Highway is 90 per cent. Despite the talk about the need for "balance" in our transportation network, public support of alternative means of transportation is very much out of balance, at every level of government.

President Kennedy drew the nation's attention to this situation in 1962, when he said that our national welfare "requires the provision of good urban transportation, with the properly balanced use of private vehicles and modern mass transport to help shape as well as serve urban growth." Since that time, "balance" has been a shibboleth at the highest levels of government. But a balanced transportation system is no nearer reality. Nearly six years after Kennedy's admonition, New York Planning Commissioner Joseph Leiper warned that considerably more public funds must be made available for mass transit in our major urban areas if our planning is to result in "more than just talk." A long-time advocate of increased spending for mass transit, Representative Jonathan B. Bingham of New York, says if we mean to honor our "commitment" to the goal of a balanced transportation system, the federal government must provide "fairer, more flexible, and more equitable" allocation of funds among the various kinds of transport.

In the next breath, Representative Bingham told why this is more easily said than done. The problem, he said, is one of "constituencies." Highways have an obvious constituency: truckers, builders, automobile companies, building materials products, oil companies, and so on. The mass-transit supporters, said Mr. Bingham, are the notoriously unorganized "consumers" and, to a less extent, the railroad industry. But the ranks of the mass-transit supporters are even thinner than that. The consumer supporting mass transit is the less affluent consumer who has no choice in his method of transportation. And the interest shown by the railroad industry in reviving mass transit could hardly be described as ardent.

The key to public funds for balanced transportation lies in Washington. As long as the federal government is willing to dole out highway money to the states on a 50-50 basis for continuing programs, and on a 90-10 basis for the Interstate program, state and local governments quite naturally prefer to build highways. Many observers feel that the citizens of San Francisco have rocks in their heads: for every dollar they have invested in their Bay Area Rapid Transit System, the federal government has contributed seven cents; if they had invested that dollar in highways, the federal government would have matched it with nine dollars. The source of our present imbalance in public commitment to transportation is in federal appropriations.

Local governments—badgered at every turn for more money to improve education, provide jobs and housing, support health and welfare programs, and dampen the fires that threaten to destroy the city—lack the resources needed to put transit on its feet. State legislatures have their eyes fixed on the federal highway dollar, and the legislators themselves, as often as not, are part of what Representative Bingham called the highway constituency. Further, legislators from rural districts are usually unsympathetic to the problems of the city. During recent debate in the Pennsylvania Senate on a proposal to appropriate the munificent sum of $9.6 million to aid mass transit, one senator from a rural area complained, "People in rural America are being asked to bail out the people in the cities, and we can't afford it. There isn't any such thing as a free ride these days. This is the start of a very expensive urban program, and I am not going to vote to tax my people to give people in the cities a free ride."

In the spring of 1968, New Jersey Transportation Commissioner David J. Goldberg proposed a $1.2 billion bond issue for the state, to be repaid from increased tax on gasoline. Of this money, $1 billion would be spent on highways, and $200 million on improving railroad commuter lines. This imbalance of 5 to 1 in favor of highways would provide for additional and improved lanes of asphalt leading into the already choked tunnels and bridges at the threshold of Manhattan, an island whose need for more automobiles is questionable. *The New York Times* deplored the imbalance of funds, stating that it "would continue the long emphasis on rubber over rails that has caused so many difficulties in metropolitan transportation in the past; but any drastic change would be considered politically suicidal in New Jersey." Or, apparently, anywhere in the United States, with the possible exception of San Francisco.

Thomas T. Taber, chairman of the Board of Public Transportation of Morris County, New Jersey, stated flatly that the 5-to-1 ratio in the proposed bond issue showed the hand of the "all-powerful high-way lobby," and it showed a lack of enthusiasm at the state level for solving the worsening rail transportation problem for the benefit of the users of the service. Further, he said, those in the state who rep-resented the public interest and the users of mass transit had been ignored in the preparation of the proposal. "Is it not time," he asked, "that the rights, needs, and desires of the users of public transporta-tion service be recognized, for a change?"

In November, 1967, the voters in the state of New York approved the largest single bond issue ever proposed by a state or local govern-ment: $2.5 billion, the money to be used for transportation. Of the total, $1.25 billion was earmarked for highways, $1 billion for mass transit, and $250 million for airports. This was the first time that any state government had ever agreed to share the responsibility for urban mass transit. Although the $1 billion for mass transit was a notable political victory, there were those who, conscious of the abject poverty of transit and the opulence of highways, complained that too much was allocated to the latter. *Business Week* magazine pointed out that, when federal and local contributions were added in, the figures would be more like $3.6 billion for highways and $1.3 billion for mass transit.

New York City Councilman Edward I. Koch bitterly criticized the bond issue. This proved, he said, that "the power of the highway establishment is even greater on the state level than on the Federal level." He charged that state officials were planning to "divert as much of that $1 billion as possible away from rapid transit uses." The people of New York, he said, "have been defeated by the highway establishment." They would have to fight that establishment to prevent the $1.25 billion portion of the bond issue from being used to build "still more freeways into our choked city," and, when the federal Interstate program comes up for renewal, the people must see to it that some of the billions from the Highway Trust Fund are allocated to mass transit.

The November, 1968, ballots in three major cities—Washington, Atlanta, and Los Angeles—included proposals for bond issues to build mass transit networks. Washington voted Yes; Atlanta and Los Angeles said No. The Atlanta bond issue would have helped to finance a 40-mile, $750-million system. The plans for the sprawling Los Angeles area were for an 89-mile rail system to cost $2.5 billion.

Oil companies, construction firms, automobile clubs, and car dealers spent heavily in a successful campaign to defeat the bond measure in Los Angeles. This defeat is particularly poignant in the face of a statement issued just three months earlier by sixty members of the UCLA medical faculty: "Air pollution has now become a major health hazard to most of this community during much of the year. Anyone who does not have compelling reasons to remain should move out. . . ." Despite the most vigorous air pollution control measures of any community in the nation, Los Angeles still is being strangled by some 12,000 tons per day of automobile exhaust pollutants, which comprise at least 80 per cent of the air-borne poisons in that unhappy land. Says the Los Angeles County Medical Association: "Air pollution is becoming increasingly worse and may lead to great lethality in this community." More and more citizens of Los Angeles will be killed by automobile exhausts, according to Arie J. Haagen-Smit, chairman of the California Air Resources Board, until the community attacks "the root of the problem, the excessive use of the car at the expense of other less polluting means of transportation." For Los Angeles, that means the bicycle or the pogo stick.

The federal role in mass transit so far has been limited by funds allocated under the Urban Mass Transportation Act of 1964, amended in 1966. Congress appropriated $60 million for this program in 1965, and this figure has increased slowly over the years, to $130 million for 1968 and $175 million for fiscal year 1969. This kind of money could fall through the cracks in the floor of any self-respecting highway program. These days, $175 million can be swallowed up in building just ten miles of an urban expressway. In one project in northern New Jersey, $350 million is being spent to widen the Jersey Turnpike from six to twelve lanes. Where the additional six lanes of cars will go when they reach the two tunnels and the George Washington Bridge into Manhattan is anybody's guess. As *The Wall Street Journal* editorialized recently: ". . . it takes no economic genius to figure out that Washington could use a more balanced approach to transportation."

In commenting on the use made of federal money for mass transit Congressman Bingham has remarked that deliberate efforts were made to award grants which would "placate" some of the earlier enemies of the program. Applications for grants by local committees were judged on a first-come, first-served basis, and little or no effort was made to encourage or to stimulate major transit undertakings or truly innovative projects. Thus, in the first year or so of its existence, the federal role was "carefully limited and self-disciplined," calculated to alleviate fears of "federal intervention" and "Main Street buses being run from Washington." Since then, action has been slightly less circumspect, but $175 million per year is just about enough to keep a tourniquet on the bleeding stump. Meanwhile, the federal government spends more on new highways than it does on public housing, rent supplements, the Model Cities program, and the so-called war on poverty all combined.

After the Urban Mass Transit Act of 1964 was passed, interest in transit experienced a boom, and there was a quick flurry of activity and hope. But the funds allocated were entirely too meager, and after several years, transit advocates soured. By the middle of 1967, equipment manufacturers were still looking for the promised market. Said one car-maker, "Sure, there's a tremendous market predicted for the next decade, but the question is, when does the decade begin?" Asked another, "What good is talk of a boom when you're almost starving, waiting for the darned thing to arrive?" *The Wall Street Journal* reported that the "long-heralded" boom in mass transit systems "apparently has bogged down in a frustrating traffic jam of skimpy municipal budgets, endless planning sessions, and lethargic city administrations."

The Philadelphia Bulletin gloomily predicted that, even if the city's "maximum option" for transit spending is realized, the proportion of Philadelphia commuters using mass transit will fall from the present figure of 57 per cent to 44 per cent by 1985. The bleak meaning of these figures, said the newspaper, is that the center of the city is in for more inundation by auto, more street congestion, more real estate given over to the automobile with low or no tax yields, more air pollution and noise. "There is no certainty," the *Bulletin* concluded, "that the city can stand it."

In a summary of the 1967 construction year, the weekly trade magazine *Engineering News-Record* called the federal aid program for mass transit "low-key" and observed that it had "few dramatic accomplishments to show for the money and effort thus far expended."

Three months later, *The Iron Age* reported disillusioned comments overheard at the Third International Conference on Urban Transportation, in Pittsburgh, G. R. Schaefer, Westinghouse Air Brake Co., said that his firm finally had to cut back promotion. "The people who say this is going to open up whole new industries do not have a grip on the problem." Westinghouse, he said, has gone through an "agonizing re-evaluation." A representative of U. S. Steel said that the program, after nearly four years, "hasn't gotten off the ground." *Iron Age,* noting a "general simmering down of enthusiasm" at the conference, said that the problem was simply lack of spending for any type of transit. Federal funds for mass transit, it predicted, will remain at $230 million a year through 1970. "That compares with $1.2 billion for the supersonic transport and $4 billion for highways."

An engineer for Sperry Rand Corporation was asked why engineers, in the face of widespread resentment of the antisocial aspects of the SST, "go submissively about the job of designing the monster." The reason, he replied, is that they are being paid to do just that, "and there is no one in sight to pay them to design rapid transit."

Woefully inadequate as the federal support for mass transit is, there are still some who believe it is excessive. In the fall of 1967, Senator Gordon Allot of Colorado, the ranking Republican on the Senate Appropriations Subcommittee, remarked that the mass-transit program had accomplished "relatively little" and that he would expect to get some "hard facts as to what has actually been accomplished in the program" before voting it any more money.

One method of increasing federal support for mass transit has been suggested by Congressman Bingham. In January, 1967, he introduced a bill that would give the governor of any state the power to decide how to use the money allocated to his state from the Highway Trust Fund; the governor could use the money for highways or mass transit. The bill was assigned to the Committee on Public Works, whose chairman, Congressman George H. Fallon of Maryland, is a charter member of the highway establishment. It was he, in the fall of 1966, who had denounced President Johnson's partial freeze of federal highway allocations as "economically shortsighted" and likely to "spell death and injury to the thousands of people who will be involved in accidents." It was he, together with Jennings Randolph, his counterpart in the Senate, who had hurriedly called joint hearings to pressure the President into releasing the highway funds. Congressman Bingham's bill is still tightly locked in committee.

In July, 1968, during debate on that year's highway bill, Representative William F. Ryan of New York attempted to introduce an amendment giving state governors the option of using allocations from the Highway Trust Fund for highways or mass transit. Fallon rose to declare that the amendment was out of order. Questioned by the chair, Ryan replied that he had offered a similar amendment two years before to the 1966 highway bill, but "it was ruled out of order on the ground that it related to mass transportation and not highways." Ryan had been told to try again when a mass-transit bill reached the floor. Several months later, following instructions, he offered the same amendment to the mass-transit bill, "and it was ruled out of order on the ground that it related to highways and not to mass transportation."

"We cannot have it both ways," Ryan complained to his fellow Congressmen. "It must be in order one place or another." But ap-

parently not—the chair ruled once again that Ryan's amendment
was out of order. Three strikes and out.

The thought of raiding the Highway Trust Fund to help mass
transit raises the blood pressure of all devoted highway builders and
their friends in the automobile and allied industries. William E. Pat-
terson, American Trucking Associations, says that the "most unreasonable" of all the proposals for easing our transportation bind is the
one "to more or less abandon the urban highway networks in favor
of building one or more forms of mass transit facilities. Highways
and streets in the area would be allowed to stagnate while a 'pie in
the sky' transit facility is built with public funds."

Trucking firm executive Mark Robeson is adamant. "Lest there be
any doubts," he says grimly, "I should announce to anyone who con-
templates slicing off a chunk of federal highway money to subsidize
nonhighway transportation, that there is a big red light on this one.
Any hint of siphoning off these funds in other directions, however
noble, raises the highway user's hackles."

U. S. Rubber Company's H. E. Humphreys, Jr., says that if "balanced" transportation "means taking taxes paid in good faith by highway users for *roads* and then using those taxes for another form of
transportation, or for studies of another form, or for purchasing
rights-of-way for the benefit of another system—then highway users
emphatically do *not* agree." (Humphreys' italics.) No one, he added,
"should be forced to pay higher car use taxes or subsidize mass transit
used by someone else." One wonders whether, if Mr. Humphreys is
childless, he refuses to pay his school taxes.

Kermit B. Rykken, official of the American Automobile Association, is understandably reluctant to see anyone forsake his automobile for a subway or railroad train. "We who represent the passenger car owners of America," he implores, "say to all who are in positions of responsibility: Give us the facilities we need and for which
we are paying our fair share and then some; do not withhold from us
the streets and highways in urban areas we require, for the purpose
of fostering some Blue Sky form of transportation, or some form of
transportation which for the most part has gone the way of the black-
smith; do not use our special taxes to finance these deficit-ridden
means of getting about."

Mr. Rykken's plea to those in "positions of responsibility" is being heard. Speaking to a gathering of the American Road Builders Association in March, 1967, Federal Highway Administrator Lowell K. Bridwell was very reassuring: "Let me go on record here as being adamantly and unalterably opposed to the growing trend toward raiding highway funds . . . to finance mass transit programs. Our highway users who foot the bill for highway services have every right to expect their user taxes will be used for highway purposes. To do otherwise is to break faith with a major segment of our population."

Mr. Bridwell's assertion that highway users "foot the bill" for highways helps to perpetuate the myth that prevents calm discussion of this question. Highway advocates insist that taxes paid by highway users make highway construction a pay-as-you-go proposition, and that tax money given over to mass transit systems amounts to a subsidy. The truth of the matter is that the automobile driver is also heavily subsidized. Out of taxes comes the money to buy the right-of-way; build the road, the bridges, and tunnels; repair and maintain these once they are built; cut the grass in summer; plow the snow in winter; install and maintain traffic signals and signs; buy and maintain a fleet of highway patrol cars and pay the salaries of the police force; and, in the city, build and maintain thousands of storage areas for cars, along the curbs and in garages. A large hidden cost is the loss of taxes from the land used for all this.

Taking the Interstate system as an example, even when it is granted that all the money in the Trust Fund comes from the highway user, this money is used only to obtain the right-of-way and build the highway. There is no money in the fund for maintenance, which, by the time the system is completed, will be costing the states more than a quarter-billion dollars a year. Granted, some of this money will be collected from highway users at the state and local level. On the whole, however, studies on this question point to heavy subsidies of highway facilities from tax money not contributed by highway users.

In one year in Philadelphia, total city expenditures for highway-user facilities and services came to $46 million, but collections from motorists totaled only $30 million. And this does not include the large loss of taxes from the land occupied by the highways. When this and other costs are added, Philadelphia estimates that it spends about $50 *more* per year per automobile than it receives; Milwaukee estimates this annual subsidy of each motorist at $90.

Since urban land is more expensive to buy than rural land, the tax loss is higher, and since more lanes are needed to handle large rush-hour loads, the subsidy is much higher for urban freeways. One estimate puts it at ten cents per mile per motorist. Officials in Washington, D. C., estimate that every time another commuter decides to use his car to make the daily drive into the city, the additional cost to the city is $21,000.

None of this can justify the use of highway tax money for subsidizing mass transit, of course. But it does serve to adjust the perspective on the problem. Both the highway user and the mass-transit user must be subsidized by public funds. Both systems are *public* systems. Mass-transit systems cannot be operated by private enterprise at a profit in the face of competition from tax-supported highway systems. On the other hand, if the users of urban freeways were required to pay all the costs incident to the construction, operation, and maintenance of those freeways, the competitive position of mass transit would be considerably improved.

The question of where to spend the public funds that are available for transportation should be answered on the merits of the various forms of transportation, not on the source of the funds. Just as childless couples should be required to pay school taxes, so the highway user should be expected to subsidize mass transit with his fuel taxes, if that is in the best interest of the community as a whole. There can be little doubt that it is. Our preoccupation with highways threatens to destroy our cities and gobble up our countryside. We must restore balance to our transportation system. This means far less highway construction and far more mass-transit construction. The money now being devoted to one must be transferred to the other.

15

Packing the Pork Barrel

If ever there was any doubt that the Congress, and especially the Public Works Committee of the House, is owned and operated by the highway lobby, the Federal Aid Highway Act of 1968 dispelled that doubt. Under the provisions of that law, signed by President Johnson on August 23, 1968, the Congress weakened federal protection for park lands, wildlife preserves, and historic sites; it commanded that a disputed freeway network for the District of Columbia be built over the objections of the local citizens; it added to the still-incomplete Interstate system 1,500 miles of highway for which no need had been shown; and it told the President that money appropriated by Congress for building roads is to be used forthwith for just that purpose, and any "freezing" of funds by the Executive will not be tolerated.

Newspapers across the land, appalled by the arrogance of what one called this "legislative abomination," urged the President to veto it. *The New York Times,* dubbing the bill "monstrous" and a "lobbyist's delight," slapped the brand of "porkbarrel politician" on Representatives John C. Kluczynski and William C. Cramer, chairman and ranking minority member, respectively, of the House subcommittee on roads. *The St. Louis Post-Dispatch* angrily told Congress that it "needs a reminder of concern" for where roads should be built. Said *The Washington Daily News,* the bill "is part pork-barrel, part toady to the billboard lobby, and part arrogance. . . . About the only sensible course for President Johnson is to veto the whole shebang."

Two years before this destructive law was passed, conservation interests in Congress, led by Senator Henry M. Jackson of Washington, had wrung from Congress a commitment to protect open lands and historic areas from further highway intrusion. Section 4(f) of the 1966 Act creating the Department of Transportation prohibits the building of highways on any land from a public park, recreation area, wildlife and waterfowl refuge, or historic site unless "there is no feasible and prudent alternative to the use of such land."

This section of the law had been under attack by the highway establishment ever since its enactment. John O. Morton, president of the American Association of State Highway Officials, told the Senate Public Works Committee in 1968 that "we believe that there is over-emphasis and over-enthusiasm in administering Section 4(f) of the Transportation Act of 1966, to the point that needed highway improvements are being delayed and complicated." In the writing of the 1968 Highway Act, this section was all but destroyed in the House and then only partially restored by the Senate.

The House bill, first of all, spoke only of protecting "federally owned" land, thus yielding to the bulldozer all city and state parks and historic sites, and all privately owned recreation areas and wildlife refuges. Further, the House bill no longer prohibited road-building unless "there is no feasible and prudent alternative"; instead, it stated merely that the plans for using a federally owned park for highway construction "must include feasible and prudent alternatives to the use of such land." There was no stipulation that the alternatives must be used, only that they be "included" in the planning process, whatever that might mean.

Representative Richard D. McCarthy of New York, fighting the bill on the House floor, asked, "What does 'consideration of alternatives' mean? How much consideration of what kinds of alternatives?" Such language, he stated, might permit a highway engineer to glance at an alternative to a proposed highway—an alternative that is more costly but does not slice through a park—and reject the alternative because use of park land will keep down his acquisition costs.

Senate conferees fought successfully to bring this section of the law back from the grave, but its state of health is still uncertain. In place of "federally owned" land, the bill signed by President Johnson says "publicly owned." Protection is therefore lost for privately owned recreation areas and historic sites, and for such lands as wildlife refuges owned by the National Audubon Society and the Nature Conservancy. Further, the issue is clouded by the provision that protection will be offered only to publicly owned land "of national, State, or local significance as determined by the Federal, State, or local officials having jurisdiction thereof." What does this mean? It appears to say that a city park, for example, can be protected only if the city official having jurisdiction over the park declares it to be of local "significance" and thus worth saving. So far, so good. But suppose the local official declines to make this declaration and opens his park to the bulldozer? Can a federal official override this decision by declaring the park to be of "national" significance? This is no trivial question: as we have seen on a number of occasions, citizens having appealed to Washington to prevent bulldozing authorized by "development-minded" local officials.

Opinion on this question is split. During the floor debate on the final bill, anxious Senators repeatedly questioned Jennings Randolph, chief Senate conferee, on this point, and he repeatedly assured them that he interpreted this language to mean the federal official *does* have the power of veto over local decision. "Under any circumstances," he maintained, "the Secretary of Transportation does not have to accept the local approval of use of parklands. He has authority . . . to exercise his independent judgment and oppose the use of parklands." There is at least one dissenting voice. In the report of the conference committee, the House conferees state that "the Congress does not believe . . . that clearly enunciated local preferences should be overruled on the basis of this authority."

Russell E. Train, president of the Conservation Foundation, has no doubts as to the meaning of this section of the law. "The public has now learned," he says, "that the conservation gains of recent years simply cannot be taken for granted." Mr. Train deplores "the highway lobby's success in eroding existing environmental safeguards."

Long before the 1968 highway measure reached Congress, it was clear that a showdown would one day materialize between the highway establishment and the advocates of increasing support for mass transit, led by Transportation Secretary Boyd. That power struggle developed, appropriately enough, over the proposed expressway system for the nation's capital city, and it reached its climax in the debate on one provision of the highway bill.

Washington has perhaps the most primitive and inadequate system of public transportation of any city its size in the nation. Buses compete fiercely with automobiles for space on the congested streets. Each working day, 350,000 commuters are wheeled into the city from surrounding suburbs, more than 60 per cent of them by private automobile. Downtown Washington is the largest employment center in the nation lacking rail rapid transit. The rush hour scene is ludicrous. The four bridges bringing commuters across the Potomac from Virginia are known locally as the "car-strangled spanners."

Since World War II, Washington has spent half a billion dollars building expressways, and it plans to spend as much again within the next few years. A 1965 report of the District of Columbia Highway Department predicts that highway building by the end of the decade will take an additional 694 acres of land, including 180 acres of homes, 50 acres of stores, 176 acres of factories, 247 acres of parks and government-owned land, 24 acres of schools, and 17 acres of tax-exempt institutions such as churches and cemeteries. There are now parking spaces for 50,000 cars in the central business district, where 60 per cent of the land is devoted to moving or storing automobiles. The plan for more expressways has been called a "license to destroy the city."

Opposition to rampant expresswayism grew in Washington among those threatened with eviction, those who believe more balance is needed in the city's transportation system, and those who fear a general degradation of the quality of life in the nation's capital. Influential citizens' groups formed to fight the freeways, and the National Capital Planning Commission began to drag its feet, stating that it would withhold approval of additional freeways until overall studies showed a distinct need for them and until progress was made on a long-sought subway system.

In 1965, after Congress finally authorized construction of a subway system, the highway establishment discovered a new tool for pressuring the Planning Commission: it would hold the subway for ransom. Representative William H. Natcher of Kentucky, chairman of the House Appropriations Subcommittee for the District of Columbia, told the antifreeway forces that he would allow no appropriations for the subway until all proposed highway routes were approved. Expressway opposition in the Planning Commission thereupon collapsed, and the routes were approved in the spring of 1967.

But later that year the battle broke out anew. Outraged citizens threatened with eviction, supported by more than thirty civic groups, petitioned the U. S. District Court for an injunction to stop highway construction, charging that the condemnation procedures used by the highway department in acquiring land were illegal and that the public hearings had been inadequate. One citizens' group calling itself "Niggers Incorporated" circulated handbills calling for "No more white highways through black bedrooms." Transportation Secretary Boyd threw his weight behind the aroused residents of Washington's black ghettos whose homes were menaced by the highway bulldozer. "We're going to have to find a better way to build freeways," he said, "than by disrupting those without political clout."

The District Court denied the petition. Several months later, however, the U. S. Court of Appeals reversed the decision and issued a restraining order halting expressway construction until proper hearings could be held.

Meanwhile, however, Boyd had taken his stand. He announced that he disapproved construction of the so-called Three Sisters Bridge across the Potomac, a key element in the freeway system which will feed commuter traffic from Arlington and points west into downtown Washington. At the same time, Boyd declared that the entire system would be "tremendously expensive, and inadequate" to solve the city's transportation problems. "It's a question," he added, "of whether you go ahead and build expressways because they're planned, or take a whole new look at the city's whole transportation picture in light of the latest thinking on urban planning." Boyd was in favor of taking another look before laying down more concrete.

The issue was joined. The Administration and Congress were on a collision course. Representative Kluczynski sputtered that he would introduce legislation to force construction of the Washington expressway system, despite court decisions, despite the Secretary of Tranportation, despite opposition from citizens and local officials. Representative Natcher once again raised his club of no highways, no subway. *The New York Times* observed that the highway establishment viewed this confrontation as "the Dienbienphu of the long guerrilla war between themselves and the anti-freeway forces."

All over the country, freeway battlers ceased fire momentarily and leaned on their weapons to watch the fur fly in Washington, knowing full well the implications for their own communities: if Kluczynski succeeded in marching Congress roughshod over local opposition to force construction of expressways in Washington, he could do it anywhere.

It was a pushover. In writing the 1968 highway bill in his House roads subcommittee, Kluczynski simply added a section directing that, not later than thirty days after enactment, work must begin on the remainder of the expressway system for the District of Columbia, "notwithstanding any other provision of law, or any court decision or administrative action to the contrary." In bringing his bill before the House, Kluczynski said that it "breaks the deadlock on construction of needed links of the interstate system in the District of Columbia. . . . I told you last year that we would bring before you a highway bill that would try to solve these problems, and I think we have done it." Said Republican Cramer, "I believe it is time for the District of Columbia to get on with the job of building highways. . . . I, for one, cannot sit idly by and see the District of Columbia not complete its system because it has a few problems." It was a bipartisan effort.

In the House-Senate conference on the bill, a few of the racially sticky routes were deleted from this section, but three legs of the expressway system, plus the Three Sisters Bridge, remain in the final version, which also directs the Secretary of Transportation to come up with recommendations about the rest of the system within eighteen months.

A more high-handed, arrogant abuse of power is hardly conceivable within a system of representative government. Local officials had clearly been ignored. A letter to Kluczynski from Walter E. Washington, mayor of Washington, and John W. Hechinger, city council chairman, expressed their "great disappointment" with the forced rape of their city. "It is our feeling," the two officials wrote, "that the transportation system within an urban community, especially in the nation's capital, should be decided by the local government after an expression by the citizens of the community." The action by Congress "would remove self-determination from our city government's authority. It is also regrettable that Congress would direct that a specific freeway system be built in *any* of the urban centers of our country."

Condemnation of this dictatorial affront to the nation poured in from all quarters. Representative Richard D. McCarthy of New York said, "It is difficult to imagine any legislation that is more conducive to disrespect for law and order in these troubled times in our nation's capital." In overriding the wishes of the people, their local government officials, the federal courts, and the responsible Cabinet officer, Congress had bludgeoned through a highway system that would "mutilate the nation's capital" and "establish a precedent for forcing urban highway construction" anywhere in the country.

Senator Majority Leader Mansfield told Congress that it was usurping the role of the highway engineer. "I am not convinced in my own mind that the members of Congress are the proper ones to be planning and dictating the construction of highways and freeways," he said. John Sherman Cooper was more direct. "It is wholly wrong for the Congress to direct a political subdivision to make a certain choice of roads," he said. "It is wrong."

Congress, concluded *The New York Times,* had "yielded pliably to the wishes of the highway lobby" in its "high-handed dictation of freeway routes in the capital." Even the bible of the construction industry, *Engineering News-Record,* called the Congressional action "irresponsible." This and other features of the bill, said the magazine, "mirror exactly the high-handedness that has produced a backlash of enraged opposition to highways in big cities and wilderness areas alike."

Members of Washington's City Council vowed they would reject the unwanted freeways, despite the will of Congress. When Representative Natcher repeated his threat to withhold mass transit funds until freeway construction begins, City Council Vice Chairman Walter E. Fauntroy cried "blackmail."

Residents of Washington's black ghettos whose homes lay in the

path of the bulldozer threatened to "start a revolution." Said T. H.
Booker, chairman of "Niggers, Incorporated," black citizens of the
nation's capital should "take up arms to defend their neighborhoods"
against the highway invasion.

Under pressure from the press, from some members of Congress,
and some officials of his administration to veto the 1968 highway
bill, President Johnson waited until the last possible moment before
reluctantly signing it into law. One section of the bill, he said, would
"remove the protection we have given in the past to many park lands
that should be preserved for the families and children in America."
This was "unfortunate, ill-considered, and a setback to the cause of
conservation." The section forcing construction of Washington expressways, the President went on, was "inconsistent with a basic
tenet of sound urban development—to permit the local government
and the people affected to participate meaningfully in planning their
transportation system." Also, the bill would "extend the interstate
system by 1500 miles without any serious study of the type of major
highway program we will need after we complete the present system
in 1974." Despite all this, the President concluded that "the good in
this bill outweighs the bad," and he signed it.

The highway bill, according to columnist Drew Pearson, was "one
of the most lobby-dominated bills" of that session of Congress. To
Pearson's charge that Representative Kluczynski had "bowed to the
lobbies" in pushing the bill through Congress, the roads subcommittee
chairman replied, "I don't associate with lobbyists and I don't accept
contributions from them and I didn't yield anything to the lobbyists
on this bill." Evidence appeared to contradict this sweeping declaration of purity. During the deliberations on the bill, the normally
smooth and silent workings of the highway lobby erupted briefly
into the public eye.

An enterprising reporter with *The Des Moines Register* obtained
and published a detailed listing of the "contributions" given to members of the House Public Works Committee by a "nonpartisan committee" of trucking operators. Gifts were listed for fifteen members
of the committee, ranging in size from $500 to $3,000. Kluczynski
was reportedly at the top with $3,000.

Wishing to explore the truth of these charges, Representative

Fred Schwengel of Iowa dispatched a letter to the House ethics committee suggesting an inquiry. When he repeated his request on the
floor of the House, heated words flew and fists were shaken in red-
dened faces. Representative John Dingell of Michigan asked angrily,
"Is the gentleman charging that any of his colleagues in this body
engage in any practice that is not fully ethical? You have made a lot
of charges and I want an answer."

Dingell, who reportedly was on the truckers' list for a gift of
$1,500, waved his fist under Schwengel's nose, shouting, "You're a
liar and a coward. If I see you in the alley, I'll plant my fist where
your glasses are." Although not a member of the Public Works Committee, Dingell is a member of the Subcommittee on Transportation
and Aeronautics of the Committee on Interstate and Foreign Commerce, and thus eligible for the kind attentions of trucking operators.

The Senate-House conference committee that hammered out the
final compromises on the highway bill lasted thirteen days, during
which House conferees adamantly defended their lobby-dominated
version against efforts by Senate conferees to soften some of the more
objectionable features. Senator Jennings Randolph later said that it was
the most difficult conference committee he had ever served on during
his twenty-four years in the capital. Senator John Sherman Cooper,
another conferee, deplored the intransigence of the House members. "I
have never found a conference committee more adamant, more insis-
tent on its manifest intention to maintain its position," he later told the
Senate. "It seemed to me that the bill they presented to the conference
was more anticonservationist than any other bill I have seen come
before this body. In at least three major sections, it attempted to
strike down legislation which had been enacted by Congress in an
effort to protect the natural resources and beauty of this country.
The Senate conferees struggled manfully against these efforts; we
succeeded in some respects and failed in others."

As in most contests with the highway establishment, the failures
outnumbered the successes.

Highways or People?

Many of those who have viewed with mounting horror our present orgy of highway building have taken some comfort in the belief that, with the completion of the Interstate system in 1974 or 1975, the frenzy will subside. On the contrary, once the expenditures for the Vietnam War are ended, we are more likely to see an increase in the tempo of black-topping.

Despite one of the most agonizing budgetary reappraisals of recent memory, federal funds for roads go marching on unabated. The Federal Aid Highway Act of 1968 provides $4 billion per year for the next several years for the Interstate system, plus $1.1 billion per year for "regular" federal-aid construction, plus nearly $300 million per year for miscellaneous road-building on federal lands in forests, parks, and so on. This rate of spending, about $5.4 billion per year of federal-aid money, will set new all-time records and kick off an unprecedented wave of highway construction in the spring of 1969.

But this will be only the beginning. The automobile population is growing faster than the human population, and, under the doctrine that the machine must be served, the highway advocates are already laying plans for an accelerated effort to blanket the nation with asphalt. "Today," says Francis C. Turner, director of the Bureau of Public Roads, "Americans drive 97 million cars, buses, and trucks. Ten years from now we'll be operating 120 million vehicles—and the number goes up from there. In 1967 we drove 960 billion miles. We'll hit a trillion in 1968. Better roads and highways are vital to our social and economic welfare and to national defense."

John De Lorenzi, public relations director for the American Automobile Association, states that "the highway needs of this country in the decade 1975–1985 greatly exceed those of the previous decade." City Planner Alexander Ganz envisions "more than a doubling of route miles of urban freeways by 1985, over and above that now scheduled for the urban portion of the interstate system."

A study by Wilbur Smith and Associates for the Automobile Manufacturers Association concludes that, except for the largest and smallest cities, one mile of urban freeway should be provided for every 10,000 city dwellers. Thus, by the year 1980, about 16,000 miles of urban freeways will be required, but present programs will supply only about 9,600 miles. "Accordingly," says the Smith report, "a continued and accelerated program of express highway construction, particularly in urban areas, should follow completion of the Interstate System."

Other loyal members of the highway establishment echo this demand. Senate Public Roads Subcommittee Chairman Jennings Randolph says, "After this interstate system has been built we will have another. . . . This is a fact of life." The Asphalt Institute, noting that expenditures on highway construction, as a percentage of the gross national product, have declined slightly since World War II, concludes that "our road program is not keeping pace with our economic growth and vehicle registration. This lag, coupled with the burgeoning number of cars flowing from Detroit every year . . . calls for an inescapable conclusion. To keep our roads adequate to the needs of the motoring public in the years to come, there must be more roads built and more existing roads improved." The present program of road-building "is not the final answer to our ever-growing traffic problem. Even more and better roads will continue to be needed as our population continues to grow and as we produce more and more vehicles to carry our goods to market and move more people from one place to another."

It has always been dogma among the members of the politically powerful American Association of State Highway Officials (AASHO) that highway appropriations are insufficient. As long ago as 1964, before the Interstate system was even half-completed, AASHO officials were preparing recommendations to Congress for vast new programs. Addressing the 1964 annual meeting, AASHO President J. Burch

McMorran urged rapid completion of an AASHO study of highway needs following 1972, which was then the target year for completion of the Interstate system. "Our evaluation of highway needs will be the most sweeping in the history of highway building," he told his fellow highway officials. "Our studies must be developed so that no drop-off or gap in highway designs and construction will ensue, regardless of how early the Interstate Program achieves completion. Highway construction has become such an important part of American life and economy that it must flow forward uninterruptedly to carry the ever-increasing load of motor traffic without interruption."

Although some differences have developed between AASHO and the Federal Department of Transportation on the allocation of highway funds and the procedures for approving routes, there *is* agreement that spending for highways must increase. Three years after McMorran's pronouncement, Federal Highway Administrator Lowell K. Bridwell told a meeting of highway officials that "we are not spending enough on highway construction and improvement today. And I do not expect any development in the field of transportation is going to measurably counter our increasing national need for more and better roads over the next two or three decades." These words were an effort to placate the state highway officials who feared that talk of "balanced" transportation at the federal level portended reduced appropriations for highways. No such thing, said Bridwell. Even if increased support should develop for mass transit, highway construction should still proceed at an accelerated pace.

In June, 1967, noting that it is "absolutely necessary that highway development continue without interruption" after the Interstate system is completed, the officials of AASHO presented recommendations to Congress for the decade 1975–1984. Despite recent moves to improve other forms of transportation, said the report, "most of these proposals will not go much beyond demonstration project status for a considerable time, and even in the northeastern corridor, where new modes will first have practical applications, these other transportation forms will not materially decrease highway needs for many years."

If the advice of AASHO is taken, it is doubtful that travel by high-speed rail will ever supplant any substantial portion of highway travel. The report states that AASHO is "not prejudiced toward any other mode of transportation," but, on the other hand, "we feel that in the United States, the transportation agencies must furnish transportation in line with the public's desires, instead of imposing some transportation system on the public that would require their regimentation and realignment of their travel habits and some system that someone thinks might be better for the public or more efficient in the long run." Despite these efforts at "regimentation," the report concludes, "highways will be a dominant force and a major transportation mode in all areas of the United States for years to come."

A study of the wishes of the public, financed by AASHO at a cost of $285,000, shows clearly that the man in the street wants to drive his car where and when he wishes. Results of a questionnaire and interviews with 5,000 families show an overwhelming preference for the automobile as a form of transportation—a not unexpected conclusion.

Some of the findings of the AASHO study are:

"The automobile is by far the most important mode of travel to the American household. . . . Nearly all changes in family situations and community developments tend to increase the use of the automobile, leading to the conclusion that the automobile will become even more important in the years ahead.

"There appears to be close 'ego-involvement' with the automobile as a way of life.

"The attitudes toward existing public transportation services and facilities tend to be generally negative, rather than positive."

The AASHO report frowns upon any effort to achieve "balance" in our transportation system at the expense of the plain wishes of the people: "We believe that it is academic and indisputable that highway improvement and the role of highways in any so-called balanced total transportation system must be based on documented highway needs and upon the public's desires in regard to transportation. We do not believe that highway development can be based on some arbitrarily assigned role of highways in relation to total transportation as developed solely by a theoretical financial investment return concept which would artificially retard highway transportation and artificially fertilize other modes." So much for any suggestion that transportation be looked upon as anything but a system for moving automobiles.

The AASHO report recommends that, during the 1975–1984 decade, a total of $78 billion be pumped into federal-aid highway construction, two-thirds of the money from the federal government and one-third from the states. A later report, issued in June, 1968, gives strong support to a ratio of three-quarters federal to one-quarter state contributions. The 1968 report also increases the estimated yield from the Highway Trust Fund from $54 billion to $60 billion for the decade. Thus the figure of $78 billion for federally aided highway construction would be nearer to $90 billion. Even this staggering sum, says AASHO, will "only take care of the most pressing needs." If Congress in its wisdom should decide to spend more, "the justification for such expansion is well established and justified."

One more thing, says the report: state highway departments have been subjected to an annoying series of "increasing requirements and reviews" from federal officials that "complicate" the job of building highways. The federal government should stick to its job of disbursing the money and leave it to the states to build the highways where and how they feel best. Otherwise, "if the threat of penalties continues and more complications are introduced, it might cause a reappraisal of the desirability of federal aid in our highway programs."

One cheery note in the AASHO report is the statement that most of the $90 billion or so to be spent on federal-aid highways during the post-interstate decade should be spent on improvements in existing highways rather than construction of new ones. This program, say AASHO, "will probably not add more than 10 per cent to the existing public road and street mileage of the nation." Since existing roads and streets total about 3,600,000 miles, that would mean an addition of 360,000 miles during the ten-year period. If this mileage is all just four-lane road, using what AASHO considers to be the desirable minimum width of 12 feet per lane, that would mean an additional 3,200 square miles of the United States would disappear under the asphalt shroud, an area larger than the states of Rhode Island and Delaware.

So in the face of wholesale degradation of our environment by the pavers, the prospect is for more of the same. The only effective center of political power that offers any hope of change, the Federal Department of Transportation, has so far provided only palliatives. It dares not question the wisdom of building more highways; instead it makes recommendations to ease the associated pain and minimize the damage. It is treating symptoms, not the disease.

The most recent such effort is a set of regulations proposed by the Federal Highway Administration late in 1968, just before the change in Administrations. If adopted, these regulations would require two public hearings instead of only one: the first to announce the general corridor for the highway, and the second to give design details and the exact location of the right-of-way. The regulations also would give any citizen opposing the highway the right to appeal his case in Washington.

These proposals were welcomed by conservationists and city planners, who saw in them an opportunity for the ordinary citizen to gain some leverage. The highway lobby attacked the proposals as an attempt by the federal government to dominate highway planning and to burden the process with so much red tape that construction would be all but impossible.

Reaction to the proposed regulations underlined the schism that has developed between the various levels of government on the question of transportation. This alignment finds the federal government and the cities on one side, the states on the other. The U. S. Conference of Mayors and the 3,000-member National League of Cities strongly supported the regulations. The governors of all fifty states, speaking through the National Governors' Conference, opposed them. The state officials complained that the regulations would "remove the decision-making responsibility and power from the levels of government closest to the people and place it in the Federal bureaucracy." In the governors' eyes, the level of government closest to the people is the statehouse. The mayors have other ideas. Often, they look to Washington for help that is denied them by rural- or lobby-dominated state legislatures.

The federal-state partnership for building highways, once a perpetual honeymoon between the state highway officials and the Federal

Bureau of Public Roads, has been soured in recent years by efforts in the new Department of Transportation to curb the rampaging bulldozer and gain support for other modes of transportation. State highway officials have grown increasingly resentful of so-called "planners" in Washington. A. E. Johnson, executive director of AASHO, recently heaped scorn on the "attorneys, economists, budgeteers, scientists, academics, and politicians" in the "multi-layered management levels of the new Department of Transportation . . . who have very little going for them to qualify them as experts to administer the big highway program." These people, says Johnson, are "anti-highway." With them in charge, "it is getting more difficult to build a road."

So bitter has the relation become that some states talk of mutiny. If the proposed new federal regulations are adopted, Texas has threatened to pull out of the federal-aid highway program entirely. Mr. Johnson recommended to the states that they amass sizable highway funds of their own so that they would not be forced to become "subservient" to Washington. He advised the states to re-examine the federal-aid program to see whether it is worth continuing, "or whether the major highway programs should again become state-oriented." If it is necessary for the states to go it alone, he said, they are going to need "the support of the highway industry."

Those whose sympathies are on the side of the federal government in this wrangle are not encouraged by the tone of the new Administration. President Nixon's Secretaries of Transportation, Interior, and Housing and Urban Development are all former governors who oppose the new regulations. Former Governor John A. Volpe of Massachusetts, the new Secretary of Transportation, was a multimillionaire contractor and builder before he became the first Federal Highway Administrator under President Eisenhower. One of his last acts as governor was to send a 200-word telegram to Secretary Boyd asking him to "withdraw" the proposal. The regulations, he said, were "a slight to the dedication, sincerity, and integrity of our state highway officials and the career employees of the Bureau of Public Roads." Planning of highways, he said, should be left in the hands of "professional highway planners," and the proof of their all-around competence is best seen in the quality of the highway system completed to date. Adoption of the proposed regulations, said Volpe, "is not in the best interests of our highway program." If the regulations are adopted, it will be Volpe's duty to enforce them.

The recommendation for two public hearings instead of one presumably will result in twice as much talk before the bulldozers move in. The introduction of the "design concept team" (comprising engineers, architects, city planners, economists, and sociologists to pool their talents in selecting the routes for urban freeways) presumably will give the sociologist a voice in deciding whether the highway will cut through a park, a school, or someone's bedroom. The idea for "joint development" and "multiple use" of urban highway corridors, which suggests that office buildings, apartments, and homes be built along the corridor above, below, and around the highway, symbolizes perfectly the central place of the highway in our culture. It would assuredly reduce the horrendous waste of urban land, provided the money can be found for such development, and provided we can evolve a race of city dwellers with high tolerance for incessant fumes, noise, and hurtling steel. One such suggestion for the proposed Crosstown Expressway in Philadelphia stalled out for lack of funds. The high cost of putting buildings on top of the expressway, which was estimated at $12 to $15 per square foot, discouraged private builders, who said they could put the same buildings on nearby land for less than $10 per square foot. The expressway, if built, will thus be an open ditch through the city.

The latest self-delusion is the suggestion that we put our faith in the black magic of "systems analysis" to solve our highway problems for us. This cannot save us: our failure is not in our methods of analysis, but in our values that put the machine first and man second. As architecture columnist Michelle Osborn writes, the best that these modern techniques of systems analysis, electronic data-processing, cost-benefit analysis, and all the rest can do for us is to "force more sophisticated justifications for the pork barrel."

None of these recommendations go to the central problem, which is to restore some semblance of balance to our transportation system. As long as the federal government continues to support highway construction at the rate of $5 billion to $6 billion per year, it is extremely doubtful that any balance can be achieved, since the availability of funds of this magnitude for improving mass transportation facilities is not in the cards. Since the Highway Trust Fund is the only pie in sight, the only solution is to slice it differently. For several years, Congress has ignored bills to permit each state government to choose how it would spend its slice of the pie—whether for new highways or new mass-transit facilities. Such legislation would, in effect, transform the Trust Fund from a highway fund to a transportation fund. This should be done.

Highway buffs oppose any such move with great vigor; they protest that all the money in the Trust Fund cannot build enough highways to handle the traffic demand. Of course, they are right. Our society has already proved beyond doubt that expenditures for highways and neglect of public transportation increases the population of automobiles and decreases the population of trains and subways, thus, in turn, increasing the demand for more highways and decreasing demand for trains and subways. The imperative need now, if we are to have any hope of salvaging human qualities in our environment, is to reverse the movement on that circle. That means not only increasing support for mass transit but *decreasing* it for private automobiles. It means not only encouraging use of mass transit, but *discouraging* use of the private automobile. It means replacing freeways with subways; parking lots with parks.

In the city, which is where most of us live and where the problem is keenest, this means doing everything within reason to take the streets away from the private automobile and give them back to the people. Special express lanes, for example, might be designated for trucks, taxis, and buses, the movement of which are in the public interest, so that they take precedence over private automobiles. Instead of widening streets at the expense of sidewalks, we should do just the opposite: give people more walking space and cars less running space. Pedestrian malls should be established in shopping districts. Also, scattered through the residential sections, streets should be closed off entirely to automobile traffic and made available for playgrounds, grass and trees, block parties, or whatever. Take from the machine to give to the human. It is just possible that these steps might give ghetto residents reason to hope that our society prizes a black human being above a Cadillac.

All such efforts to make life more difficult for private automobiles in the city must be matched by sweeping improvements in our public transportation facilities, all in the spirit of making movement of human beings easier and movement of automobiles more difficult.

The Greater London Council recently asked Parliament for permission to take a number of steps to make life more difficult for the automobile in London. Instead of encouraging new buildings in London to provide for ample parking space, the Council proposes to require *fewer* parking spaces. More parking meters will be installed on all heavily traveled streets to eliminate long-term parking. New parking areas will be provided outside London at railway, subway, and bus terminals. In a predictable response, the Royal Automobile Club called these proposals "an objectionable threat of traffic dictatorship." Just so. It is about time we began to dictate to the automobile.

For too long, the automobile has dictated the shape of our cities and dominated the quality of our lives. The highway establishment points to the torrent of new cars pouring off the assembly lines in Detroit and demands that we build the highways that are needed to accommodate them. This is community planning by knee-jerk.

The AASHO questionnaire, in an effort to give the acid test to the citizen's dedication to his automobile, pointed out that cars disgorge most of the air pollution that is strangling him, create nerve-destroying traffic congestion, kill 50,000 persons every year, displace tens of thousands of home-owners every year, and eliminate precious and irreplaceable open space. Yet 85 per cent of the 5,000 families questioned replied that Yes, that was so, but it was all worth it. Some volunteered the information that it is drivers, not automobiles, that kill people. We must stop catering to this perverse and destructive devotion.

If past trends are simply extended into the future, the road builders are right—we can never build enough highways. There are now nearly 100 million motor vehicles on the roads; by 1984 we will have 144 million. There is now one vehicle for every 2.2 persons; by 1984 there will be one vehicle for every 1.8 persons. If we simply drift with the tide of what Detroit can do and what the American citizen can assimilate, all this will come to pass. We must decide *now* whether our environment twenty years hence will be shaped willy-nilly by the insatiable demand for highways, or whether the city and the countryside shall be made fit for human habitation.

Some extreme proponents of human rights, observing the corrosive, brutalizing effects of rampant freewayism on the city, propose that all private automobiles should be barred from city streets. Frank Stead, in his book *Cry California,* says that the only effective way to make the air in that tormented state fit for assimilation into the delicate tissue of the human lung is "to serve legal notice that after 1980 no gasoline-powered motor vehicles will be permitted to operate in California."

The highway-ridden citizen acquired a new weapon from the 1968 decision in a precedent-shattering lawsuit. A New York businessman had built himself a retreat in the Adirondack Mountains overlooking Lake George, where he soaked himself in the healing silences between weekly stints in the city. But his haven was destroyed when the state of New York used part of his land on which to build an exit for a six-lane freeway. Infuriated, he sued the state for loss of privacy, destruction of his scenic view, and intrusion of traffic noise. The court stunned all observers by awarding him $37,000. In his decision, Judge Kenneth Keating deplored the damage wrought by highway construction "to the quiet beauty of many once remote and inaccessible areas, as well as the intrusion of the seemingly endless lines of asphalt and concrete into the enclaves which many have sought as surcease from the hustle and bustle of modern-day life."

The decision sent shock waves of anxiety through the highway establishment.

Another weapon may be taking shape in the form of a voracious micro-organism that has been chomping through highways in Australia. The tiny bug *Desulfovibrio desulfuricans* consumes the oily substance in bituminous materials, leaving the highway dry and brittle and subject to quick destruction by the elements. This heroic bug can eat a quantity of road material equal to its own weight every five seconds, and under ideal conditions one bug can multiply itself 17 million times in twenty-four hours. Here is an adversary worthy of the most zealous road builder.

The rebellion of our youth and our poor is rooted in the deep conviction that technology is in the saddle, that the system and the machine will be served, and people must somehow adapt and fit themselves in, or be cast aside. They see billions spent for a supersonic transport while children cry themselves to sleep with empty bellies. They see grass and trees and houses and shops steam-rollered to make way for highways and the dehumanizing roil and roar of high-velocity steel. With their flowers, bells, and dreams, they drop out of an America in which everything made of plastic, cement, and aluminum is cunningly shaped and made to work, while human flesh must adjust and follow along somehow.

There is deep irony in Wilbur Ferry's estimate of the chances for success of the Department of Transportation in its assigned mission to "untangle, to coordinate, and to build the national transportation system that America is deserving of." Under what authority? Mr. Ferry asks, and by what means? "The mind wanders to the lengths of asking what would happen if the new department might one day soon feel itself compelled to limit by fiat the manufacture of cars and trucks; to coerce car owners by tax or otherwise to use public transportation; to close state and city borders to visitors approaching by cars; to tear up rather than to build freeways, garages, bridges, and tunnels."

Our society would judge such steps to be insane, and any official who advocated them would be instantly flattened by the avenging hammer of the highway establishment. Yet, such steps as these must some day be taken if we hope to save ourselves. Population grows, asphalt spreads, and land diminishes, and there is a finite end to it all. Long before the limit is reached, the environment will have become utterly hostile to human life.